Frederick Arthur Crisp

The Parish Registers of Ongar

Frederick Arthur Crisp

The Parish Registers of Ongar

ISBN/EAN: 9783337132491

Printed in Europe, USA, Canada, Australia, Japan

Cover: Foto ©Andreas Hilbeck / pixelio.de

More available books at **www.hansebooks.com**

THE

PARISH REGISTERS

OF

ONGAR,

ESSEX.

PRIVATELY PRINTED FOR

FREDERICK ARTHUR CRISP.

1886.

CONTENTS.

		PAGES
BAPTISMS	. . .	3-74
MARRIAGES		75-90
BURIALS	. .	91-138
INDEX	.	139-184

Private Circular.   *January*, 1892.

LIST OF

PARISH REGISTERS

AND OTHER

Genealogical Works

EDITED BY

FREDERICK ARTHUR CRISP.

(FOR PRIVATE CIRCULATION ONLY.)

BERKSHIRE.

Catholic Register of Ufton Court, Berkshire, & Woolhampton. 1764 to 1828. Fifty copies printed, numbered and signed, bound in vellum; subscription price, twelve shillings and sixpence. Price of remaining copies, one guinea.

BUCKINGHAMSHIRE.

Catholic Registers of Weston-Underwood.—Twenty-five copies printed.—*No copies remaining.*

ESSEX.

Sepulchral Memorials of Bobbingworth.—Monumental Inscriptions in Church and Churchyard, Pedigrees, Wills, Woodcuts of Arms, &c. One hundred copies printed, numbered and signed, bound in vellum; subscription price, two guineas.

In the Press. **Registers of Greensted,** near Ongar.—Baptisms, Marriages and Burials, 1558 to 1812. Fifty copies will be printed, numbered and signed; subscription price, ten shillings and sixpence.

Registers of Moreton.—Baptisms, Marriages and Burials, 1558 to 1759. Fifty copies printed, numbered and signed; subscription price, one guinea.

Registers of Ongar.—Baptisms, Marriages and Burials, 1558 to 1750. One hundred copies printed, numbered and signed; subscription price, one guinea and-a-half. Price of remaining copies, two guineas.

In the Press. **Registers of Stapleford Tawney.**—Baptisms, Marriages, and Burials, 1558 to 1752. Fifty copies will be printed, numbered and signed; subscription price, ten shillings and sixpence.

Of the following no copies remain:

Registers of Bobbingworth.—Thirty copies printed.
Registers of Lambourne.—Fifty copies printed.
Registers of St. Leonard's, Colchester, 1670 to 1671.—Twelve copies printed.
Registers of Stifford.—Thirty copies printed.

GLOUCESTERSHIRE.

Registers of Kempsford.—Baptisms, Marriages and Burials, 1653 to 1700. Fifty copies printed, numbered and signed; subscription price, ten shillings.

₊ *Copied from a MS. in my possession, made and certified by the late W. H. Black, Esq., F.S.A., of Her Majesty's Record Office.*

KENT.

Registers of the French Church at Dover.—Fifty copies printed. *No copies remaining.*

LEICESTERSHIRE.

Registers of Newton-Linford.—1677 to 1679. Ten copies printed. *No copies remaining.*

LINCOLNSHIRE.

Registers of Stubton.—1577 to 1628. Twelve copies printed.—*No copies remaining.*

Registers of Irby-upon-Humber.—1558 to 1785. Fifty copies printed, numbered and signed; subscription price, one guinea. Price of remaining copies, one guinea and-a-half.

MIDDLESEX.

Monumental Inscriptions in the Church and Churchyard of St. Olave, Jewry.—Fifty copies printed, numbered and signed; subscription price, five shillings. Price of remaining copies, ten shillings.

₊ *This church has been closed, and will shortly be pulled down.*

Registers of Staines.—1644 to 1694. Thirty copies printed —*No copies remaining.*

SOMERSETSHIRE.

Somersetshire Wills.—Six Volumes. One hundred and fifty copies printed. Price of remaining copies, nine guineas.

₊ *Abstracts of about four thousand wills made by the late Rev. Frederick Brown, M.A., F.S.A.*

SUFFOLK.

Registers of Carlton.—Baptisms, Marriages and Burials, 1538 to 1886. Fifty copies printed, numbered and signed; subscription price, one guinea. Price of remaining copies, two guineas.

Registers of Chillesford.—Baptisms, 1740 to 1812; Marriages, 1754 to 1812; Burials, 1740 to 1812. No earlier Register existing. One hundred copies printed, numbered and signed; subscription price, ten shillings.

Registers of Culpho.—Baptisms, Marriages and Burials, 1720 to 1886. No earlier Register existing. One hundred copies printed, numbered and signed; subscription price, seven shillings and sixpence.

Registers of Frostenden.—Baptisms, 1539 to 1791; Marriages, 1538 to 1754; Burials, 1538 to 1791. Fifty copies printed, numbered and signed; subscription price, one guinea and-a-half. Price of remaining copies, two guineas.

Registers of Kelsale.—Baptisms, 1538 to 1812; Marriages, 1538 to 1868; Burials, 1538 to 1812. Fifty copies printed, numbered and signed, bound in vellum; subscription price, four guineas. Price of remaining copies, five guineas.

Registers of Pakenham.—Baptisms, Marriages and Burials, 1563 to 1766. Fifty copies printed, numbered and signed, bound in vellum; subscription price, three guineas. Price of remaining copies, four guineas.

Monumental Inscriptions in the Church and Churchyard of Ellough.—Fifty copies printed, numbered and signed; subscription price, seven shillings and sixpence. Price of remaining copies, ten shillings.

* *During the restoration of the church two brasses were found, facsimiles of which are given in the volume.*

Of the following no copies remain:

Registers of Brundish.—Thirty copies printed.

Registers of Ellough.—Fifty copies printed.

Registers of Tannington.—Fifteen copies printed.

SURREY.

Catholic Registers of Woburn-Lodge and Weybridge.—1750 to 1874. Fifty copies printed, numbered and signed, bound in vellum; subscription price, one guinea. Price of remaining copies, one guinea and-a-half.

WORCESTERSHIRE.

Catholic Registers of the City of Worcester.—1685 to 1837. Fifty copies printed, numbered and signed, bound in vellum; subscription price, two guineas. Price of remaining copies, three guineas.

WALES.

Registers of Kegidog, *alias* **St. George, near Abergele.**—Thirty copies printed.—*No copies remaining.*

To F. A. Crisp,

        Grove Park, Denmark Hill, London, S.E.

Sir,

    Please send me,_____

_____

for which I enclose*_____

              *Name*_____

              *Address*_____

£   :   :

* *Cheques should be crossed "Bank of England," and made payable to F. A. Crisp.*

A true Register of the names of
all such Persons as haue been Baptized,
maried, and Buried wthin the parish of
Chepingonger in the Countie of Essex,
wth the daie & yeare of ey such
Baptisme, mariage & Buriall,
since the beginning off the
raigne of o^r Soaigne
Ladie Queene Eli-
zabeth, according
to an Iniunction made to that end in a Synode holden
at London, in the XI^{tith} yeare of her Maties Raigne. A° D.
1597.
written out of the old boke by me
Hugh Ince, Preacher
and Pasto^r of this
Church.
1590.

Memorandū : That ye Church-yard was railed and paled in in y^e
year 1701 at ye charge of ye Parish of Chip: Ong^r Philip
Trahearn and ffrancis Sadler being then Church [wardens].
Wit. Joⁿ Campe Minis^{tr}.

Memorandum that the Church yatd towards the Glebe was
paled in the year 1735 at the Charge of The Parish of
Chip : Ongar, Robert Wrenn & Thomas Royston being
then Church Wardens.
Witness, Thomas Velley, Rector.

Baptisms.

Christenings.

Aº. D. 1558, & a 17º Novembr̄ eiusdem anno, quo die
Serenissima Regina nr̄a Elizabetha regnare cepit.

Aº.D. 1558. Anne, Daughtr of - Wiłłm Calys, was baptized 20ᵗʰ of
Decembr̄.
Grace, the Daughtr of Robert ffinch, was baptized the same
Daie.
Ellin Courtney, of Grensteed, was baptized 20ᵗʰ Januar̄.
George, sonne of Richard Graehawe, was bapt. 4º febr̄.

Aº.D. 1559. Elizabeth, the Daughtr of Robert Duckett, was bapt. 22ᵗʰ
Januar̄.

Aº.D. 1560. John, sonne of Hugh Abbott, was bapt. 15º Octobr̄.
Nicolas, sonne of Jeffrey Alsopp, was bapt. 24ᵗʰ Noueb̄.
eodē Aº.
Alice fyfield, daughtr of John fyfield, was bapt. 21º Decembr̄.

Aº.D. 1561. Joane fox, daughtr of John fox, was bapt. 4º Maie.
Edmond Willand, sonne of Wiłłm Willand, was bapt. 1º
June.
James Adams, sonne of Tho. Adams, was bapt. 6º Julij.
Stephen, sonne of Robert fynch, was bapt. 11º August.

A.D. 1562. Nathaniel, sonne of John Alsopp, was bapt. 1º Martij.
Robert, sonne of John Turnish, was bapt. 10º Maij.
Thomas, sonne of John ffosten, was bapt. 1º Junij.
Elizabeth, Daughtr of Tho. Saling, was bapt. 1º Aug.
Robert, sonne of Robert Duckett, was bapt. 6º Septembr̄.
Joane, daughter of Thomas Brainwoode, was bapt. 19º
Sept.
Richard, Sonne of Thomas Rand, was bapt. 19º Nouembr.

1564. Alice, Daughtr of Jeffrey Alsopp, was bapt. 28º Maij.
William, sonne of Henry Ting, was bapt. 7º June.
Joane, Daughtr of Henry foster, was bapt. 16º Julij.
George, sonne of John foston, was bapt. 2º Julij.
William Edmunds was bapt. 3º July.
Nathaniel, sonne of John Alsopp, was bapt. 6º Aug.
Joseph, sonne of John Hansaker, was bapt. 8º Octob̄.
John, sonne of Tho. More, was bapt. 5º Sept.
Grace, Daughtr of Tho. Brainwood, was bapt. 18º Sept.

5

1564. Jeffrey Butler was bapt. 2° Octob.
Thomas Saling was bapt. 30° Octob.
Mary, Daught' of Wiłłm. Thomas, minist', was bapt. 20 March.

1565. Elizabeth, Daught' of John Questell, was bapt. 19 Aug.
Joan, daught' of Tho. Adams, was bapt. 14° Octob.
John, sonne of John foston, was bapt. 16 Decemb.
Thomas, sonne of Henry Ting, was bapt. 26° Decemb.
Jane Ducket was bapt. 19° Januar.
John Symson was bapt. 24° March.

1566. Wiłłm. Barwicke was bapt. 11 Aug.
Elizabeth Edmunds was bapt. 18 August.
Dennis, Daught' of Robart ffinch thelder, was bapt. 1° Septemb.
Robart Siluester, base borne, was bapt. 14° Sept.
Elizabeth, Daught' of Willm̄ Thomas, Clerk, was bapt. 18° Octob.
Giles Ailett was bapt. 1° Decemb.

1567. James, sonne of John Questell, was bapt. on East' day, viz. 30° March.
Anne, Daught' of James Morice, Esquier, was bapt. 20 Aug.
Josua, sonne of Willm̄ Thomas, clerk, was bapt. 9° March.

1568. John Morrice, sonne & heire of Ja : Morice, Esq', was bapt. 17° Octob.
Rebecca Ward was bapt. 24° Octob.
James, sonne of Robart fynch theld', was bapt. 21 Nouĕb.
James Glascock was bapt. 27 Decemb.

1569. Thomas Ailett was bapt. 7 Octob.

1570. Edward, sonne of Ja : Morice, Esq', was bapt. 4 May.
Anne, Daught' of Jo. Glascock, was bapt. 6 Aug.
Joan, Daught' of Jo : foston [blank] Octob. was bapt.
Thomas Trappes [blank] Octob. was bapt.
John, sonne of Robart Cole, was bapt. 26 Nouemb.
Elizabeth, Daught' of Tho. Ailett, was bapt. [n. d.]
Joan, Daughter of Richard Rogers, was bapt. 21 Januar.
frauncis, sonne of George Wittam, was bapt. 2° febr̄.
Jane, daught' of Jo : Questell fre denison was bapt. 2° febr.
Anne, daught' of Jo : Glascock, was bapt. 27 Decemb.

1571. Jane (or Joane) Questell was bapt. 30° Januar.

1572. Jane Brainwood was bapt. 12 febr.
Robart Roffe was bapt. 8 June.

1573. Mary Barnard was bapt. 28 Octob.

1574. Margett Questell was bapt. 16 Jañ.

1575. Henry, sonne of Ja : Morice, Esq., was bapt. 14 Sept.
Elizabeth, Daught' of Tho : Morice, clerke, was bapt. 15 Octob.
Grace Cole was bapt. yᵉ same daie.
Thomas, sonne of Ric. Clerke, was bapt. 13 Nouĕb.
Alice, daught' of Jo : Glascock, was bapt. 30 Nouĕb.
Richard, sonne of Henry Barnard, was bapt. 15 Jañ.
Mary, daught' of Jo : Questell, was bapt. 12 febr̄.

1576. John, sonne of George Wittham, was bapt. 25 March.

6

1576. Margett, daught' of Hugh Abbott was bapt. 10 June.
John, sonne of Jo : Crabb, was bapt. 22 Julij.
Jane, daught' of Tho : Pomfrett, was bapt. 12 Aug.
Jane, daught' of Tho : Morice, pson, was bapt. 10 Nouemɓ.
Bennett Wailett, of Highong', was bapt. here 2° febr̃.
Reg. Regi. Eleno', daught' of Jo : Questell, was bapt. 17° febr̃, & R.
Eliz. 19.   Eliz. 19°.
Susan, daught' of Giles Small, was bapt. 6 Octob.
1577. Anne, daught' of Tho : Morice, pson, was bapt. 1 deceɓ.
1578. Elizabeth, Daught' of Jo : Glascocke, was bapt. 1 Jañ., R.
    Eliz. 20°.
John, sonne of Jo : Questell, was bapt. 16 Maij.
Margaret, daught' of Ric. Clerke, was bapt. 20° Aprill.
Elizabeth, daught' of Giles Small, was bapt. 26 Sept.
1579. Jeffrey, sonne of francis Alsop, was bapt. 28 June. R.
El. 21.   Eliz. 21.
Katherine, daught' of Jo : Questell, was bapt. [n. d.]
William, sonne of Giles Small, was bapt. 1° Sept.
George, Sonne of Henry Ting, was bapt. 8 Noueɓ.
Elizabeth, daught' of Joseph Bury, was bapt. 12 Noueɓ.
Joan Oliu', was bapt. 22 Jañ. R. Eliz. 22.
Jane, daught' of John Louett, bapt. here 12 Januar̃.
John, sonne of Jo : Glascocke, was bapt. 25 Jañ.
John, sonne of Jo : Grange, was bapt. 21 febr̃.
Edward, sonne of Jo : Crabb, was bapt. 25 febr̃.
1580. Joan, daught' of Jo : Wailett, 15 Maij.
James, sonne of Ric. Derrington, was bapt. 2 Octob.
Thomas, sonne of Jo. Palɱ, was bapt. 13 febr̃. R. Eliz. 23°.
Robert, sonne of Willɱ Lambert, was bapt. 11 March.
1581. Katherine, daught' of Ric. Clerk, was bapt. 30 Aprill.
Katherine, daught' of frauncis Alsop, was bapt. 21 Maij.
Morice, sonne of Willɱ Bourne, gent., was bapt. 28 Maij.
Rebecca, daught' of Jo : Questell, was bapt. [blank] Sept.
Agnes Mallery, daught' of Phill : Mallery, was bapt. 31 Jul.
Anne, daught' of Henry Ting, was bapt. 29 Octob.
Henry, sonne of Ja : Morice, Esq., was bapt. 28 deceɓ. R.
Eliz. 24.
1582. Elizabeth, daught' of Jo : Weldon, was bapt. 6 Maij.
Thomas, sonne of Tho : Clerk, was bapt. 21 Octob.
Phillip, sonne of Phillip Mallery, was bapt. 20 Jañ. R.
Eliz. 25.
Anne, daughter of Richard Derington, was bapt. y° 12 of ffebr.
Robart, sonne of Jo : Crabb, was bapt. 27 febr̃.
1583. Bennet, daught' of Ric. Clarke, was bapt. 28 Aprill.
Mary, daught' of Jo : Weldon, was bapt. 2° June.
Mary, daught' of Jo : Turnish, was bapt. 29 Junij.
Jane, daught' of Tho : Wiatt, was bapt. 30 June.
Willɱ, sonne of Hugh Ince, Pastor here, was bapt. 15 Sept.
Jone King, base borne, was bapt. 13° Octob.
Grace, daught' of fr : Alsopp, was bapt. 24 Noueɓ. R.
Eliz. 26.
Elizabeth, daught' of Willɱ Bourne, gent, was bapt. 1° deceɓ.
Anne, daught' of Jo : Questell, was bapt. 3° deceɓ.

7

1583. Henry, sonne of Edw: Wailett, was bapt. 8 deceb.
frauncis, daught' of Jo : Browne, was bapt. 5 Jañ.
Marian, daught' of Andr : Spranger, was bapt. here 2° febr.
Andrew, sonne of Raffe Grange, was bapt. 9° febr̄.
Joan, daught' of Jo : Cheston, was bapt. 22 febr̄.

· 1584. Richard, sonne of Phil : Mallery, was bapt. 16 Aug.
Robart, sonne of Jo : Crabb, was bapt. 4 Octob.
Mary, daught' of Jo : Browne, was bapt. 1 Jañ R. Eliz. 27.
Mary, daught' of Jo : Weldon, was bapt. 14 March.

1585. John, sonne of Jo : Turnish, was bapt. 1 Aug.
Alice & Grace, Twinnes, daught'ʳ of Gy : Small, were bapt.
15 Aug.
Richard, sonne of Jo: Cheston, was bapt. 3 Octob.
John, sonne of Jo. Questell, was bapt. 10 Octob.
Mary, daught' of Henry Ting, was bapt. 5 Deceb.
Margaret Lamborne, of Highong', was bapt. 2 Januar̄.
Thomas, sonne of fr: Alsopp, was bapt. 9 Jañ.
Alice, daught' of Tho: Clerk, was bapt. 13 febr̄.
Mary, daught' of Ric. Derrington, was bapt. 20 febr̄.

1586. Andrew, sonne of Jo: Oliu', was bapt. 17 Aprill. R.
Eliz. 28.
Thomas, sonne of Tho: Wiatt, was bapt. 10 Julij.
John, sonne of Jo: Weldon, was bapt. 30 Octob.
Anne, daught' of Jo: Browne, was bapt. yᵉ same daie.
Rebecca, daught' of Hugh Ince, Pastoʳ here, was bapt. 1
Noueb.
John, sonne of Jo: Cheston, was bapt. 27 Noueb. R. Eliz.
29.
Anne, daught' of Ric. Clerke, was bapt. yᵉ same daie.
Willm̄, sonne of Giles Small, was bap. 5 March.

1587. Henry, sonne of Jo: Crab, was bapt. 30 July.
Morice, sonne of Edw: Turno', gent., borne 9 feb., bapt.
18° thereof. El: 30.

1588. Henry, sonne of Phil: Mallery, was bapt 5 Maij.
Cornelius, sonne of Giles Small, was bapt. 25 Aug.
Richard, sonne of Raffe Grange, was bapt. yᵉ same daie.
Jane, daught' of Ric. Deryngtō, was bapt. 22 Sept.
John Ince, sonne of Hugh Ince, pastor, was borne 24 Octob.,
bapt. 27 thereof.
Anne, daught' of John Weldon, was bapt. yᵉ same instant.
Arthur, sonne of Edw: Turno', gent., was bapt. 19 Jañ. R.
Eliz. 31.

1589. Henry, sonne of Tho: Wiat, was bapt. 15 June.
Tho:, sonne of Jo: Cheston, was bapt. 17 August.
Willm̄ & Elizabeth, twinnes of fr. Alsopp, were bapt. 12
Octob.
Auger, sonne of Jo: Weldon, was bapt. 7 decemb.

1590. Elizabeth, daught' of Barthol Deringtō, was bapt. 13 Aprill.
R. El : 32.
Thomas, sonne of Giles Small, was bapt. 17 Maij.
John, sonne of Jo: Browne, was bapt. 28 June.
John, sonne of Willm̄ Graue, ·was bapt. 16 Aug.
Samuel, sonne of Willm̄ Grapes, was bapt. 6 Sept.

8

1590. John, sonne of Ric. Hutley, was bapt. 8 Noueb.
Martha, daught^r of Ric. Derringtō, was bapt. 10 Jañ. Eliz.
33.
Isaac, sonne of Robert Champnes, was bapt. 17 Jañ.
Elizabeth, daught^r of Jo: Weldon, was bapt. 21 febr̃.
1591. Bartholomew, sonne of Barth: Deringtō, was bapt. 15 Aug
Grace, daught^r of Willm̃ fynch, was bapt. 29 Aug.
Prudence, daught^r of Giles Small, was bapt. 3 Octob.
Martha, daught^r of Hugh Ince, pastor here, was bapt. 28
Noueb. .
Josua, sonne of Thomas Ramsey, was bapt. 6 febr.
1592. Mary, daught^r of Jo: Cheston, was bapt. 2 Aprill.
Thomas, sonne of Peter Deringtō, was bapt. 9 Aprill.
Richard, sonne of fra: Alsop, was bapt. 25 Aprill.
Elizabeth, daught^r of Jo: Browne, was bapt. 27 Aug.
Richard, sonne of Barth. Derington, was bapt. 22 Octob.
Elizabeth, daught^r of Ric. Hutley, was bapt. 19 Nouemb.
R. Eliz. 35.
Robart, sonne of Willm̃ fynch, was bapt. 3 Decemb.
Samuel, sonne of Jo: Weldon, was bapt. 28 Janû.
George, sonne of Willm̃ farrington, was bapt. 14 March.
Priscilla, daught^r of Peter Deringtō, was bapt. 11 March.
Debora, daught^r of Rob: Champnes, was bapt. 18 March.
1593. Elizabeth, daught^r of Tho: Turnish, was bapt. 6 Maij.
Elizabeth, daught^r of Edm. Willand, was bapt. 21 June.
James, sonne of H. Ince, pastor here, was borne 26 June
bapt. 1 July. R. El. 35.
Willm̃, sonne of Willm̃ Barnard, was bapt. 23 Deceb.
Willm̃, sonne of Henry Gladwin, of High Ong^r, bapt. here
16 March.
1594. Mary, daught^r of Edm. Willand, was bapt. 4 Aug.
frauncis, sonne of fr. Alsop, was bapt. 18 Aug.
Theophilus, sonne of Ric. Deringtō, was bapt. 16 Octob.
Sara, daught^r of Jo: Browne, was bapt. the same time.
Em̃a fynch, daught^r of Willm̃ finch, was bapt. 10 febr. R.
Eliz. 37.
1595. Lidia, daught^r of Giles Small, was bap. 15 June.
Henry, sonne of Tho. Ting, was bapt. 4 Sept.
Elizabeth, daught^r of Willm̃ Barnard, bapt. 8 febr. Eliz. 38.
Morice, sonne of Brian Tuke, gent., was bapt. 18 febr., borne
9 febr.
George, sonne of peter deringtō, was bapt. 6 March.
1596. Elizabeth, daught^r of Georg Pechie, was bapt. 16 Maij.
Margaret, daught^r of Georg Parmeter, bapt. ye same houre.
Elizabeth, daught^r of John Morice, Esqr, borne 4 Maie, bapt.
1° June.
Prudence, daught^r of Edm. Willand, was bapt. ye same daie.
Samuel, sonne of Jo: Butch^r, was bapt. 24 July.
John, sonne of John Spilmā, was bapt. 12 deceb.
1597. Katherine, daught^r of George Goodwin, Clerk, was bapt. 25
March.
Willm̃, sonne of Willm̃ fynch, was bapt. 28 March.
Elizabeth, daught^r of Georg wrath, gent., was bapt. 3 July.

1597. James, sonne of Jo : Morice Esq', was borne 24 Aug., bapt.
1° Sept.
John, sonne of fr : Alsopp, was bapt. 4 Sept.
Elizabeth, daught' of Willm Bilt, was bapt. 18 Sept.
Rebecca, daught' of Jo : Browne, was bapt. 23 Octob.
Mary, daught' of Willm Barnard, was bapt. 29 Jan.
Eliz. 40.
1598. Margaret, daught' of Robert Batsford, was bapt. 30 Aprill.
Gilbert, sonne of Peter Deringtō, was bapt. 30 July.
Mary, Daughter of George Pechie, bapt. 6° Aug.
Richard, sonne of Edm. Willand was bapt. 1° Octob.
1599. Thomas, sonne of John Weldon, was baptized 25° Martij.

Hugh Ince, pasto'. Churchwardens $\left\{\begin{array}{l}\text{Williā fynch.}\\\text{John Weldon.}\end{array}\right.$

Williā, sonne of Rob. Jones, was bapt. 3° Junij, A¹⁴ βdc.
Thomas, sonne of Tho. Anzer, was bapt. 17 June, A¹⁴ βdc.
Nicolas, sonne of Henry Clerk, was baptized 15° July,
An¹⁴ βdc.
James, sonne of John Pennymā, was baptized 29° July,
A¹⁴ βdc.
Richard, sonne of Willm finch, was baptized yᵉ same daie.
John Willand, sonne of Edmund Willand, was bapt. 25°
Noueb. 1599.
Richard, sonne of Willm Bilt, was baptized 6 Januaī,
A¹⁴ pd.
Marie & Margaret, twinnes daughters of Zachary Batemā,
were bapt. 12° Januaī.
William, sonne of Willm. forrington, was bapt. 10 febr.
Marie, Daught' of Georg Pechie, was bapt. 16ᵗʰ March, A¹⁴ pd.
1600. Katharine & Damaris, daughters of Will. Barnard, bapt.
[*blank*] Aprill.
frauncis, sonne of Barth. Derington, bapt. 13° July. ·
Catherine Willet, Daught' of Ric. Willett, was bapt. 7°
Septeb. ·
Thomas, sonne of Wᵐ Graue, bapt 14° Septeb.
Lettice, Daught' of Henry Clerke, bapt. 5 Octobr.
Catherine, Daught' of Ro : Batsford, was bapt. 4° January.
Zachary, sonne of Zachary Batemā, baptiz. 11 Januaī.
Willm, sonne of Willm. Batsford, bapt. 6 Martij.
Willm, sonne of John Stane, baptiz. 15 Martij.
Timothy, sonne of John Weldon, bapt. 22 March.
1601. Marie, Daughter of Tho : Anzer, was baptized 10 Maie, 1601.
John, sonne of Nic. Tomson, was bapt. 11° Octob.
Matthew, sonne of John Browne, bapt. 24 Noueb. Eliz. 44°.
Mary, Daught' of Zachary Batemā, bapt. 1° Januarij.
Willm, sonne of Willm. Bilt, bapt. 3° Januarij.
1602. John, sonne of Tho. Sedgewicke, was baptiz. July 25°.
Eliz. 44°.
Prudence, Daught' of Willm fynch, bapt. June 6°. A¹⁴ βdc.
Mary, daught' of Willm Batsford, baptiz. 15° Aug.
Sara, daught' of Willm Grave, baptiz. eidē die.
Mary Anzor, daught' of Tho : Anzor, was bapt. 3° Octobr.
Mary, daught' of Barth. Derington, bapt. eodē die et hora.

1602. Robart, sonne of John Weldon, bapt. 19 Deceb. Eliz. 45°.
El. 45. Elizabeth, Daught' of Alice Clerk, base borne, bapt. [*blank*] febr.
Richard, sonne of Ric. Lankford, the 5 of March bapt.
John, sonne of Willm̄ Barnard, bapt. y° same day.
1603. James, sonne of Willm̄ Batsford, baptized 28 August, 1603.
Jacobi Regis   Ja. R. 1°.
1°.   Sara, daughter of John Barrett, baptized y° last of Julij.
Edmond, sonne of Edmund Willand, baptized 16° Octob.
Marie, daught' of Nic. Tomson, baptiz. 15° January.
1604. Elizabeth, Daught' of Tho. Sedgewick, bapt. 1 Aprill, A°. d. 1604. Ja. 2°.
Margaret, daught' of Jo : Stane   } bapt. togeth' 22° July.
John, sonne of Barthol. Deringtō }
Zachary Batemā, sonne of Zachary Batemā, bapt. 12° Aug.
Mary, daughter of widow Graue, bapt. 14° Octob.
Elizabeth, daught' of Ric. Lankford, bapt. 2° Decemb.
George, sonne of Willm̄ fynch   } bapt. 23° Deceb.
Nathanel, sonne of Willm̄ Bilt   }
John, sonne of Tho : Anzor, bapt. Dec' 30°.
Mary, daughter of Tho : Prentise   } baptiz. 24° febr.
Thomas, sonne of George Haselwood   }
1605. George, sonne of Willm̄ Barnard, baptiz. 21 Aprill, 1605.
Thomas, sonne of Williā Batsford, baptiz. 28 Aprill.
Sara, daught' of Edmund Willand, bapt. 9 (?) May.
Sara, daught' of Willm̄ Duddesborow, baptiz. 23° June.
Elizabeth, daught' of Tho : Heard, bapt. 27° Julij.
Thomas, sonne of Tho : Sedgewick, baptized y° 20 of January.
John, sonne of John Barrett, bapt. 12 Januar̄.
Andrew, sonne of Willm̄ fynch, bapt. 9 febr.
1606. James, sonne of James Derington, bapt. 3° August.
Mary, daughter of Giles Miller, baptiz. 31 Augusti.
Jane, daughter of Nicolas Tomson, bapt. 14 Sept.
George, sonne of James Penimā, baptiz. 2° Noueb.
Anne, daughter of John King, baptiz. y° after noone y° same day.
John, sonne of Barthol. Chapmā, bapt. 16 Noueb.
Thomas, sonne of Nicolas Parker, bapt. 23 Noueb.
Grace, daught' of Zachary Batemā, baptized 7 deceb.
Joane Batsford, daughter of Willm̄ Batsford, baptized 25 Jañ.
Laurence, base borne sonne of Alice Clerke, bapt. . . . febr.
1607. Joseph, sonne of Ric. Lankfeld, baptiz. 19 Aprill, 1607. Ja : 5.
Martha, daught' of George Haselwood, bapt. . . . .
Thomas, sonne of Tho : Anzer, bapt. 26 Aprill.
Hugh, sonne of Edmond Willand, baptiz. . . . August.
James, sonne of Tho : Sedgewicke, bapt. 24 Jañ.
Joyce, daughter of Rob : Mott, baptiz. 20 Martij.
1608. Elizabeth, daught' of Jo : Crab, senio', baptiz. . . . June, 1608. Ja : 6.
Margaret, daught' of Giles Miller, baptized 11 Sept.

11

1608. John, sonne of John Shipton, baptiz. 11 Octob.
Thomas, sonne of Michaell White, bap. 18 Octob'.
Williā, sonne of Willm̄ Shingleton, bapt. 30 Octob.
Elizabeth, daughter of Rob. Polley, baptized 8 Noueb.
Edward, sonne of Ed : Maior, bapt. 18 deceb.
Margarett, daught' of John King, baptiz. 22° Jañ.
Giles, sonne of Willm̄ Batsford, bapt. 29° Jañ.
Thomas, sonne of Tho : foot, bapt. 12° febr.
John, sonne of Nicolas Parker, baptiz. 26 febr.
Mary, daught' of John Scampion, bapt. 5° Martij.
1609. James, sonne of Bartholomew Chapmā, bapt. 16 Aprill,
1609.
Elizabeth, daught' of James Penymā, bapt. . . . . Aprill.
Elizabeth, daught' of Nic. Tomson, bapt. . . . .
Elizabeth, daught' of George Hazelwood [bapt.] 22 Octob.
Clemence, daught' of Edmond Willand, bapt. 13° Deceb.
Robart, sonne of Tho : Sedgwick, bapt. 24 Deceb.
Marget, Daught' of Rob : Mott, bapt. last of Deceb.
Thomas, sonne of Robart Tydy, bapt. 15° Martij. Ja : 7°.
Mary, daughter of Nicolas Spark, bapt. 18 March.
1610. Elizabeth, daughter of John King, bapt. 12 Apl, 1610.
George, sonne of Michael White, bapt. 3° Junij.
Giles, sonne of Richard Lankfield, bapt. 10 June.
Mary, daughter of James Deringtō, baptized 28 July.
Samuel, sonne of John Scampion, bapt. 26 August.
Mary, daughter of Edward Maior, bapt. 23 Sept.
Mary, daughter of Willm̄ Duddesborow, bapt. 30 Sept.
Ellyn, daught' of John Shipton, bapt. 2° Octob.
Katherine, Daughter of Giles Miller, bapt. 11° Noueb.
Anne, daught' of Willm̄ Batsford, bapt. 24 febr.
Elizabeth, Daught' of Willm̄ Tiler, was bapt. 19 Janū.
1611. John, sonne of Willm̄ Howbroke, bapt. 21° Aprill, 1611.
Anna, daught' of Nic. Parker, bapt. 30 April.
John, sonne of John Small, bapt. 9° Junij.
John, sonne of Nicolas Spark, bapt. 23° June.
John, sonne of John Scampion, baptized 3° Sept.
Solomon, sonne of Robert Crab, baptiz. 8 Sept.
Edward, sonne of Ric. Lankford, bapt. Octo. [blank].
Robert, sonne of George Haselwood, 17 Noueb.
Robert, sonne of Michael White, baptiz. 15 Deceb'.
John, sonne of Thomas fote, baptiz 22 Deceb'.
John, sonne of John King, bapt. 18 febr.
Edward, sonne of Edw. Hum̄stone, bapt. 27° febr.
1612. Laurence, sonne of James Penymā, bapt. 13 Aprill, 1612.
Jac: 10. Jac. 10°.
Isaac Bilt, sonne of Willm̄ Bilt, bapt. 19 Aprill.
Phillip, sonne of Tho. Sedgewick, bapt. eodē die.
Beniamin, sonne of Andrew wamsley, bapt. 17 June.
Hugh, sonne of Phillip Eųerard, borne on St James day,
being saterdaie, & bapt. 2° Aug.
Martha, daught' of Edw. Maior, bapt. 24 August. Jacobi
10.
Agnes, daught' of Willm̄ Tyler, bapt. 4° Octobr..

1612. Robert, sonne of Rob. Crab, bapt. 11 Octob.
John, sonne of John Cliffe, bapt. 25 Octob.
Thomas, sonne of Tho: Champnes, bapt. 8° Noũeb.
John, sonne of James Derington, bapt. 6 Jañ.
Phillip, sonne of Willm̃ Batsford, bapt. 24 Jañ.
Thomas, sonne of Nicolas Sparke, bapt. 24° febr.
1613. Isaac, sonne of Willm̃ Howbroke, bapt. 5 Aprilis, 1613. R
Ja: 11.   Ja: 11°.
Robert, sonne of John King, bapt. 13 April.
Thomas, sonne of Jo. Shiptõ, bapt. 25 Aprill.
Robert, sonne of Rob. Tydy, bapt. 9 Maij.
Beniamin, sonne of Andrew Wamsley, bapt. 27 May.
John, sonne of Edward Harris, was bapt. 15 Junij.
Matthew, sonne of Avery Lasy, bapt. 19 Julij.
John, sonne of Michael White, bapt. 2 July.
Thomas, sonne of Tho: Stracy, bapt. 11 Sept.
Mary, daught'' of Philip Euerard, bapt. 20 Sept.
Elizabeth, daughter of John Rivers . . . . Lond, bapt. 9°
January.
Elizabeth & Henry, Twinnes Children of John Small, bapt.
6 febr.
1614. Jeremy, sonne of John Scampion, was bapt. 14 Aprill, 1614.
Ja. 12.   Ja. R. 12.
Edward, sonne of Jo: King, bapt. 25 Aprill.
Thomas, sonne of Willm̃ Best, bapt. 2° Octob.
Sara, daught'' of Tho: Platt, bapt. 28 Octo.
Mary, daught'' of Ed: Barefote, baptised Noueb̃. 7°.
John, sonne of Philip Euerard, bapt. 4° Deceb̃'.
Mary, daughter of Robert Watson, bapt. eidẽ die, of
Staford.
Mary, daught'' of Tho: Sedgewick, bapt. 18 Deceb̃.
Robert, sonne of Willm̃ Batsford, bapt. 1° Jañ.
Joseph & Dorothey, Twins of Nicolas Spark, bapt. 9° febr.
John, sonne of Robert Crab, bapt. the same instant togeth''.
1615. Elizabeth, daught'' of Avery Lacy, bapt. 10 Aprill, 1615.
Ja. R. 13. Joane, daught'' of Giles Horwood, bapt. 19 Maij.
Willm̃, sonne of Jo: Shipton, bapt. 28 Maij.
Ellin, daught'' of Jo: Champnes, bapt. 29 Maij.
Thomas, sonne of Rich: Lankfield, bapt. 16 June.
Richard, sonne of John Stoddard, of Shelly, bapt. 20
August.
Elizabeth, daught'' of John Scãpion & Eliz. his wife, bapt.
4° Sept.
Richard, sonne of Willm̃ Tiler & Anne his wife, bapt. 26
July.
Sara, daught'' of Willm̃ Hardmã & Martha his wife, bapt. 12°
Sept.
Ruth, daught'' of James deringtõ & Eliz. his wife, bapt.
eodẽ mometo.
Elizabeth, daught'' of Ed: Harris & Zephora his wife, bapt.
26 Sept.
Martha, daught'' of Mich: White & Margaret his wife, bapt.
26 Noueb̃.

13

1615. Dorothie, daught' of John King & Eliz: his wife, bapt. 28 Noueb.

Tho:, sonne of Rob. Tidy, bapt. 25 febr.

1616. Sara, daught' of Phillip Euerard & Martha his wife, bapt. 7°
Ja: 14. Aprll, 1616. Ja. 14.

James, sonne of James Brainwood, bapt. 17 July.

Martha, daught' of Henry Scampion, bapt. 25 Aug.

Edward, sonne of Edward Peacoke, bapt. 6 of Noueb.

Easter, daught' of Nicolas Sparke, bapt. 9° Octob'.

Elizabeth, daught' of Richard Samuel, bapt. 11° Noueb.

1617. Henry, sonne of Robt. Crab, bapt. 8° Junij, 1617.
Ja: 15. Daniel, sonne of Water Corby, bapt. 12 June.

Joseph, sonne of John King, bapt. 1° Julij.

James, sonne of Phillip Euerard, bapt. 20 Julij.

Lidia, daught' of Williā Smale, was bapt. 29 September.

Samuel and Robert Griffin, twins, the sons of John Griffin,
bapt. 20 Novemb'.

Elizabeth Parsons, the daughter of Rodolph Parsons, bapt.
30 of November.

Elizabeth, the daughter of William Batsford, bapt. the 25 of
January.

Michael, son of Michael White, bapt. the 15 of March.

An. 1618. Thomasyn, yᵉ daughter of Richard Langfield and Katherin
Jac. 16. his wife, was bapt. May 10.

Sara, daughter of Edward Mare and Mary his wife, bapt.
Aug. 9.

Elizabeth, daughter of Joshua Haggar and Rose his wife,
bapt. Octob' 14.

William, son of Edward Peacock and Elizabeth his wife,
bapt. Novemb' 10.

Richard, son of Richard Samuel and Mary his wife, bapt.
Decemb' 22.

Anna, daughter of Robt. Tydie and Katherine his wife, bapt.
17 of Jan.

Thomas, sonne of John King and Elizabeth his wife, bapt.
23 of february.

Anna, daughter of Edward Jacob and Anna his wife, bapt.
27 febr.

An. 1619. Daniel, yᵉ son of Phillip Everard and Martha his wife, bapt.
Ja. 17. 29 of March.

Thomas, sonne of James Derington and Elizabeth his wife
was baptized yᵉ 15 of Aprill.

Margaret, yᵉ daughter of Robt. Crab and Margaret his wife,
bapt. Aprll.

Mary, yᵉ daughter of John Shipton and Katherin his wife,
bapt.

Willm̄, yᵉ sonne of George Hasley and Elizabeth his wife,
bapt.

Mary, daughter of Rodolph Parsons & Mary his wife, bapt.

William, son of William Smal & Sarah his wife, baptized
Sept.

William, sonne of Nicolas Spark & Thomasyn his wife,
baptiz. ffebr the 20ᵗʰ day. I say yᵉ 20 of febr.

14

1619. Martha, daughter of William Tyler and Agnes his wife, bapt. ffebruary 27. I say ffebr. 27.
Margaret, daughter of John Roberts and [*blank*] his wife, baptized March 12. I say March 12.

[1620] Joan, yᵉ daughter of Philip Everard & Martha his wife, bap-
[Ja. 18] tized May 24.
Elizabeth, daughter of Nathaniel Hewet & Alice his wife, baptized yᵉ 25 of June.
Alice, daughter of Thomas Plat & Elizabeth his wife, bapt. August 28.
ffrancis, son of John Hore & Anne his wife, baptized Octobʳ 3.
ffrancis, son of John Glascock & Mary his wife, bapt. Octobʳ 15.
Andrew, yᵉ son of Andrew Grange & Anne his wife, baptized Novembʳ 1.
Margaret, daughter of Richard Langfyeld & Katherin his wife, bapt. 10 of December.
Dorothey, yᵉ daughter of Richard Samuel & Mary his wife, bapt. decembʳ 27.
Joyce, yᵉ daughter of Robert King & Anne his wife, bapt. Jan. 21.
John, yᵉ sonne of Robert Ruck & Elizabeth his wife, bapt. ffebr. 18.
Margaret, daughter of Rodolph Parsons & Mary his wife, bapt. March 11.

An. dom. 1621. Willm, sonne of Willm Smale & Sarah his wife, bap-
Ja. 19. tized yᵉ second day of Aprill.
Timothy, sonne of Edward Mare & Mary his wife, bapt. Aprill 23.
Mary, yᵉ daughter of John Crab, deceased, & Mary his wife, baptized Aprill 30.
Steven, sonne of Edward Peacock & Elizabeth his wife, baptized May 15.
Sarah, daughter of Willm Bennet and Ann his wife, baptized yᵉ 20 day of June.
ffrancis, sonne of John King and Elizabeth his wife, baptized August 22.
Joseph, son of Edward Harris and Zipporah his wife, bapt. Septembʳ 20.
William, yᵉ son of Robert Crab & Margaret his wife, bapt. Novembʳ 25.
Newland, yᵉ son of Simon Burrell and Jane his wife, bapt. yᵉ 4ᵗʰ day of Decembʳ, 1621.
Samuell, yᵉ son of Robt. Tydie and Katherine his wife, bapt. December yᵉ 9ᵗʰ day.
Mary, yᵉ daughter of Henrie Mallery & ffrances his wife, bapt. yᵉ 17 day of ffebruary.
Phillip, yᵉ son of Phillip Everard & Martha his wife, bapt. ffebr. 24 day.
Stephen, son of John Shipton and Katherine his wife, bapt. March 17, 1621.

·15

An. Dom. 1622.   Henry, ye sonne of Barnabas Peacock and Margaret
regni Jac. 20.   his wife, bapt. April 7th.

Robert, sonne of Thomas Plat & Elizabeth his wife, bapt.
on Easter Tuseday, Aprill 23.

Mary, daughter of Thomas Prentice and Mary his wife,
bapt. May 1 day.

James, the sonne of Thomas Graves, pastour of Cheping
Ongar, and Agnes his wife, baptized ye tenth day of
June, an: dom: 1622, regni Jac. 20.

Katharine, ye daughter of Andrew Grange and Anne his
wife, baptized the same day.

Anne, daughter of John Roberts and Joyce his wife, bapt.
Octob^r 27.

Jane, daughter of Robert Basse and Jone his wife, bapt.
Octob^r 28.

Mary, ye daughter of Robert King and Anne his wife, bapt.
Novemb^r 14th.

Anne, daughter of John Nicolson, Shoemak^r & Elizabeth his
wife, bapt. ye 11 of December.

Matthew, son of Richard Samuel & Mary his wife, baptized
on ye apostle Matthias day ffebr. 24.

Adam, ye son of Robert Ruck and Elizabeth his wife, baptized ye first day of March.

Abigail, ye daughter of Willm̃ Heardman and Martha his
wife, bapt. ye 12 of March.

Anno domini   John, ye son of Rafe Parsons and Mary his wife, bapt.
1623   ye 14th of Aprill.

anno regni   Robert, ye son of Robert Barker and Jone his wife, bapt.
Regis Jacobi   ye 20th of Aprill.

21.   Jonathan, ye son of Philip Everard and Martha his wife
was baptized ye 5 of July, 1623.

Samuel, son of Willm̃. Smal and Sarah his wife, was baptized
ye 31 day of August.

John, the sonne of Avery Lacy & Jane his wife, baptized y^e
seventh of October.

Elizabeth, ye daughter of John Wulpit & Mary his wife,
bapt. 8 of October.

Ellen, ye daughter of Charles Bloomer & Anne his wife,
bapt. 10 of October.

ffrances, ye daughter of Henric Mallery & ffrances his wife,
baptized ye 8 of November.

Thomas, ye sonne of Edward Peacock & Elizabeth his wife,
ye 9th of November bapt.

Martha, daughter of Edward Mare & Mary his wife, bapt. y^e
18 of November.

Katherine, daughter of Robert Basse & Jone his wife, bapt.
ye second of Decemb^r, 1623.

Thomas, ye son of Christopher Beard and Agnes his wife,
bapt. 14 of December.

Millesant, ye daught^r of John Nicolson & Elizabeth his wife,
was bapt. ye sixt day of January.

Elizabeth, daughter of John Keel & Thomasyne his wife,
bapt. ye 17th of January, 1623.

16

1623. Jeffery, yᵉ son of Jeffery Collins, a musitian, & Mary Bales, bapt. yᵉ 1 of ffebruary.

Abigail, yᵉ daughter of John King and Elizabeth his wife, bapt. yᵉ 9ᵗʰ day of March, 1623.

John, yᵉ son of Richard Langfyeld & Katherin his wife, bapt. yᵉ 14ᵗʰ of March.

Anno Domini
1624
anno regni
regis Jacobi 22.

Jane, yᵉ daughter of Simon Burrell & Jane his wife, bapt. yᵉ 25 of March.

George, yᵉ son of Thomas Glascock & Alice his wife, bapt. yᵉ 18ᵗʰ of April, 1624.

Thomas, son of Thomas Prentice, baily, & Mary his wife, bapt. April 25.

Walter, yᵉ son of Robt. Crab & Margaret his wife, bapt. May 17, 1624.

. . . . son of Christofer Whetstone & Elizabeth his wife, bapt. May 23.

. . . . son of Andrew Grange and Anne his wife, bapt. yᵉ 30ᵗʰ of May, 1624.

Andrew, yᵉ son of Michael White and Margaret his wife, bapt. June 13ᵗʰ.

By me Thomas Graves, pastor of Cheping Ongar in Essex.

By me Auery Lacy, John Parker. Churchwardens.

Anno domini
1624
anno regni
Regis Jacobi
22.

Willm̃ yᵉ sonne of Barnabe Peacock & Margaret his wife, bapt. yᵉ fift of September.

Abigail, yᵉ daughter of Thomas Graves, minister of Cheping Ongar, and Agnes his wife, bapt. yᵉ 14ᵗʰ of Septembʳ, 1624.

Jasper, yᵉ son of Jasper Smyth, a smith, & Elizabeth his wife, bapt. yᵉ 24ᵗʰ day of October, 1624.

Jacob, yᵉ sonne of Rafe Parsons and Mary his wife, bapt. Jan. 9ᵗʰ.

ffrancis, yᵉ son of John Shipton & Katherin his wife, bapt. ffebr. 20ᵗʰ.

ffrancis, yᵉ son of ffrancis Derrington & Katherin his wife, bapt. ffebr. 24ᵗʰ.

Anno domini
1625,
Annoq regni
regis Caroli 1°.

Henrie, son of Henrie Mallery & ffrances his wife, bapt. yᵉ 8 day of May.

Jone, yᵉ daughter of Willm̃ Smal and Sarah his wife, bapt. June 26.

Thomas, yᵉ son of Thomas Plat & Elizabeth wife, bapt. Octobʳ 6ᵗʰ.

Jonathan, the son of Jonathan Pope and Mary his wife, bapt. Novembʳ 15ᵗʰ.

Willm̃, yᵉ sonne of Michael White & Margaret his wife, bapt. decembʳ 18ᵗʰ.

Nathan, the sonne of Avery Lacy & Jane his wife, baptized the 14ᵗʰ of ffebruary.

Jone, the daughter of John Sammon and Anne his wife, bapt : ffebr : 26ᵗʰ.

Anno domini
1626,
annoq̨ regis
Caroli 2°.

Mary, the daughter of Richard Samuel, deceased, & Mary his wife, bapt. April 24ᵗʰ.

Jane, yᵉ daughter of Samuel Poulter & Thomasyn his wife, bapt. May 29ᵗʰ.

17   d

1626. Willm̃, y° son of Robt. Barker and Jone his wife, bapt. the second of July.

Mary, yᵉ daughter of John Roberts and Joyce his wife, bapt. July 23, 1626.

John, yᵉ son of Christopher Beard and Agnes his wife, bapt. August 13ᵗʰ.

Willm, the son of Edward Mayor & Mary his wife, bapt. August 14ᵗʰ.

John, yᵉ son of Barnabe Peacock and Margaret his wife, bapt. October 4ᵗʰ.

Abdiel, the son of ffrancis Derington and Katherin his wife, bapt. Decembʳ 18ᵗʰ.

Mercie, the daughter of John Nicolson and Elizabeth his wife, bapt : Jan : 1 day.

Anno domini 1627, annoq regis Caroli 3°.

John, the son of John Sammon and Anne his wife, bapt. the first day of May, 1627.

Jone, yᵉ daughter of Simon Burrel & Jane his wife, bapt. June 5.

John, the sonne of John Anjer & Sarah his wife, bapt. the first of July.

Anne, daughter of Thomas Plat & Elizabeth his wife, bapt. yᵉ second of July.

Anne, the daughter of Robert King and Anne his wife, bapt. the 14ᵗʰ of August, 1627.

Elizabeth, yᵉ daughtʳ of John Parker, wine coup, & Alice his wife, bapt. Aug. 19ᵗʰ.

Edmund, y° son of Edmund Mace & Mary his wife, bapt. Octobʳ 25.

Dorothey, daughter of Thomas Alsop and Elizabeth his wife, bapt. Decembʳ 26.

Mary, the daughter of ffrancis Alsop & Mary his wife, bapt. Jan. 8, 1627.

Sarah, yᵉ daughter of Daniell Stepping and Sarah his wife, bapt. ffebr : 12ᵗʰ.

Sarah, daughter of Henrie Mallery & ffrances his wife, bapt. March 11ᵗʰ.

Elizabeth, daughtʳ of Jonathan Pope and Mary his wife, bapt. March 18ᵗʰ.

Anno Dómini, 1628, annoq. regni regis Caroli 4°.

Willm̃, yᵉ son of Benedict Mathewes & Sarah his wife, bapt : March 31ˢᵗ.

Anne, y° daughtʳ of Nicolas Babb and Anne his wife, bapt. April yᵉ eight day.

Margaret, daughter of Thomas Wennell and Mary his wife, bapt. April 14ᵗʰ.

Hannah, daughter of Rafe Parsons and Mary his wife, bapt. July yᵉ first day.

Margaret, daughter of Michael White & Margaret his wife, bapt. Septembʳ 9ᵗʰ.

Rebecca, daughter of George Wright & Rebecca his wife, was bapt. Octobʳ 21.

Thomas, yᵉ son of ffrancis Derington & Katherin his wife, bapt. Novembʳ 25.

1628. Josiah, son of Christopher Beard and Agnes his wife, was
bapt. ffebr : 5 day.
William, y⁸ sonne of Averie Lacy and Jane his wife, bapt.
ffebr : 11ᵗʰ day.
John, y⁸ sonne of John Pepper and Martha his wife, bapt.
ffebr : 16ᵗʰ.
David, y⁸ son of John Roberts and Joyce his wife, bapt.
March 8 day.
Theophilus, y⁸ son of Thomas Barrison and his wife Tem-
perance, was bapt. March 23.
Margaret, y⁸ daughter of Willm̃ Smal & Sarah his wife, bapt.
March 24ᵗʰ.

Anno domini 1629.   Mary, y⁸ daughter of Anthony Harwood, & Mary
Annoq regni regis   his wife, bapt. April 14ᵗʰ.
Caroli 5⁰.   Anne, y⁸ daughter of Richard King & Anne his
wife, bapt. May 5 day.
Elizabeth, y⁸ daughter of Robert King & Anne his wife,
bapt. May 21.
ffrancis, y⁸ sonne of ffrancis Alsop and Mary his wife, was
bapt. June 2 day.
Theophilus, sonne of Thomas Graves, pastour of Cheping
Ongar, & Agnes his wife, was bapt. y⁸ 8 day of June.
John, the sonne of John Niccolson & Elizabeth his wife,
bapt. y⁸ 16 day of June.
George, y⁸ son of George Penyman and Mary his wife, bapt.
Aug. 16ᵗʰ.
Sarah, y⁸ daughtʳ of John Anjer & Sara his wife, bapt. y⁸
same day.
         By me, Thomas Graves, pastour of Cheping
                  Ongar in Essex.
         Jacob Archer, } Churchwardens.
         Jonathan Pope, }

Anno dom : 1629.   Benjamin, y⁸ son of Barnabas Peacock and Mar-
Annoq regni   garet his wife, bapt. Sept. 21.
regis Caroli 5⁰.   John, y⁸ son of Richard Parnbe and Sarah his wife,
bapt. Sept. 29.
Simon, y⁸ son of Simon Burrell & Jane his wife, was bapt.
October 8 day.
Mary, daughter of Thomas Renalds and Susan his wife, bapt.
Novemb. 17ᵗʰ.
Mary, y⁸ daughter of Robt. Barker and Jane his wife, bapt.
y⁸ 8 day of Decemb.
Mary, y⁸ daughter of Thomas Anjer and Mary his wife, bapt.
Jan. 17ᵗʰ.
William, y⁸ sonne of Thomas Plat & Elizabeth his wife, bapt.
ffebr. 21.
James, y⁸ sonne of James Batsford and Jone his wife, was
bapt. March 9ᵗʰ.

Anno domini, 1630.   Robert, son of Benet Mathewes & Sarah his wife,
Annoq regni regis   bapt. March 30ᵗʰ.
Caroli 6⁰.   ffrancis, son of ffrancis Archer and Mary his wife,
bapt. May y⁸ second day.

1630. Phillip, son of Henric Mallery & ffrances his wife, bapt.
May y⁰ 17ᵗʰ day.

Thomas, sonne of Thomas Wennell and Mary his wife, bapt.
May 31 day.

Matthew, an infant left in y⁰ shambles on Ongar faire day at
night, bapt. Sept. 26.

John, y⁰ sonne of Charles Breach and Elizabeth his wife,
bapt. October 4ᵗʰ.

Jane, the daughter of George Wright & Rebecca his wife,
bapt. Octobᵣ 26.

Elizabeth, y⁰ daughtᵣ of Anthony Harwood and Elizabeth
his wife, bapt. Novembᵣ 9.

John, y⁰ son of Richard Parnbe & Sarah his wife, bapt. Decembᵣ 1.

Sarah, y⁰ daughtᵣ of George Penyman and Mary his wife,
bapt. Jan : 2 day.

Mary, daughtᵣ of Michael White and Margaret his wife, bapt.
ffeb. 15ᵗʰ.

John, sonne of Gregorie Wallis and Mary his wife, bapt.
ffeb : 20.

Willm̃, y⁰ sonne of Jonathan Pope & Mary his wife, bapt.
March 6 day.

Anno domini   John, y⁰ sonne of John Beard and Katherin his wife,
1631.   bapt. April 12.

annoq regni   Jone, y⁰ daughter of Rafe Parsons & Mary his wife,
regis Caroli 7⁰.   bapt. July 17ᵗʰ.

Mary, y⁰ daughter of Robt. Barker and Jone his wife,
bapt. Octobᵣ 18ᵗʰ.

Willm̃, sonne of ffrancis Alsop and Mary his wife, bapt.
Novembᵣ 15ᵗʰ.

Mary, daughter of John Anjer and Sara his wife, bapt.
Novembᵣ 28.

Thomas, sonne of Thomas Anjer and Mary his wife, bapt.
ffebr : 5.

Richard, y⁰ sonne of Richard King & Anne his wife, bap.
ffeb : 20ᵗʰ.

Anno domini   John, y⁰ son of John Niccolson and Elizabeth his wife,
1632.   bapt. Aprill 17ᵗʰ.

annoq regni   Mary, y⁰ daughter of James Hurrell and Mary his wife,
regis Caroli 8⁰.   bapt. Aprill 19 day.

Thomas, y⁰ son of Thomas Renalds and Susan his
wife, bapt. July 10ᵗʰ day.

Thomas, y⁰ son of Jacob Archer and Margaret his wife, bapt.
July 12ᵗʰ day.

Marye, daughter of Anthony Harwood and Elizabeth his
wife, bapt. Aug : 19ᵗʰ.

Elizabeth, daughter of ffrancis Archer and Mary his wife,
bapt.

John, son of Simon Burrell and Jane his wife, bapt. Sept.
13 day.

John, son of John Broun & Margaret his wife, bapt. Octobᵣ 23.

Thomas, son of John Beard and Katherin his wife, bapt.
Novembᵣ the 13 day.

1632. Richard, son of George Penyman and Mary his wife, bapt. Decemb. 2.

Margaret, daughter of Barnabas Peacock and Margaret his wife, bapt. Jan. 8.

John, sonne of Edward Sanford and Anne his wife, bapt. ffebr. the 10th day.

Elizabeth, daughter of Nicolas Northey and Mary his wife, bapt. ffebr. 26 day.

John, son of Thomas Wennell and Mary his wife, bapt. March 10th day.

Anno Domini 1633. Abigail, daughter of Willm Read & Elizabeth his wife, bapt. Apr. 14th.

annoq regni regis Caroli 9°. Margaret, daughter of Willm Small & Sarah his wife, bapt. Aprill 27th day.

Willm, son of Willm Betty & Susan his wife,
Richard, son of Richard Choppin & Elizabeth his wife, } both bapt. May 19th.

Mary, daughter of Christopher Beard & Agnes his wife, bapt. Aug. 18.

Judeth, daughter of ffrancis Alsop and Mary his wife, bapt. Octob. 30.

Anne, daughter of John Sedgewick and Anne his wife, bapt. Novembr 17th.

Mary, daughter of Gregory Wallis and Mary his wife, bapt. Novembr 24th.

Anne, ye daughter of Thomas Anjer and Mary his wife, bapt. Decemb. 9.

Robert, ye sonne of Robert King and Anne his wife, bapt. decemb. 10 day.

Ellen, ye daughter of John Anjer and Sara his wife, bapt. Decem. ye 16.

Margaret, daughter of Henry Mallery and ffrances his wife, bapt. Decembr 22 day.

Thomas, ye son of Thomas Renalds and Susan, bapt. ffebr. 25.

By me, Thomas Graves, parson and pastor of Cheapen Ongar.

Jacob Archer, Willm Stanes, } Churchwardens.

Anno Domini 1634. Robert, son of Robert Stane and Rebecca his wife, bapt. March 30.

annoq regis Caroli 10°. Joshea, son of John Beard and Katherin his wife, bapt. Aprill 1.

Elizabeth, daughter of John Niccolson & Elizabeth his wife, bapt. Aprill 8 day.

Sara, daughter of James Batsford and Jone his wife, bapt. April 17th.

Jone, daughter of Anthony Harwood and Elizabeth his wife, bapt. May 18th.

John, ye son of Willm Tabor and Elizabeth his wife, was bapt. ye 23 day of Decembr.

James, the sonne of Richard King and Anne his wife, bapt. ye 30 of Decemb.

21

1634. Elizabeth, yᵉ daughter of James Stone & Elizabeth his wife,
       bapt. ffebr. 22.
       John, yᵉ son of Jacob Archer and Margaret his wife, bapt.
       March 5.
       William, son of Simon Burrell and Jane ⎫
          his wife,   ⎪ both were bapt.
       Robert, son of Robt. Stane and Rebecca ⎬ March 10ᵗʰ day.
          his wife,   ⎪
       Elizabeth, daughter of Richard Granjer and Jone his wife,
          bapti. March 24ᵗʰ.
Anno Domini   Mary, daughter of George Penyman and Mary his wife,
    1635.   bapt. April 5.
annoꝗ regni   Mary, daughter of ffrancis Archer and Mary his wife,
regis Caroli 11°.   bapt. May 31 day.

Anno 1635.   Julye.

       Jane, the daughter of Richard & Elisabeth Chopping, bab-
          tized Julye the xjᵗʰ.
       Jane, of Mʳ James Darvile. 20ᵗʰ.

                              Septemb.

       Elisabeth, of Rob. & Elisab. White. 29ᵗʰ.

                               Octob.

       George, of Henry & ffrances Mallery, bab. 19ᵗʰ.
       Jane, of Thomas & Mary Osborne. 20ᵗʰ.

                              December.

       John, of Thomas & Mary Anjer. 15ᵗʰ.
       John, of Jôhn & ffortune Nicolls.

                              January.

       Anne, of Edward & Anne Samford, ⎫ ₃ᵈ.
       ffrances, of Robert & Anne Childs, ⎭
       John, of Wᵐ & Elisabeth Read. 12ᵗʰ.

                             ffebruarye.

       Wᵐ, of Wᵐ & Elisabeth Tabor. 9ᵗʰ.
       Daniell, of Mʳ James Sedgwick and Elisabeth his wife.
          22ᵗʰ.

                               March.

       Jane, of Anthonye and Elisabeth Harwood.   12ᵗʰ.
     . Elisabeth, of ffrances & Mary Alsop. 20ᵗʰ.

September.

Ellin, of Thomas & Mary Wennell. 25th.
Rebekah, of Robert & Rebekah Staine. Octob. 2^d.
Alice, of Edward and Alice Parker. Octob. 23.
. Thomas, of John & Sarah Anjer. 16.
Elisabeth, of John & Katherin Beard. 31.
James, of George and Mary Pennyman. [*no date.*]

January.

Mary, of James and Elisabeth Stone. 5th.
Daniell, of James and Elisabeth Darvile. 16.
Daniell, of Daniell and Cordelia Joyner. 19.
  borne Jan. 5, circa hora sextū post mer. diem. Dan :
  Joyner.

Anno 1637. Regis 13⁰.

Aprill.

William, of Richard & Anne Kinge, bapt. Aprill 2^d.
Jacob, of Richard Grainger and Joane his wife, babt.
  Ap. 23.

June.

John, of John & Mary Clark. 11.

August.

Mary, of Nath : & Mary Built. August 21.
Grace, of Robert & Anne Childs. 24.

November.

Thomas, of Thomas and Ellin Wood. 21th.
John, of Richard and Elisabeth Chopping. 26th.
Richard, of Richard and Elisabeth Bora^r, of High Ongar,
 . baptized in o^r parish of Cheping Ongar, Novemb^r 28th.

December.

Robert, of Edward and Alice Parker. 24th.
Joseph, of Jacob and Margarett Archer. 28th.

January.

Josiah, of W^m & Elisabeth Read. 2.
Jane, of Thomas and Mary Angier. 30th.

ffeb :

Anne, of Anthonye Harwood & Elisabeth. 4th.

Anno. 1638.

George, of George & Elisabeth Babbs. June 24ᵗʰ.
William, of Richard & [*blank*] Johnson, of High Ongar,
    babtized in oʳ parish July 7ᵗʰ.
Margarett & Jane, daughters of Andrew & [*blank*] Hawes,
    Citizen of London, babtized in oʳ parish August 5ᵗʰ.

Septemb:

Thomas, of Ralph & Mary Parsons. 27ᵗʰ.
John, of John & Elisabeth Williams. 28ᵗʰ.

Decembʳ.

David, of James & Elisabeth Darvile. 17ᵗʰ.
Elisabeth, of Wᵐ & Elisabeth Tabor. 18ᵗʰ.
Daniell, of Philip & [*blank*] Poole.

January.

Lydia, of Christopher & Lydia Preston. 13.
Margarett, of ffrances & Mary Alsop. 30.

ffeb:

Anne, of Anthonye & Elizabeth Harwood. 19ᵗʰ.
Robert, of Bennett & Mary Tomson. 19ᵗʰ.
Isaac, of Dan : & Cordelia Joyner. 21ᵗʰ.

March.

John, of George & Mary Penÿman. 19ᵗʰ.

Anno Domini
1639.

May.

Martha, of Gregory and Mary Wallis. May 7ᵗʰ.
Sarah, of James & Elisabeth Stone, babtized August 11ᵗʰ.

September.

Judeth, of Christopher & Judeth Glascock, 22ᵗʰ.

October.

Rebekah, of John & Margaret Lavendar, babtized in oʳ
    parish Octob. 8ᵗʰ.
Mary, of John Newton & [*blank*], October 24ᵗʰ.

December.

Robert, of Robert & Rebekah Stanes. 2ᵈ.

January.

Richard, of Richard and Anne Kinge. 19ᵗʰ.

24

ffebruary.

Katherine, of Richard & Elizabeth Choppinge.   4th.
Thomas, of Thomas & Mary Osborne.   11th.
. . . . . of Simon & Jane Burrell.   13th.

March.

Katharine, of Nathaniell & Mary Bilt.   8th.
James (or Joane), of James & Elisabeth Darvile.   9th.
Mary, of Thomas & Mary Wennell.   15th.

Anno domini, 1640.

Thomas, of Richard & Elisabeth Borã, of High Ongar, bapt.
    in o^r Parish, Aprill 7th.
Philip, of Joseph & Anne Lankfield.   26th.

May.

. . . . . of [*blank*] & [*blank*] Burton xth.
. . . . . of Richard & Joane Granger.   13th.
Abraham, of Thomas & Mary Angier.   17th.

September.

Robert, of Robert & Elis. White.   25th.

November.

. . . . . of John & [*blank*] Newton.   1st.
James, of Philip & [*blank*] Poole.   8th.
John, of Robert & Rebekah Stane.   10th.

September (*sic*).

Elisabeth, of Xtopher & Judeth Glascock.   21.

January.

Daniell, of Richard & [*blank*] Johnson.   16th.

ffeb:

Mary } of W^m and Elisabeth Tabor.   3^d.
Anne }

March.

Elisabeth, of James and [*blank*] Batsford.   11th.

Anno dom. 1641.

Thomas, sonne & heir of Edward Sedgwick, gent. & of
    Susanna his wife, baptized the twelfth of Aprill, 1641.
Elisabeth, the daughter of James Sedgwick, gent., & of
    Elizabeth his wife, baptized 7° Maij, 1641.
Anne, of Dan. & Cordelia Joyner.   May 12.

Anno dom. 1641.   June.

Benjamin, of Jacob and Margaret Archer. 9th.
Sarah, of ffrances & Mary Alsop. 22th.

July.

Jane, of James & Elisabeth Darvile. 2^{d}.

August.

Margarett, of Anthony and Elisab^{h} Harwood. 24th.

January Babtized.

Joane, of George & Mary Pennyman. 2^{d}.
Elisabeth, of Richard & [blank] Hutton. 9th.
Ellin, of John and Sarah Angier. 22th.

ffebruary.

Margarett, of Joseph and Anne Lankfield. 27th.

March.

Anne, of Gregory and Mary Wallis. 6th.
Jane, of Thomas and Mary Osborn. 10th.
Mary, of Phillip and Eliz : Batsford. 13th.
Jonas, of Richard and Anne Kinge. 2th.
Jane, of Robert and Elis : White. 23th.
James, of James and Elisabeth Stane. 24th.

Anno Dom. 1642.   March.

Robert, sonne of [blank] Waters and [blank] his wife, lately
  come out of Ireland, babtized March 30th.
George, of George Wood, of ffifield, Tanner, babtized in o^{r}
  parish Aprill 12th.
Robert & } Read, of W^{m} & Elisab. Read, babtized Aprill 24th.
Elisabeth }
Elisabeth, of Thomas and Mary Anger. Aprill 30th.

June.

Robert, of Robert & Rebekah Stane. 27th.

July.

Sarah, of John & Sarah Waylett. 3^{d}.
Susanna, of Edward Sedgwick, gent., & of Susanna his wife
  13th.
Margarett, of Xtoph^{r} and Judeth Glascock. 18th.

26

Anno dom. 1642.   August.

Thomas, of Edward and Anne Samford.   Aug.   ,
Nathaniell, of Nath. & Mary Bilt.   27th.

December.

John, of Gamaliell and [*blank*] Burton.   4th.

January.

Jacob, of Jacob and Margarett Archer.   24th

ffebruary.

ffrances, of John & [*blank*] Clarke.   7th.

Anno Dom. 1643.   March.

George, of Thomas & Mary Wennell.   27th

May.

Sarah, of James & Elisab. Darvile.   5th.

June.

Clemence, of Xtph^r & Judeth Glascock.   20th.

July.

George, of George & Joane Haines.   10th.
Elisabeth, of Edward Sedgwick, gent., & of Susanna his wife,
    Baptized 27th July, 1643.

August.

Clemence, of W^m & Elisabeth Tabor.   27th.
Elisabeth, of Laurence & Kath. Morton.   30th.

Novemb.

Dulcibella, of Anthony & Elisabth Harwood.   14th.
Robert, of Richard & Elisabth Borã, of High Ongar.   21th.

[*The following entries between* 1644 *and* 1659 *are interspersed in various
places in the original.   They are here collected in chronological order.*]

Christopher, of Phillip & Elizabeth Batsford, bapt. June
    16th, 1644.
Henery, of Robert & Elezabeth White, babtized Aug. 18th,
    1644.

Rebecka Aker, daughter of William & Mary Aker, borne
    Aprill ye 9th, 1646.

27

Abigaill, Daughter of Mr George Bound and Abigail his
wife, was borne the 23th day June, Anno Dom. 1647.
John, son of Samuell King and Anna his wife, baptised
July 24 [1647]?
Isaak, of Nath. Bilt, Augst 15th, 1647.
James, of Robert & Elezabeth White, baptized Aug. 18th,
1647.
1647. September. Babtized Ann Lukas [of] Daniell and
Ann his wife.
Mary Aker, dag^h of W^m and Mary Aker, was borne Nouemb^r
ye 20th, 1647.

Horatio, the sonne of Edward Sedgwick, of London, Esquire,
& of Susanna his wife, was borne the fowrth day of July,
& baptized the nynth day of the same month of July,
Anno Dñī, 1648.
John Durentone, sune of John Durringtone, was Borne the
24 of febewari, 1648.

Joane Aker, da. of W^m & Mary Aker, was Borne May ye 4th
day, 1649.
1649. July. Thomas, ye sonne of Rob. Platt & Margarett
his wife, babtized 25th.
1649. Witt. of Nath. Bilt, Jan. 3.
1649. Joyce, ye Daughter of Dorothee Parish, was baptized in y^e
Parish Church of Willingale, Doe Octob. 9, 1649.
Elizabeth, ye Daughter of John King, was baptized 29th of
Novemb.

W^m, of Phillip & Elezabeth Batsford, baptized June 11th,
1650.
Robert, of Robert & Elezabeth Whyte, baptized Jan. 6th,
1650.

Elizabeth Pledger, of Elias & Elisab. Pledger, Julie 1, 1651.
Susanna Ennyver was Babtized the 27th day of December,
1651?
Hannah, of Tim. Major, ffebr. 24, 1651.
Richard, of Nath. Bilt [ffeb.] 25, [1651].

1652. Aprill 11th. Jane Peacock, of Edw. & Jane Peacock.
    „   13. Anne & Francis, of John & Francis Samon.
    1652. Babtized Christian Lukas, the daughter of Daniell &
Ann his [wife], Bab : the 30th of July in ye yeare aforesaid.
Elizabeth, Daughter of Thomas Gouldesburgh and Elizabeth
his wife, was baptized the Twentieth day of October,
1652, and was borne the xxxth of Sept.
                         Tho. Gouldesburgh.

Thomas, of Thomas & Mary Babs, was borne August ye 20th,
1653.

1653. Babtized Elizabeth Lukas, daughter of daniell & Ann his [wife] Bab : in y⁰ latter end of Nouember in y⁰ yeare aforesaid.

Sarah Ennyveer was borne y⁰ 16ᵗʰ day of december, 1653.

Robert Plat, of Thomas & Winnifred Plat, borne May 19, 1654.

Ellen Ward, The daughter of Edward & Mary, Baptised the 6 of July, 1654.

Elizabeth Branwood, the daughter of Jeane (*sic*) & Elizabeth, baptised y⁰ 19 day of July, 1654.

On October the 9ᵗʰ, 1654, Elizabeth Lacey, the daughter of Jonas and Joane, was bourn and baptised.

1654. James Lacy, of Henery & Ruth Lacy, was borne 29 of Nouember.

Aprill the 15ᵗʰ, 1655. Babtized Rebecka Grubb, y⁰ Daughter of John Grubb and Sarrah.

Aprill 17ᵗʰ, 1655. Baptized Joseph, sonne of George Haynes & of Jane his wife.

1655. Joyce Thurgood, the son of ffrancis and Mary his wife, baptized the 20 day of May.

A.D. 1655. Elizabeth Martin, the daughter of Thomas Martin, minister of Chipping Ongar, and Katherine his wife, Born the 17 day of July, and baptised the 17 of August following.

December the 20, 1655. Jonah Lacey, the son of Jonah and Joan, was Baptized.

1656. Babtized Charles Lukas, sonne of daniell & Ann his wife, Bab : in the begininge of Aprill in ye yeare above written.

1656. Francis, y⁰ daughter of Danell & Mary Hull, bapt. y⁰ 29ᵗʰ of Aprill.

„ Marah, of James & Rebecka Clift, baptised y⁰ 7ᵗʰ of May.

John Ennyveer was borne the 11ᵗʰ day of May, 1656.

William Bridges was borne y⁰ 29ᵗʰ of Nouember, 1656.

A.D. 1656. John, y⁰ son of Thomas and Katherine Martin, Born y⁰ 29 day off January, & baptised y⁰ 26 off ffebruary.

Anne Platt, of Thomas & Winnifred Platt, borne Aug. 4ᵗʰ, 1657.

1657. Ruth Lacy, of Henery & Ruth Lacy, borne 18ᵗʰ of August.

Septembʳ y⁰ 16ᵗʰ, 1657. Anne, the Daughter of Thomas Anger and Anne his wife, was baptized.

Elizabeth, daughter of James Batsford and Elizabeth his wife, borne the 27ᵗʰ day of ffebruary, 1657.

William Parkes, the son of Will : and Jone his wife, was baptized March ye 23, 1657-8.

29

Borne Elizabeth Thurgood, daughter of William and Elizabeth Thurgood, the 11th day of June, in the yeare of our Lord God, Anno 1658.

William Ennyveer was borne ye 23 day of June, 1658.

1658. September. Babtized Elizabeth, of Josiah and Ann Beard, the 15 day.

William, sonne of W^m and Hañah Lacey, bab: ffeb: the first day, 1658.

Sarah, daughter of Thomas and Mary Babs, was babtized the 16 of March, 1658.

Elizabeth, daughter of Nickholas and Eliz : Horsnaylle, was borne the second day of May, 1659.

An : Dom : 1659, Babtized William, sonn of W^m & Susan Stane, was Bab : September the 29 day in ye yeare aboves^d.

October ye 6th, 1659. Thomas, Sonne of Thomas Anger & Anne his wife, was baptised.

1659. Sarai, the daughter of ffrancis Warner and Sarai his Wife, born ye Wedensday, December the Seauenth, in the yeare of o^r Lord one Thousand Six hundred fifty Nine.

Sarah, of John & Sarah Bridges, Babtized ffebuary the 26th.

William, of George & Ann Write, Baptized March 11th, 1659.

Josiah, of Josiah and Ann Beard, Baptized March ye 18th, Anno 1659.

Anno 1660. Easter, daughter of Wm Smith & Jone his wife, Aprill the 8th.

Anne, the daughter of Mr Thomas Gouldsburgh, was Babtized the 25th day of Aprill, 1660.

Rebecka Cliffe, daughter of James & Rebecka, babtized July the 20, 1660.

Mary Babs, daughter of Thomas & Mary, babtized August ye 5, 1660.

Israell Lukas, Daug. of Daniell and Ann Lukas, babtized August ye 12.

John Thurowgood, sonne of ffrancis & Mary Thurowgood, bab. Aug : ye 17.

Hannah Lacey, daug^r of W^m and Hannah Lacey, Bab. ye 12 of October.

John, ye sonne of George and Roase Pepper, bab : October 31th.

Edward, sonne of Edward and Marey ffibs, was borne the 20th day of Nouember, and babtized the same day.

John, of James & Mary Kinge, bātized the 28 day of Nouember.

Katherine, daughter of Richard & Jane Choppinge, bab : ye 23th De^r.

January, 1660. John, of Edmunde and Joane Kendall, babtized the 6 day.

Sarah, the Daughter of James Lewis and Joane his wife, was baptised Febru : 12th.

30

1660. Susannah, the Daughter of William Stanes and Susannah
his wife, was baptised Febru : 20th.
Mary, the Daughter of Will : Parkes and Joan his wife, was
baptised March 5th.
Nicholas, the sonn of Nicholas Horsenayle and his wife,
was baptised March 12th.
Sarah, the Daughter of Jeames Batsford and Elizabeth his
wife, was baptised March 14th.
Elizabeth, the Daughter of Robert Chaplin and his wife,
baptised March 11th.

1661.

ffrancis Warner, Sonn of Francis Warner & Sarah his wife,
bapt. July ye 23th, 1661.

Baptized.   An. Dom : 1661.

John ye sonne of Jeffery Throughgood and his wife.
March 26.
Edward, the sonne of Timothy Mayer and his wife.
Aprill 4.
Elizabeth, the Daughter of John Chopping and his wife.
April 15.
Mary, the daughter of Richard Tyler and his wife. May 6.
Francis, the Sonne of Francis Warner and his wife. July 23.
Sarah, the Daughter of Edward Peacock and his wife.
July 26.
William, the sonne of William Godfry and his wife.
Octob : 18.
William, the sonne of William Spranger and his wife.
Octob : 28.
William, the sonne of Edward Ward and his wife.
Decem : 4.
Avery, the sonne of Will : Lacy and his wife. Decem : 26.
Francesse, the Daughter of John Bridges and his wife.
Jan. 19.
John, the Sonne of John Taber and his wife. Jan. 31.
Jeames, the Sonne of Jeames Lewis and his wife. Febr : 4.
Sarah, the Daughter of George Pepper and his wife.
Febr : 21.

Baptized.   1662.

Thomas, the sonne of Thomas Anger and Sarah his wife.
April 1.
John, the sonne of Josias Beard and his wife. April 20.
Margaret & Rebeccah, Twins of William Stone and his
wife. Octob : 8.
Edmund, the sonne of Edmund Kendale and his wife.
Nov : 14.
Robert, the sonne of John Innyver and his wife, Nov : 24.
Virgine, the daughter of Thomas Babs and his wife, Nov :
26.

.31

John, sonne of John & Eliz : Chopping, Decr 28.
Jane, da. of Rich. & Jane Choping, Feb. 20.
Joana, da. of W^m & Joane Parkes, Feb. 10.
Ann, Da. of Jeffery & Ann Thrgood, Feb. 17.

An. dom : 1663.

George, sonn of Edward & Mary Fipps, Mar. 25th.
Mary Wanner, Daughter of Francis Wanner & Sarah his
    wife, bap^t Ap^{ll} the 22th 1663, & borne the first of
    March.
John, sonn of Nictas & Eliz. Horsnaile, Ap. 23.
Margerett, da. of Will : & Eliz. Thurgood, Ap. 29.
Elizabeth, da : of Edward and Mary Ward, babtized May
    the 12th.
Abigayle, of Rebeca & James Clift, May the 20.
Thomas, sonne of Tho : & Margrett Crafts, June ye 8.
Rebecka, Da. of Tim : & An Mayor, July 26.
Robert, sonne of James & Ka : Sigersgill, Aug. 3.
Elizabeth, ye da. of Richard & Priss : Tyler, Aug. 3.
Mary, da. of W^m & Mary Spranger, Octo^r 1.
Elizabeth, da. of Tho : & Penellipe Norington, Nov. 3.
Katherine, of Josias Beard and Ann his wife, 17.
Thomas, the sonne of Thomas Gouldsburgh, Gent., and
    of Elizabeth his wife, was baptized Novem^r the 24th,
    1663.
Rebeckah, the daughter of John and Sarah Bridges, Bab-
    tized March ye 20th, 1663.

Annoq : 1664.

Samuell, the sonne of Samuell and Dorathy Whitheade, bab-
    tized May ye 5^t.
Abygaile, the Daughter of James and Joane Lewis, babtized
    June the 6.
Elizabeth, daughter of George Stokes & Mary his wife, July
    11th.
Lydia, daughter of William Smith & Joaña his wife, July
    24th.
Anne, daughter of Thomas Crofts and Margaret his wife,
    August 28th.
Anne, the daughter of ffrancis Thurgood & Mary his wife,
    September 4th.
Anne, daughter of Thomas Sell & Hellen his wife, October
    30th.
John, of John Carter & Alice his wife, November 27th.
William, of John & Elizabeth Tabor, december 5th.
Katherine, of James & Elizabeth Branwood, Decem : 5th.
John, of William Parks & Joanna his wife, Decem : 15th.
John, of ffrancis & Sarah Warner, January 2^d.
Thomas, of Thomas & Elizabeth Malcott, Jan : 10th.
Sarah, of Thomas & Sarah Anger, January 18th.
Nymphas, of Timothy & Anne Mayor, January 23th.

Elizabeth, of Thomas & Jane fford, ffebruary 13th.
William, of William & Katherine Tabor, ffebruary 14th.
Elizabeth, of Richard & Jane Chopping, ffebruary 28th.
John, of William & Susaña Stanes, March 1º.

Baptized 1665.

Mary, of Edward & Mary Phips, March 27th.
Anne, of John & Sarah Grubb, Aprill 4th.
James, of John & Elizabeth Chopping, May 14th.
Anne, of Thomas & Mary Babs, July 10th.
Mary, of Nicholas & Elizabeth Horsnaile, No^{ber} 2^d.
Jeffry, of Jeffry & Añe Thurgood, Decem^{ber} 8th.
Abigail, of Richard & Priscilla Tyler, Jan. 29th.
Mary, of Henery & Joanna White, ffeb: 5th.
Marget, of Edward & Mary Ward, ffeb: 15th.
Jane, of W^m & Hañah Lacy, ffeb: 27th.

James Crooke, Rector.

John Burrill, } Churchwardens.
William Spranger, }

1666.

John, of James & Rebecca Cliffe, March 28th.
Thomas, of Samuel & Dorothy Whitehead, Aprill 12th.
John, of Thomas & Elizabeth Malcott, Aprill 26th.
Andrew, of ffrancis & Sarah Warner, Aprill 29.
John, of William & Joanna Smith, Aprill 29.
Agnes, of W^m & Elizabeth Thurgood, May 1.
Margaret, of Thomas & Margaret Crofts, May 2.
Elizabeth, of John & Susan Iñivere, June 25.
Mary, of Thomas & Jane fford, July 29th.
Mary, of James & Mary King, August . . .
Susan, of W^m & Susaña ffrancis, 7^{ber} 24th.
Elizabeth, of Lawrence & Winifred Pickerine, January 27th.
Richard, of W^m & Susan Stanes, ffeb. 6th.
John, of W^m & Katherine Tabor, ffeb. 19th.
John, of Edward & Mary Phips. March 12th.
Jane, of John & Elizabeth Chopping. March 24th.

Baptized 1667.

Jonas, of W^m & Hañah Lacy. June 3^d.
William, of Thomas & Mary Babs, June 6th.
William, of Henery & Joaña White, 7^{ber} 24.
Anne, of Thomas & Sarah Anger, 8^{ber} 3.
Jane, of Daniel & Jane Chapman, Janu. 16.
Michael, of Thomas & Margaret Crofts, ffeb. 10.
Thomas, of Thomas & Jane fford, ffeb. 12th.
John, of John & Sarah Lucas, ffeb. 18.
George, of George & Katherin Stanes, ffeb. 25.
Elizabeth, of John & Abigail Boram, March 8th.

f

Baptized 1668.

Mary, of Edward & Mary Ward, Aprill 8th.
Elizabeth, of W[m] & Joaña Smith, Aprill 15th.
Elizabeth, of W[m] & Susaña ffrancis, Aprill 27th.
Elizabeth Anna, of Thomas & Elizabeth Malcott, May 3[d].
William, of John & Elizabeth Chopping, July 13.
Robert, of Robert and Katherine Stains, July 25th.
Mary, of William and Katherine Tabor, August 7th.
James, of James & Rebecca Cliffe, August 26.
Dorothy, of William & Elizabeth Thurgood, Sep. 7th.
Elizabeth, of Henery & Joana White, September 18th.
Dorothy, of Samuel & Dorothy Whitehead, Sep. 29th.
Rebecca, of Edward & Mary Phipps, October 20th.
Hannah, of George & Anne Right, November 9th.
Mary, of William & Joaña Parks, December 3[d].
Ruth, of ffrancis & Sarah Warner, January 1mo.
Mary, of John & Mary Sweetapple, January 15th.
Elizabeth, of James & Elizabeth King, January 26th.

Baptized 1669.

. . . n, of John & Abigail Boram, Aprill 25th.
George, of John & Elizabeth Tabor, June 7th.
William, of Nicholas & Elizabeth Horsnail, September 5th.
William, of Robert & Katherine Stains, September 20th.
Susaña, of Thomas & Sarah Anger, October 6th.
John, of Thomas & Jane fford, October 10th.
George, of George & Jane ffrancis, October 20th.
Daniel, of Daniel & Jane Chapman, Nove[ber] 16th.
Sarah, of Henery & Joaña White, December 14th.
William, of Thomas & Mary Babs, January 4th.
Robert, of James & Rebecca Cliffe, January 5th.
Añe, of Thomas & Margaret Crofts, January 5th.
Thomas, of Thomas & Hellen Sell, January 24th.
John, of John and Anne Waylet, March 1st.
Abigail, of Mr Benjamin Stepping & Abigail his wife, March 8th.
William, of William & Susaña ffrancis, March 13.
James, of Edward & Mary Ward, March 17th.

1670.

James, of Mr Thomas & Mrs Elizabeth Malcott, March 29th.
Thomas, of William & Katherine Tabor, June 15th.
Katherine, of George and Katherine Stains, July 7th.
Elizabeth, of John & Mary Sweetapple, September 21th.
Richard, of Richard & Mary Talcot, September 21th.
October 15th, 70. Margaret & Joane, daughters of Henry & Joane White.
23. Mary, daughter of ffrancis & Sarah Warner.
Ann, of Jeames & Ealizabeth King, January 8th.
Richard, of John & Ealizabeth Choppin, March 5th, 70.

34

1671.

Ann, daughter of Thomas & Susan Chaucke, of Duddinghurst, Aprill 30th, 1671.

Nathaniell, sonn of Benjamin & Abigall Stepping, July 23th, 1671.

John, son of Thomas and Mary Babbs, July ye 31st, 1671.

Eliner, daughter of William and Elizabeth Thurgood, Nouem^r the 7th.

Nathaniell, of Nathñell and Mary Allen his wife, Octo. 26th, 1671.

Elizabeth, Daughter of Thomas & Sarah Anger, Oct. 29th, 1671.

Mary, daughter [of] Edward and Mary Phipps, December 6th, 1671.

Mary, daughter of Thomas and Mary Readmel his wife, Bap: Decemb: ye 18th, 1671.

Robert, Sone of Robert and Katherine Stanes, babtised January 17th, 1671.

Sarah, Daughter [of] John & Elizabeth Choppen, Baptised ffebuary ye 8^d, 1671.

Samuell, Sone [of] William & Sarah Godfrie, Baptised ffeb. 26th, 1671.

George, son of William and Susan Francis, Baptized March ye 6, 1671.

Baptized 1672.

July the 21 Katherine, Daughter of George & Katherine Stanes.

September the 9th, Sarah, the Daughter of John Waylett and Anne his wife.

John, sonn of John and Mary Sweateapple, Baptized October ye 15, 1672.

John, ye son of John and Jaine Anger, Baptized November ye 19.

William, sonne of ffeby Reese, bease born, January the 5.

Roberd, son of John and Elizabeth Taber, January the 16.

Susen, daughter of Benjamin and Abigell Steabing, was baptized febuary 21.

Baptized 1673.

Mary, daughter of John and Elizebeth Choping, was baptized April ye 29th.

Thomas, of Thomas and Mary Redman, May 4.

Elizebeth, daughter of Samuell and Ann King, May 18.

John, ye sonne of Richard & Mary Talcut, was baptized June 25.

Thomas, sone of Nicolas and Elisebeth Horsnaill, was bap. Julie 2.

Elizebeth, daugter of John & Elizebeth Martin, September the 3^d, 1673.

John and Rebeckah, son and daughter of John Lucke and Rebeckah his wife, were Baptized Septem. 1.

Mary, daugter of Georg & Katerine Stanes, baptized Nouember 24.

Henery, son of Henery & Jone White, baptized december 1.

Elizabeth, the daughter of Thomas and Elizabeth Sells, babtized december ye 14.

Daniel, of Daniel & Elizebeth Alsup, baptized 20th of Janv^{ry}, 167¾.

1674.

Edward, son of Mary and Edward Fips, Baptized Aprill 6.
Grace, daugter of John & Elizebeth Wells, May 13th.
Ann, daugter of John and An Wailet, May 24.
Ann, daugter of Benjamin and Abigall Stebing, August 20th.
Mary, daugter of Robert & Mary Hungate, baptised September 16.
Mihill, son of Mihill & Marthe Turner, Baptised September 29.
Katerine, dufter of John & Jane Angier, Baptised Nouember 3th.
Katerine, daf. of William Whitehead and Elisebeth his wife, Nouember 22th.
Decem: 10th, 1674. Baptized Anne, daughter of William Munday & of Anne his wife.
Sarah, of Thomas and Sara Houte, ffebruary 1th, 167$\frac{4}{5}$.

1675.

Richard, of James and Elizebeth King, was Baptized Aprill 5th, 1675.
William, of Daniell & Elizebeth Alsop, Bap. Aprill 20.
Robert, son of Jone Aker, baseborn, Baptized Aprill 22.
Thomas, sonn of Richard & Mary Talcut, Bap. May 6th.
Mathew, of Mathew & Margeret Broun, May 20th.
Elizabeth, of William and Susan Frances, bap. May 22°.
William, y[e] son of Philip Thrayen [Trayherne] & his wife, June 21.
Susanna, daugter of Georg & Katerine Stanes, Sept 26th.
Margarett, the daughter of John Martin and Eliz: his wife, was borne the 23[d], and Baptized the 27 following of the month of September, Anno dñi 1675.
Elizabeth, daughter of M[r] Tho: & Sarah Velley, Baptised November 7th, 1675.
Agatha, daughter of Benjamin & Abigall Stebing, Novemb[r] 20th.
Ann, daughter of John & Ann Wailet, O[br] 28. (?)
Elisebeth, daufter of William & Kathrine Tabour, November 23th.
Thomas, son of John Stanes and Maryon his wife, Bap: dece: 1th.
An, daufter of William Mundey and Ann his wife, Bap: decem: . . .
James, son of Henry and Joane White, was baptized Jan. 23, 167$\frac{4}{5}$.
Thomas, son of Robert and Katherine Stanes, was baptized feb. 2, 167$\frac{4}{5}$.

Baptized A.D. 1676.

Mary, daughter of James and Mary Scambler, was baptized June 19, 1676.
Sarah, daughter of Thomas and Sarah Holt, was baptized July 2[d], 1676.
Thomas, son of Thomas and Elizabeth Sell, was Baptized Aug. 27, 1676.
Benjamin, son of M[r] Benjamin Stebbin and Abigail his wife, was baptized Octob: 19th, 1676.
John, son of Edward Phips and Mary his wife, was baptized Octob: 24, 1676.
Elizabeth, daughter of William Skinner and ffrances his wife, was bapt. decem: 3th, 1676.

36

Martha, daughter of Michael Turner and Martha his wife, was bapt. decem: 24, 1676.

Rowland, son of Philip Trayherne, was baptized decem: 27, 1676.

Elizabeth, the daughter of daniell Allsop and Elizabeth his wife, was baptized Jan: 16, 167$\frac{6}{7}$.

Sarah, daughter of William Smith and Joan his wife, was baptized Feb: 26, 167$\frac{6}{7}$.

Elizabeth, daughter of John Anger and Jane his wife, was baptized Feb: 26, 167$\frac{6}{7}$.

Catherine, daughter of John Choping and Elizabeth his wife, was baptized March 5, 167$\frac{6}{7}$.

Anna, daughter of Henry White and Joan his wife, was baptized March 7th, 176$\frac{6}{7}$.

Sarah, daughter of George Haines and Sarah his wife, was baptized March 11, 167$\frac{6}{7}$.

1677.

Mary, daughter of Richard Sarrett and [blank] his wife, was baptized Apr: 18, 1677.

William, Son of Will. Munday and Anne his wife, was baptized Apr: 18, 1677.

Mary, daughter of Will: Munday and Anne his wife, was baptized Apr: 18, 1677.

Mary, daughter of Daniell Chapman and Jane his wife, was baptized July 9th, 1677.

Martha Haines was baptized July 9th, 1677.

George, Son of Nathanaell Allen and Mary his wife, was baptiz: July 16, 1677.

Thomas, Son of Will: Francis and Susanna his wife, was baptiz: Septem: 7, 1677.

Daniel, Son of John Waylet and Anne his wife, was baptized August 28, 1677.

Martha, daughter of John and Sarah Williamson, was baptized Octob: 15, 1677.

John and William, Sons of John and Susanna Freshwater, were baptized Octob: 23, 1677.

Elizabeth, daughter of Richard Cary and Elizabeth his wife, Jan. 30, 167$\frac{7}{8}$.

Sarah, daughter of Thomas Spicer, was baptized Feb. 5, 167$\frac{7}{8}$.

Robert, Son of Will: and Elizabeth Whitehead, was baptized Feb: 12, 167$\frac{7}{8}$.

Martha, daughter of Will: Smith, was baptized March 10, 167$\frac{7}{8}$.

1678.

Elizabeth, daughter of George Stanes and Katharine his wife, was baptized April the first, 1678.

Samuell, Son of Samuell Eve and Elizabeth his wife, was baptized May 21, 1678.

James, Son of James Scambler and Mary his wife, was baptized June 10th, 1678.

Daniell, Son of John and Ann Wailett, was baptized June 28, 1678.

Sarah, daughter of John Young and Sarah his wife, was baptized July 4th, 1678.

Grace, daughter of Henery White and Alice his wife, was baptiz : July 28, 1678.

Olive, daughter of Philip Traherne and Sarah his wife, was baptiz : Aug : 19, 1678.

Sarah, daughter of Georg Peg and Rebekah his wife, was baptized Sept : 2, 1678.

Judith, daughter of Daniel Alsop, was baptized Octob : 3, 1678.

Marian, daughter of John Stanes and Marian his wife, was baptized Octob : 17, 1678.

Theophilus, Son of Benjamin Stebbing and Abigail his wife, was baptized Octob : 18, 1678.

Sarah, daughter of John Mead and Sarah his wife, was baptized Novem : 5, 1678.

Mary, daughter of George Haines and Sarah his wife, was baptized Novem : 14, 1678.

Elizabeth, daughter of Michael Turner and Martha his wife, was baptized Novem : 17, 1678.

William, Son of James Cornell and Elizabeth his wife, was baptized Novem : 21, 1678.

John, Son of John Anger, was baptized decem : 2, 1678.

Samuell, Son of Samuell Kempton, was baptized decem : 28, 1678.

Elizabeth, daughter of William Munday and Ann his wife, was baptized Jan : 27, 167$\frac{8}{9}$.

John, Son of John Wells, was baptized March 6, 167$\frac{8}{9}$.

William, Son of Edward Phips, was baptized March 17, 167$\frac{8}{9}$.

1679.

Richard, Son of John Chopping, was baptized June 16, 1679.

Joseph, Son of John Williams, was baptized July 1, 1679.

Thomas, Son of William Whitehead, was baptized June [1] 30, 1679.

Elizabeth, daughter of John Waillet, was baptized July 20, 1679.

John, Son of John Roffe, was baptized Sept : the 18, 1679.

Mary, daughter of Richard Cary, was Bapt: Sept : 7th, 1679.

Elizabeth, daughter of Will. Wood and Sarah his wife, was baptized Octob : 26, 1679.

Thomas, Son of George Peg, was baptized Novem : 3, 1679.

William, Son of William and ffrances Skinner, was baptized Jan : 6, 167$\frac{9}{80}$.

Susan, daughter of George Haines, was baptized Jan : 25, 167$\frac{9}{80}$.

Elizabeth, daughter of William Munday, was baptized ffeb : 1, 167$\frac{9}{80}$.

Elizabeth, daughter of John Young, was baptized ffeb : 12, 167$\frac{9}{80}$.

Daniell, Son of Daniell Chapman, was baptized March 3d, 167$\frac{9}{80}$.

1680.

Elizabeth, Daughter of James Cornell & Elizabeth his wife, was baptized May ye 6th, 1680.

Richard, son of Will : Frances, baptized May ye 25th, 1680.

[1] Altered from July to June.

38

Westenn, son of Westenn Norden, was Baptized June 29, 1680.
Mary, Daughter of Daniel Alsop, Baptized July y⁶ 13, 1680.
Katherine, Daughter of Tho : Spiser, Baptized July 18, 1680.
Thomas, the Son of John Anger, was Babtised the 22 day of August.
Katherine, Daughter of Jnᵒ Williamson & Mary his wife, Baptized
    Octobʳ 19ᵗʰ, 1680.
John, Son of John Meade and Sarah his wife, was babtised Desember
    the 11, 1680.

1681.

James, Sonne of Joseph Bedle, Rector, & Elizabeth his wife, was borne
    May the 13ᵗʰ & baptized on Whitsunday, being May the 22ᵗʰ, An :
    1681.
John, Son of James Scambler & Mary his wife, Baptized July y⁶ 4ᵗʰ,
    1681.
Jane, daughter of Will : Smith & Sarah his wife, Baptized July 14, 1681.
Katherine, Daughter of Rich : Cary & Eliz : his wife, Baptized July y⁶
    27, 1681.
Susanna, daughter of Wᵐ Whitehead & Elizabeth his wife, baptized
    August the 18ᵗʰ, An : 1861.
Charles, Sonn of Charles Hawers & Mary his wife, Baptiz : Sepᵗ 5ᵗʰ,
    1681.
Sussanna, Daughter of George Haynes and Sarah his wife, Baptᵈ Septʳ
    11ᵗʰ, 1681.
Eliz., the Daughter of Ben : Stebbing & Abigeiall his wife, baptized
    Septʳ 18, 81.
John, Sonn of James Branwood & Ann his wife, Bapt : Octobʳ 4ᵗʰ, 1681.
John, Sonn of Wᵐ Skiner & ffrancis his wife, Baptᵈ Nouemᵇʳ 3ᵈ, 81.
Thomas, Sonn of Thomas Leuerett & Mary his wife, Baptiz : Nouʳ 14ᵗʰ,
    1681.
Nouember 16ᵗʰ, 1681. Baptized John, Sonn of John Young and Sarah
    his wife.
John, Sonn of Weston Norden & Elizabeth his wife, Baptized Nouemᵇʳ
    17ᵗʰ, 1681.
John, Sonn of Jeffery Till & Sarah his wife, Baptiz : Nouembʳ 19, 1681.
Daniell, Sonn of Daniell Browne and Ann his wife, Bapt. ffebʸ 28ᵗʰ,
    1681.
Jane, Daughter of John Williamson & Mary his wife, Bapt. March 1ˢᵗ,
    168½.

1682.

Elizabeth, Daughter of George Staines & Kathēr his Wife, Bapt. March
    y⁶ 27ᵗʰ, 1682.
Abraham, Son of Abr͠m Griffinhoffe & Martha his wife, Bapt. Apˡˡ 11ᵗʰ,
    1682.
Joseph, Sonn of Joseph Pegrome & Sarah his Wife, Bapt. May 28ᵗʰ,
    1682.
Mary, Daughter of George Guy & Martha his Wife, Bapt. July 9ᵗʰ,
    1682.
Elizabeth, Daughter of William Bridges & Eliz : his Wife, Bapt. August
    y⁶ 14, 1682.

Mary, Daughter of Michall Turner & Mary his wife, Bapt. Octo͏ʳ 2ᵈ, 1682.

W͏ᵐ, the Sonn of W͏ᵐ Whitehead & Elizabeth his Wife, was Bapt͏ᵈ Occtober y͏ᵉ 26͏ᵗʰ, 1682.

Nathaniell, Sonn of Nath : Rachell & Margrett his wife, was baptiz : 9͏ᵗʰ of No͏ᵇʳ, 1682.

Isaac, the Sonn of John Wells and Eliz : his Wife, was bapt. the 23͏ᵗʰ of No͏ᵇʳ, 1682.

Thomas, Sonn of Charles Hauers, was baptized y͏ᵉ 22͏ᵗʰ of January, 1682.

Elizabeth, Daughter of Tho : Spicer and Sarah his Wife, was bapt͏ᵈ y͏ᵉ 30͏ᵗʰ of January, 1682.

ffeb͏ʳ y͏ᵉ Seauenth was Baptized Sarah, the Daughter of Daniell Allsop and Elizabeth his Wife. 1682.

Sarah, the Daughter of Benjamine Stebbing and Abbegeirle (sic) his Wife, was Bapt : ffeb͏ʳ 14͏ᵗʰ, 1682.

Mary, the daughter of George Stoakes, Jun͏ʳ, and Jone his Wife, was Baptized the 26͏ᵗʰ of ffebruary, 1682.

1683.

Richard, the Son of Tho : Leverick, was Baptized March 11, 1683.

Sarah, the Daughter of Will : Munday & Sarah his Wife, was baptized Aprill 1͏ˢᵗ, 1683.

Will : the Son of Henry Bridge & Johannah his Wife, was Baptized Aprill y͏ᵉ 3, 1683.

Sammuell, y͏ᵉ Son of Sam͏ᵘ Brazier & Sarah his Wife, was Baptized Aprill y͏ᵉ 3, 1683.

Joseph, Son of Joseph King and Ann his wife, was Baptised August 23͏ᵗʰ, 1683.

James, y͏ᵉ Son of James Cornell and Elizabeth, was baptised Octo : 29͏ᵗʰ, 1683.

Martha, y͏ᵉ daughter of Abraham Griffinhoofe & Martha his wife, was baptised Nou : the 7, 1683.

Mary, y͏ᵉ daughter of James Brandwood, was baptised dece : the 31, 1683.

Elizabeth, y͏ᵉ daughter of Westin Northen and Elizabeth his Wife, was baptised Jan : the 31, 8¼.

Sarah, y͏ᵉ daughter of Joseph Pegram and Sarah his Wife, was baptised ffeb : the 18, 168¼.

George Stoakes, y͏ᵉ Son of Georg Stoakes & Johannah his Wife, was baptized March 19͏ᵗʰ, 168¼.

1684.

Hannah, y͏ᵉ daughter of Daniell Chapman & Jean his Wife, was baptized y͏ᵉ 26͏ᵗʰ of March, 1684.

Mary, daughter of John Mead & Sary his wife, by me was Baptized Aprill 17͏ᵗʰ, 1684.

Aprill 29͏ᵗʰ, 1684. Baptized Loue White, daughter of Henry White & of Grace his wife.

40

October 6th, 1684. Baptized John, Sonn of John Roaffe & Mary his Wife.

1684. Baptized Elizabeth, da: of Will: & Elizabeth Whitehead. Octo: 26th.

1684. Baptized Hannah, da: of Will: & Jane Porter. No: 10th.

Elizabeth, ye daughter of Abraham Griffinhoof and Martha his wife, was baptized ye 13th of Novemb: 1684.

Sarah, da. of Jeames & Mary ffogg, No: 25th [1684].

Baptized, ye 15 of decem: 1684, Ann Leveritt, daughter of Tho. & of Mary his wife.

19th of Janū, 168⅘. Baptized Ann King, Daughter of Joseph & of Ann his Wife.

Baptiz: John Hauers, ye Sonn of Charles & of Mary his Wife, ye 8 of March, 168⅘.

12th of March, in same yeare, Baptized Elizabeth, daughter of George Stoakes & of Jone his Wife.

1685.

May 17, 1685. Baptized Will: Spicer, sonn of Thomas Spicer & of Sarah his Wife.

July ye 5, 1685. Baptized Ann Emsonn, daughter of Tho: Emsonn & Ann his Wife.

Aug: 2th, 1685. Baptized John Bridges, Sonn of Will: & of Elizabeth his Wife.

August 10th, 1685. Borne a Male Child of Mr Thomas Gouldsburgh.

Sep: 9th, 1685. Baptized William Rowse, Sonn of Simond Rowse and of Elizabeth his Wife.

Susana, da: of Rebekah & George Pegg, Baptized Sep. 24th, 1685, & was Buried 26th of ye same Moneth.

Margery, da: of Mary & Micall Turnner, Baptized Sep. 26th of ye same moneth.

Octo: 4th. Baptized George, the sonn [of] Jane & Jo: Anger.

The 18th. Baptized Sarah, da: of Richard Carie & Mary his wife.

Lidia, da: of Ann & Jeames Branwood, Jan: 6th, 168⅚.

Weston, Sonn of Elizabeth & Weston Norden, ffeb: 18th.

1686.

Jane, da. of Jone & Danniell Cock, Aprill 8th, 1686.

Mary, da. of Sarah & Joseph Pegrum, May 16th.

Tho: sonn of Sarah & Samm̃: Brasier, Baptized June 6th.

George, sonn of Sarah & George Haynes, Junior, July 16th.

Aug: 1th. Baptized John, Sonn of Ann & Joseph King.

Sep: 9th. Baptized John, Sonn of Sarah and John Meade.

Sep: 15th, 1686. Baptized Mary, da. of Martha & Abraham Griffinn-hoofe.

Octo: 4th. Baptized Margrett, da: of Susanna & William ffrancis.

Octo: 7th. Baptized Sammuell, sonn of Sarah & Jeffery Till.

No: 11th. Baptized Thomas, sonn [of] Thomas Holmes & Elizabeth his wife.

Decm̃: 5ᵗʰ. Baptized John, sonn of William Munday & Sarah his wife.
Jañ: 5ᵗʰ, 168⅘. Baptized Dorritie, da. of Auery Lane, Late deceast, &
    of Dorritie his wife.
Baptized 16ᵗʰ, Elizabeth, da : of Tho : Leueritt & of Mary his wife.
Baptized 30ᵗʰ, Elizabeth, da. of George Guy & Martha his wife.
Baptized ffebᵘ: 6ᵗʰ, Jeames, sonn of William Smith & Jone his Late
    wife; this Smith was aboue three score & tenn yeares old when
    this Child was Baptized.
Baptized 7ᵗʰ, Sarah, da : of John Roaffe & Mary his wife.
Baptized March 6ᵗʰ, ffrancis, sonn of Charles Hauers & Mary his Wife.
March 8ᵗʰ, 168⅘, Baptized Ann, da : of George Stoakes and of Jone his
    Wife.
16ᵗʰ. Baptized Phillip, Sonn of Henry Thurgood & Mary his Wife.

1687.

Aprill 3ᵗʰ, 1687. Baptized Anna, da : of Ann Rowden, a seruant, att yᵉ
    Brickt House.
May 4ᵗʰ, 1687. Baptized Mary, da : of Simon Rous & of Elizabeth his
    wife.
Baptized 29ᵗʰ [May, 1687], Mary, da : of Joseph Pegrum & of Sarah
    his wife.
Baptized 30ᵗʰ, John, sonn of Tho : Spicer & of Sarah his wife.
Baptized June 27ᵗʰ, Beniamin, sonn of Danniell Chapman & of Mary
    his wife.
Baptized July 26ᵗʰ, Steward, sonn of William Porter & of Jane his
    wife.
Sep : 4ᵗʰ. Baptized Joseph, sonn of Joseph King & Ann his wife.
The same day Baptized Griffidd, a sonn of yᵉ Widd. Waylett's.
Sep : 5ᵗʰ, Baptized Cordeliah, a daughter of Jeames Cornell's & of
    Elizabeth his wife.
Octo : 24ᵗʰ, 1687. Baptized Elizabeth, da : of George Haynes, Junior,
    & of Sarah his wife.
Baptized No : yᵉ 1, John, sonn of William Whitehead & of Elizabeth his
    wife.
Baptized Jañ 6ᵗʰ, Mary, da : of Elizabeth & Richard Carie.
Baptized 22ᵗʰ, John, sonn of Dennis & John Knight.

1688.

March yᵉ 27, 1688. Baptized Mary, da : of Jeams ffogg & of Mary his
    wife.
May 7ᵗʰ, 1688. Baptized Henry, sonn of Nathanniell Allinn & of Mary
    his wife.
Baptized 10ᵗʰ, Abraham, Sonn of Abraham Griffinhoofe & of Martha
    his wife.
June 19ᵗʰ. Baptized Mary, da : of Henry Benson & of Mary his wife.
July 11ᵗʰ. Baptized Oliue, da : of Ann & ffrancis Sadler.
Aug : yᵉ 12, 1688. Baptized Sarah, da. of Sarah & Will : Munday.
Baptized yᵉ 21. William, sonn of William Porter & of Jane his wife.
Octo : yᵉ 18. Babtized Jane, yᵉ da: of Sarah & John Meade.

42

Octo : yᵉ 22. Baptized Samm̄, sonn of Ann & Joseph King.
Baptized 31ᵗʰ, Danniell, sonn of Jone & of danniell Cock.
The 19 of No : 1688: Baptized Jeames, Sonn of Robert White, Junior, commonly called yᵉ Earle of Corcke, & of Elizabeth his wife, who was Ed. Hills his daug :, shoomaker in this prsh.
Decm̄ yᵉ 23. Baptized Samm̄, sonn of Sammuell Coe & of Mary his wife.
Jannuary 3ᵗʰ, 168⅘. Baptized Rebecka, da : of Elizabeth & Weston Norden.
The 7. Baptized Mary, da. of Elizabeth & William Bridges.
The 6 of March. Baptized Damaris, da. of George Stoakes & of Jone his wife.
The 13. Baptized William, sonn of John Rofe & Mary his wife.

1689.

Aprill yᵉ 1, 1689. Baptized William, sonn of Thomas Leuitt & of Mary his wife.
Aprll 21ᵗʰ, 1689. Baptized William, Sonn of Charles Havers & of Mary his wife.
May 28ᵗʰ, 1689. Baptized William, Sonn of daniel Chapman & of Mary his wife.
June 16ᵗʰ, 1689. Baptized Mary, Daughter of Samuel King & of Anne his wife.
July 8ᵗʰ, 1689. Baptized Sarah, Daughter of John Knight & of Denis his wife.
July 22ᵗʰ, 1689. Baptized ffrancis, Sonn of ffrancis Sadler & of Anne his wife.
July 23ᵗʰ. Baptized Anne, daughter of Richard Cary & of Elizabeth his wife.
August 11ᵗʰ. Baptized Richard, Sonn of John Sanders, Junior, & of Sarah his wife.
Sep : 26ᵗʰ. Baptized Elizabeth, daughter of Thomas Cooper & of Abigaill his wife.
Novem : 12. Baptized George, Sonn of George Guy & of Martha his wife.
Decemb : 1. Baptized Thomas, Son of Thomas ffinch & of dorathy his wife.
Jañ 12ᵗʰ, 1689-90. Baptized William, Sonn of Abraham Griffinhoofe & of Martha his wife.
ffeb. 2ᵗʰ, 1689-90. Baptized Jeffry, Sonn of Jeffry Till & of Sarah his wife.
March 2ᵗʰ, 1689-90. Baptized William, Sonn of James ffog & of Mary his wife.

1690.

April 14ᵗʰ, 1690. Baptized Jane, Daughter of Wiliiam Porter & of Jane his wife.
April 27, 1690. Baptized James, Sonn of Joseph King & of Anne his Wife.

May 19th. Baptized George, Sonn of George Stoakes & of Jone his wife.
June 1th. Baptized Rebekah, the daughter of Weston Norden & of Elizabeth his wife.
June 9, 1690. Baptized John, Son of Mary & Robert Eniver. This Child was baptized by Mr Halceter (?) of Little Lavor.
July 21th. Baptized Thomas, Sonn of Samuel Coe & of Mary his wife.
Septem. 18th. Baptized Philip, Sonn of ffrancis Sadler & of Anne his wife.
Sep. 21th. Baptized Thomas, Sonn of Nathaniel Allinn & of Mary his wife.
Sep. 24th. Baptized Susanna, daughter of Thomas Spicer & of Sarah his wife.
Octobr 5th. Baptized Katerine, Daughter of James Brandwoods & of Anne his wife.
Octobr 12, 1690. Baptized Elizabeth, daughter of James Batsford & of Anne his wife.
Novembr 25th, 1690. Baptized James, Sonn of Daniel Cock & of Jone his wife.
No: 25, quoq. 3. Baptized Elizabeth, daughter of Thomas ffinch & of Dorathy his wife.
Jañ 6th, 1690-91. Baptized Joseph, Sonn of Charles Havers & of Mary his wife.

1691.

April 1th, 1691. Baptized Abigaill, daughter of Richard Stane & of Abigaill his wife.
April 8th. Baptized Susanna, daugh : of Richard Cary & of Elizabeth his wife.
„ 17th. Baptized Sarah, daugh : of William Bridges & of Elizabeth his wife.
„ 26th. Baptized Mary, daughter of Thomas Leverett, alias Levett, & of Mary his wife.
Aprïll 24th. Baptized James, Sonn of John Mead & of Sarah his wife.
May 8th. Baptized Thomas, Sonn of George Stoakes & of Jone his wife.
June 22th, 1691. Baptized Elizabeth, Daughter of William Munday & of Sarah his wife.
Sep. 14th, 1691. Baptized Robert, Son of William Stane & of Mary his wife.
October 4th, 1691. Baptized Katherine, daughter of Elizabeth & Edward Woodhouse.
November the 1. Baptized Richard, a Child of Sarah ffoster's.
Nor 2th. Baptized William, a Child of Sarah Mallery's.
No: 22th. Baptized Richard, Son of Martha & George Guy.
December 3th. Baptized Thomas, Son of Abigail & Thomas Cooper.
Jañ 28th, 1691-2. Baptized Elizabeth, daughter of Dennis & John Knight.
ffebruary 14th. Baptized Richard, a Child of a Traveller.
March 20th. Baptized James, Son of Margrett & Nathaniell Rachell.

1692.

Aprill 12th, 1692. Baptized Elizabeth, daughter of Mary & James ffogg.

May 11, 1692. Baptized Thomas, Son of Thomas Gouldesburgh, Gentleman, & of Elizabeth his Wife.

May 15th. Baptized Jacob, Son of Mary & Charles Havers.

May 25th. Baptized Robert, Son of Elizabeth & Robert White, Junior.

July 26th. Baptized Gabriel, son of Jone & Daniel Cocke.

August 21th. Baptized Elizabeth, da. of Mary & Samuell Coe.

August ye 7th. Baptized Joseph, sonn of James Batsford and Ann his Wiffe, Annoq, Dommine, 1692.

Baptized Thomas, the sonn off William and Janne Poreter, Janneary ye 9th, 1692.

Sarah, the daughter of John Lucas, junior, and of Mary his Wiffe, ffeb : 5, 1692

Richard, ye son of Richard and Abigall Stanes, Baptized March 22^d, 1692.

1693.

John, the son of Joseph and Ann King, Baptized March ye 26, 1693.

Philip, ye sonn of William and Sarah Munday, Baptised May 23, 1693.

Rebecca, ye daughter of Weston & Elizebeth Norden, Bapt. June ye 8.

John, ye sonn of Thomas and Margett Finch, Bapt : June 13, 1693.

Abigall, daughter of Thomas & Abigall Cooper, Bap. Sep. 13, 1693.

Thomas, ye sonn of Thomas and Sarah Spicer, was Bap. Novem : 12, 1693.

Sarah, ye daughter of Thomas and Mary Leveritt, was Bap. Novem : 12, 1693.

Susana, y^o daughter of William and Susana King, was bapt. Decembr̃ 6 day, 93.

Rowlun, ye Sonn of Francis & Anne Sadler, was baptised decembr 7, 1693.

John, ye Sonn of Mr John Camp (Rector of this Parrish) and of Mrs Susanna his Wiffe, was Born ye 11 day of Janeary and Baptised ye same day Anno Dom : 1693.

William, ye Sonn of William Stanes and of Mary his Wiffe, was Baptized february ye 5th, 9¾.

William, ye Sonn of William Bridges and of Elizebeth his Wiffe, was Baptized feb : ye 7th, 169¾.

John, ye Sonn of Ed. Woodhous, and of Elizebeth his Wiffe, was Baptized feb : ye 25, 169¾.

William, ye sonn of William Peacock and of Mary his Wiffe, was baptized March ye 4th, 169¾.

1694.

Thomas, y^o Sonn of Thomas Madewell & of Sarah his Wiffe, was Baptized Aprill ye 2^d, 1694.

John, ye Sonn of Wiliiam Portor and of Jane his Wiffe, was Baptized Aprill ye 17, 1694.

Robert, the Sonn of Mr Thomas Higgs and of Mary his Wiffe, was Baptized Aprill ye 18.

Elizebeth, ye daughter of Philip Trayhern and of Elizebeth his Wiff, was
Baptiz: May ye 1st, 1694.

Elizebeth, Daughter off Philip Treyhern and off Elizebeth his Wiffe, was
Baptized May ye 1, 94.

Elizebeth, Daughter off Robert Clift and off Ann his Wiffe, was baptised
May ye 15, 1694.

William, ye Sonn of William Searl and of Sarah his Wiffe, was Baptized
July 18, 1694.

Sarah, ye Daughter of Charls Havers and of Mary his wiffe, was Bapt.
August ye 27, 1694.

John, ye Sonn of John Lucas and Mary his Wiffe, was baptized Decem.
23, 94.

James, the Sonn of James Batsford (being then Church Clerck) and of
Ann his Wiffe, was Baptised Decembr 23, 1694.

1695.

Edward, the Sonn of James and Ann Trapps, was Bapt: March 25,
1695.

Susanna, the Daughter of Richard Stanes and Abigall his Wiffe, was
Baptized Aprill ye 3^d.

John, ye sonn of Thomas Madewell & of Sarah his Wiffe, was Baptized
Apl. 29, 95.

Mary, ye Daughter of Mr Thomas Higgs and of Mary his Wiffe, was
Baptized May ye 26, 95.

Ollive, Daughter of Francis Sadler and of Ann his wiffe, was Baptized
June ye 17th, 95.

William, ye sonn of William Potter and of Elizebeth his [wife], was baptized June ye 25, 95.

Phillip, the Sonn of Phillipp Trayhern and off Elizebeth his wiffe, was
Baptized August 7, 95.

Mary, ye Daughter of Joseph Pegrum and of Sarah his Wiffe, was baptized Sep: ye 2^d, 95.

Amy, the Daughter of Calebb Baxter, penny Postman, and of Sarah his
wiffe, was Baptized September ye 17th, 95.

James, the sonn of John Knight and of Dennis his Wiffe, was baptized
September ye 22^d, 95.

John, the Sonn of John Saunders and of Sarah his wiffe was baptized
November ye 5th, 95.

James, the Sonn of Mr John Camp, Rector of y^r Parrish, and of M^{rs}
Susannah his wiffe, was Baptized Novemb^r ye 27, 1695.

Margeret, the Daughter of Weston Norden and of Elizebeth his Wiffe,
was Baptized Janneary 24th, 95.

Mary, the Daughter of William Stanes and of Mary his Wiffe, was baptized February ye 9, 95.

John, the Sonn of Thomas Cooper and of Abigall his Wiffe, was Baptized
Feb: 13, 95.

James, the Sonn of Charles Havers and of Mary his Wiffe, was Baptized
Feb: 17, 95.

Thomas, the Sonn of Thomas Read and of Ann his Wiffe, was Baptized
February 21, 95.

John, the Sonn of Samuell Coe, and of Mary his Wiffe, was Baptized
March ye 9th, 95.

1696.

William, y⁰ Sonn of William Bridges and of Elizebeth his Wiffe, was
baptized May y⁰ 10, 1696.
Samuell, the Sonn of Samuell Glascock and of prudence his Wiffe, was
Baptized May the 12ᵗʰ, 96.
Elizebeth, the Daughter of Thomas Forde and of Mary his Wiffe, was
baptized May 17.
James, y⁰ Sonn of Thomas Finch and of Marget his Wiffe, was Baptized
May y⁰ 26.
Mathew, y⁰ Daughter of Thomas Madewell and of Sarah his Wiffe, was
Baptized June 29.
Georg, the Sonn of Georg Stevens (of High Onger) and of Kathcrine his
Wiffe, was Baptized July y⁰ 30.
James, y⁰ Sonn of Georg Coward and of Ann his Wiffe, was Baptized
August y⁰ 2ᵈ.
Mary, the Daughter of John Pagett and of Mary his Wiffe, was Baptized
y⁰ 6 of Obʳ, 1696.
Sarah, the Daughter of Philip Trayhern and of Elizebeth his Wiffe, was
Baptized Obʳ y⁰ 9.
John, the Sonn of Thomas Levirit and of Mary his Wiffe, was Baptized
Obʳ 12.
John, y⁰ son of Joseph Pegrum, was Baptized Noveʳ y⁰ 2ᵈ.
John, y⁰ Sonn of Richard Stanes and Abigall his Wiffe, was Bapt. decem.
ye 8.
Sarah, the Daughter of Joseph Brown & of Olive his Wiffe, was Bapt.
Jann. ye 6.
ffrancis, the Sonn of Frances Sadler and of Ann his Wiffe, was Baptized
Jan : 27.
Edward, the Son of Edward Woodhouse & of Elizebeth his Wiffe, was
Baptized Feb : 21.

1697.

Robert, y⁰ Sonn of Robert Clifft and of Mary his Wiffe, was Bapt : Aprill
y⁰ 4. 1697.
Martha, y⁰ Daughter of Richard Cary and of Elizebeth his Wiffe, was
Baptized Aprill y⁰ 11.
A Child, born in y⁰ barn, baptized by y⁰ name of Elizebeth, y⁰ dau. of
John Smithson & Elizabeth the mother, Aprill y⁰ 7.
Olive, y⁰ Daughter of James Fogg & of Sarah his Wiffe, was Bapt : Aprill
y⁰ 27.
Henery, y⁰ Sonn of William Searll and of Eliz : his Wiffe, was Bap : y⁰
14 of May.
William, y⁰ Sonn of James Batsford, church clerk, and of Ann his Wiffe,
was Bapt : May 24, 97.
Sarah, the Daughter of Robert Stanes and Sarah his Wiffe, was Baptized
y⁰ 20 of June, 97.
William, y⁰ Sonn of Thomas Finch and of Margett his Wiffe, was Born
y⁰ 29 of June, & Baptized y⁰ same day.
Susanna, y⁰ Daughter of Thomas Williams and of Dennis his Wiffe, was
Baptized July 13.

47

John, y° Sonn of M' Thomas Goldesberg and of Susan his Wiffe, was
Bapt. July 26.
James, the son of William Munday & of Rebecka his Wiffe, was Bap.
July 26.
Edward, the Sonn of Samuell Coe and Mary his Wiffe, was baptized y°
8 of August.
Samuell, the Sonn of John Lucas and of Mary his Wiffe, was Baptized
y° 22ᵈ of August.
Edward, y° Sonn of Thomas South and of [blank] his Wiffe, was Bapt.
Sept. 15.
Mary, y° Daughter of John Knight and of Dennis his Wiffe, was Baptized
Sept. 26.
Sarah, the Daughter of Thomas Madewell and of Sarah his Wiffe, was
Baptᵈ Obʳ y° 6, 1697.
William, the Sonn of Philipp Treyhern and of Elizebeth his Wiffe, was
Baptized Obʳ 1.
Sarah, the Daughter of Susan Benten, Base born, Bapt. Obʳ 10.
Rebecka, y° Daughter of goodman Guailen, of Morton, was Baptized at
18 years of age y° 23 of 8bʳ.
Sarah, y° Daughter of John Pagett and of Mary his Wiffe, was Baptized
y° 27 of Obʳ, 1697.
Susanna, the Daughter of Georg Stephens and of Katherine his Wiffe,
was Baptized Novembʳ 7.
John, the Sonn of Samuell Glascock & of Prudence his Wiffe, was Bapt.
Janeʸ 20.
William, the Sonn of Frances Sadler & of Ann his Wiffe, was baptised
Febʷ 1.
Katherine, yᵉ Daughter of William Stanes & of Mary his Wiffe, was bap-
tised Feb. y° 6.
Elizebeth, y° Daughter of William Searl and of Elizebeth his Wiffe, was
bapt. March 9.
Mary, the Daughter of Charles Havers & of Mary his Wiffe, was Bapt.
March y° 19.

Baptized 1698.

Sarah, y° Daughter of John Saunders and of Sarah his Wiffe, was bap-
tized March 28.
Thomas, the Sonn of M' John Camp, Rector, & of Mᵐ Susanna his
Wiffe, was Baptized March 29.
Olive, yᵉ daughter of Joseph Brown and of Olive his wiffe, was Baptized
y° 1 day of May.
Elizebeth, the daughter of Calebb Baxter, Post man, & of Sarah his
Wiffe, was baptized y° 22 of August.
Rowland, y° Sonn of Philip Treyhern and of Elizebeth his Wiffe, was
Baptized y° 11 October.
John, the Son of John Skinner & of Elizebeth his Wiffe, was Bapt:
Ocbʳ 19.
Thomas, Sonn of Thomas Tiler & Mary his Wiffe, was Bapt. Obʳ 1.
(sic.)
Elizebeth, yᵉ daughter of M' Thomas Goldesberg & of Susanna his Wiffe,
was baptiᵈ yᵉ 17 of November.

Robert, y⁰ Sonn of Robert Stanes and of Sarah his wiffe, was Bapt⁴
decem : y⁰ 12.
Susanna, the Daughter of Mʳ Thomas Lacy and of Rebeka his Wiffe,
was Baptized y⁰ 27 decembʳ.
Henery, y⁰ Sonn of Thomas Finch, was Baptized Jan. y⁰ 31.
Thomas, y⁰ Son of Thomas Williames and of Dennis his Wiffe, was Baptized Febʸ 6ᵗʰ.
James, the son of Robert Clifft and of Mary his Wiffe, was Bapt. y⁰ 16
of March.

1699.

Elizebeth, Daughter of Thomas Leveritt and of Mary his Wiffe, was Bap-
tized Apʳ y⁰ 2⁴.
Mary, the Daughter of Tho : Bell and of Mary his Wiffe, was Bapt : y⁰
9 of Aprill.
Mary, the Daughter of Henery White and of Ann his Wiffe, was Baptized
y⁰ 2⁴ of May.
John, y⁰ Sonn of James Fogg & of Mary his Wiffe, was Bapt. y⁰ 11 of
June, 1699.
Samuell, Son of Samuell Glascock & Prudence his Wiffe, was Bapt. y⁰
12 of July.
Joseph, y⁰ Son of William Bridges & of Rebecka his Wiffe, was Baptized
y⁰ 16 of July.
Henery, the son of Charles Havers & of Mary his Wiffe, was Bapt. ye
6 of August.
William, y⁰ Sonn of Thomas Madewell & of Sarah his Wiffe, was Bapt. y⁰
27 of August.
Elizebeth, the Daughter of William Searll and of Elizebeth his Wiffe,
was Bapt⁴ y⁰ fifth day of Sepᵗ, 1699.
Steward, the Son of William Portor and of Jane his Wiffe, was Baptized
y⁰ 4 of Obʳ.
Ann, y⁰ Daughter of Rich : Stanes and Abygall his Wiffe, was Bapt : y⁰
18 of Obᵐ.
John, y⁰ Son of Thomas Higgs and of Mary his Wiffe, was bapt. y⁰ 10
decem :
Prudence, y⁰ Daughter of Samuell Gillett and of Susan his Wiffe, was
Bap. y⁰ 5 of January.
Treyhern, ye Sonn of Joseph Brown and Ollive his Wiffe, was Baptized
y⁰ 13 of Febuary.
Elizebeth, y⁰ Daughter of John Skinner and of Elizebeth his Wiffe, was
Baptized y⁰ 15 of Feb : 1699.
Katherine, y⁰ Daughter of Robert Stanes & of Sarah his Wiffe, was bapt.
y⁰ 18 Feb.
James, the Son of Walter Buchanan and of Mary his Wiffe, was Baptized
Feb. 19, 1699.

1700.

Ann, y⁰ Daughter of Thomas Glascock and of Ann his Wiffe, was Baptized y⁰ 1 of Aprill, 1700.
Charls, y⁰ Sonn of Mʳ Thomas Golsberg and of Mˢ Susan his Wiffe, was
baptized y⁰ 16 Aprill.

• *h*

Philip, the son of James Batsford and of Ann his Wiffe, was Baptized the seventh day of Aprill, one thousand seven hund.⁴ This James Batsford was then Church Clerk.

Aprill 13, 1700. William, the sonn of Philip Trayhern & of Elizebeth his Wiffe, was bapt.

Elizebeth, the Daughter of Thomas Finch and of Marget his Wiffe, was Bapt. Aug. 13.

Ann, the Daughter of William Crampen and of Ann his Wiffe, was bapt⁴ Aug: 28.

[blank], the Daughter of Willi: Haince and of Ann his wiffe, was bap⁴ Aug. 28.

[blank], the Daughᵗ of Thomas Williams & of Dennis his Wiffe, was baptized Noᵇᵗ 24.

John, yᵉ son [of] John Knight & of Dennis his Wiffe, was bapt. yᵉ 24 of Novembᵗ.

Ann, yᵉ Daughter of William Porter and of Jane his Wiffe, was Bapt. yᵉ 6 of December.

William, yᵉ son of Thomas Tabour & of Elizabeth his Wiffe, was Bapt: Decᵗ 30.

Prudence, yᵉ Daughter of Samuell Glascock and of Prudence his Wiffe, was Bapt: Jan. 28.

William, yᵉ son of Ed: Strutt and of Mary his Wiffe, was Bap. Jan. 29.

James, yᵉ son of Thomas Higgs and of Mary his Wiffe, was Bap. Feb. 4.

Mary, the Daughter of Robert Clift and of Mary his Wiffe, was Bapt. March yᵉ 9.

Mary, the Daughter of Henry Spunner and of Mary his Wiffe, was Baptized March 13.

Elizebeth, yᵉ Daughter of Francis Nunney & of Martha his Wiffe, was Baptized March 17.

1701.

Mary, the Daughter of James Penninton and of Mary his Wiffe, was bapt. March 26.

Mary, the Daughter of Thomas Parrish and of Mary his Wiffe, was Bapt⁴ June 28.

John, the Son of John Wennell and of Elizebeth his Wiffe, was Bapt⁴ July 6.

Stanes, the Son of Georg Stevens, of High Onger, and of Katherine his Wiff, was Bapt. July 8.

Prudence, the daughter of John Sanders and of Sarah his Wiffe, was Baptized yᵉ 21 July, 1701.

Joseph, yᵉ Son of Joseph Brown and of Ollive his Wiffe, was baptized yᵉ 30 of Augᵗᵗ.

Elizebeth, yᵉ Daughᵗ of Thom: Sell & of Mary his Wiffe, was Bapt⁴ yᵉ 7 Sepᵗ.

Nathaniel, yᵉ Son of Nathaniel Pawlson & Elizabeth his wife, was baptized Oct. yᵉ 12.

Mary, yᵉ Daughter of William Lacy & Mary his Wife, was baptized Oct. yᵉ 30ᵗʰ.

John, yᵉ son of John Thurgood and of Rachell his Wife, was Bapt. De^{br} ye 8.

John, y son of John Godfry and of Susan his Wiffe, was Bapt. December ye 10.

John, ye son of John Stanes and of Sarah his Wiffe, was Bapt. Decemb^r 17.

Mary, the Daughter of Robert Stanes and of Sarah his Wiffe, was Baptized ye 23 of Febb., 1701.

Johnathan, ye son of Johnathan Hockly and of Mary his Wiffe, was Baptized March 2^d, 1701. ·

1702.

William, ye Son of Willi: Haince and of Ann his Wiffe, was bap^t ye 1 of Aprill.

Martha, Daughter of Thomas Madewell and of Sarah his Wife, was Baptized Ap^l ye 5.

Mary, ye daughter of Walter Buchanan & of Mary his Wife, was baptized April ye 29, 1702.

Edward, Son of James Fog & Mary his Wife, was baptized June ye 8th.

Mary, ye daughter of William Potter & Elizabeth his wife, was baptized June ye 26th.

Mary, ye daughter of James Pennington & Mary his Wife, was baptized June ye 23^d.

John, ye Son of John Ennyver & of Sarah his Wife, was baptized July ye 8th.

Richard, ye Sonn of Mr Thomas Goldesberg & of Susan his Wiffe, was bapt. August ye 26.

John, ye son of Henery White and of Ann his Wiffe, was baptized ye 27 of August.

Maria, ye Daugh^r of Francis Nunny & of Martha his Wiffe, was Baptized Sep^t ye 13.

Witt, ye son of Witt Crampen & of Ann his Wiffe, was Bap^t ye 16 of Sept.

Hannah, ye Daughter of Samuell Glascock and of prudence his Wiffe, was Bapt. Sep^t ye 2^d.

Daniell, ye Son of John Chapman & Susan his Wiffe. Ob^r 11.

Thomas, son of William Stanes & of Mary his Wiffe, was bapt. Ob^r [*n. d.*].

Lydia, Daughter of Nath: Allen & of Lydia his Wiffe, was bap^t Novem : 15.

Judith, Daughter of James Batsford (church clerk) & of Ann his Wiffe, was born ye 5 Novemb^r and bapt. ye 16 of ye same.

Elizebeth, Daughter of Richard Stanes & Abigall his Wiffe, was bapt. Dec^{br} 16th.

Ann, Daughter of Mr Thomas Higgs & of Mary his Wiffe, was Bapt. ye 29 of Decem^{br}.

Thomas, Son of Robart Stanes and of Sarah his Wife, was Bapt. Jan. ye 10.

Francies, the Son of Francies Sadler and of Ann his Wife, was Babtized Jan. 14.

Ann, Daughter of John Skinner and of Elizebeth his Wife, was Bapt⁴
Feb⁻ yᵉ 3.
Robert, Son of Tho : Glascock and of Ann his Wiffe, was Bapᵗ yᵉ 8 of
Feb.
Joseph, son of Joseph Brown and of Ollive his Wiffe, was Bapt. March
yᵉ 15.
Elizebeth, the Daughter of Robert and of Elizebeth Whitehead, Baptized
Feb. 17, 170⅔.

1703.

John, son of Aron Kettle and of Martha his Wiffe, was Bapt. Apr. yᵉ 5,
1703.
Mary, Daughter of Edward Windham & of Elizebeth his Wiffe, baptized
May [n. d.].
James, yᵉ Son of John Wennell & of Elizebeth his Wiffe, was bapt.
May [n.d.].
Henery, yᵉ Son of Thomas Finch and of Marget his Wiffe, was baptized
June yᵉ 9.
Mary, Daughter of William Searll and of Elizebeth his Wiffe, was bapti :
yᵉ 28 of June, 1703.
Richard, yᵉ Son of John Stanes & of Sarah his Wiffe, was bapt. July 25.
Sarah, Daughter of Wiłł. Potter & of Elizebeth his Wiffe, was bapt.
July 29.
Ann, Daughter of John Thurogood and of Rachell his Wiffe, was bapt.
August yᵉ 15.
Mary, Daughter of John Lucas and of Mary his Wiffe, was Bapt. 7ᵇʳ 26.
Elizebeth, Daughter of Robert Clift, was Bapt. Obʳ yᵉ 7, 1703.
Georg, yᵉ Sonn of Walter Buchannan & of Mary his Wiffe, was Baptized
yᵉ 23 of Decembʳ, 1703.
Elizebeth, Daughter of Jonas Haince and of Elizebeth his Wiffe, was
Bapt. January [n. d.], 1703.
Thomas, yᵉ Son of John Knight & of Denness his wiffe, was Bapᵗ yᵉ 30ᵗʰ
Jannuary.
Elizebeth, Daughter of Henery Spooner and of Mary his Wiffe, was
Bapᵗ yᵉ 30 Jannuary.
Sarah, Daughter of Samuell Glascok & Prudence his Wiffe, was Bapt.
January yᵉ 31.

1704.

Ann, Daughter of Thomas Parrish and of Mary his Wiffe, was Bapt⁴
March 27.
Elizebeth, Daughter of Samᵘ Bowtell & of Susan his Wiffe, was Bapᵗ
May 29.
Philip, son of Joseph Brown & of Olive his Wiffe, was Bapᵗ May 3⁴.
Thomas, yᵉ Sonn of Thomas Madewell & of Sarah his wiffe, was Bapt.
yᵉ 9 of July.
Ann, Daughter of John Chapman & of Susan his Wiffe, was Bapᵗ yᵉ 9 of
July.
James, Son of Robert Whitehead and of Elizebeth his Wiffe, was bapt⁴
yᵉ 23 of July.

Elizebeth, Daug^{tr} of John Wennell & of Elizebeth his Wiffe, was Bap^t
Augst 6.
William, Sonn of William Frances & of Mary his Wiffe, was Bapt. Aug^t
ye 17, 1704.
John, Sonn of Mr Jeames Helms and of Mary his Wife, was Baptized
Sep^t 24.
James, ye son of John Andrew and of Mary his Wiffe, was Baptizd Ob^r
ye 27.
Susana, ye Daughter of Will: Russell & of Susan his Wiffe, Bap^t
Nom^{br} 5.
Mary, y^e Daug^h of John Skinner & of Elizebeth his Wiffe, was Bap^t
N^{br} y^e 8.
Mary, y^e Daugh. of Thomas Stanes and of Mary his Wiffe, was Bap^t
Jan : 1, 1704-5.
Jesse, the son of Francis Sadler and of Ann his Wiffe, was Bap^t Jan. y^e
2^d, 170$\frac{4}{5}$.
Sarah, y^e Daugh^{tr} of Richard Frances & off Sarah his Wiffe, was Bapt.
Feb^r 6, 170$\frac{4}{5}$.
John, y^e Sonn of Walter Buchanan & of Mary his Wiffe, was Bap^t y^e 14
Feb^r, 1704.
Thomas, Son of Thomas Glascok & of Ann his Wiffe, was Bap^t y^e 11
March.

1705.

Charles, the Son of John Havers and of Mary his Wife, was Babtised y^e
25 of March, 1705.
Joseph, son of Nathaniell Allen & of Lydia his Wiffe, was Bap^t Ap^{ll} ye
17, 1705.
Katherine, Daughter of William Stanes & of Mary his Wiffe, was Bap^t
May 20.

A REGISTER OF THOSE SAID TO BE BAP. BY Y^E TEACHER OF Y^E SEPARATE CONGREGATION.
1705.

The daughter of John & Hester Say, Dissent^r, born Au: 31th.
Garnet, the Son of Sam : & Eliz : Clark, born 7^{br} 8th.
Ann, the Daughter of John & Mary Phillips, born August ye 22.
Sara, Daug^t of John Phillips, bor. Jan, 10, 17 . . .
William, Son of Walter Buchanan and Mary his wife, Born Jan. y^e 22^d,
1705.
George, Son of Tho : & Eliz : Tabor, was borne y^e 12th of Noveb^r,
1706.
Samuel, Son of Samuel & Elizab : Clark, Born Decemb^r y^e 19, 1706.
David, Son of Walter Buchanan & of Mary his Wife, was B. y^e 6th day
of March, 170$\frac{6}{7}$.
Isaak, Son of Walter Buchanan, was born y^e 12 of Feb. 170$\frac{4}{5}$.
William, Son of Wather Buchanan, was born y^e 6 of March, 170$\frac{3}{4}$.

John, Son of Rob : Clift & Elizebeth his Wife, Baptiz'd July y^e 1st.

William, son of William Waskett & of Susan his Wiffe, was bap^t July y^e 30.

Harrie, Son off William Searll & of Elizebeth his Wiffe, was Bap^{td} August y^e 10.

Thomas, y^e sonn of Thomas Sell & of Mary his Wiffe, was Bap^t ye 15 Ob^r, 1705.

Elizebeth, ye daughter of William Crampion & Ann his Wiffe, was Bap^t ye 25 Ob^r.

Samuell, Sonn of Ed. Strutt and of Mary his Wiffe, was Bapt. ye 26 Ob^r.

Nov : ye 22. Joseph, the Sonn of Sarah Fogg, Widdow.

D^{br} ye 16. Elizebeth, Daug^{tr} of Samuell Glascok and of Prudence his Wiffe, Bap^t.

Joseph, Sonn of Joseph Brown and of Olive his Wiffe, was Bapt^d ye 20 D^{br}.

Dorothy, Daughter of ye Widd^w Woolly, Baptiz'd Jan : ye 20th.

George, Son of Tho : Finch & Mãrget his Wife, Bap : Feb : 3^d.

Sarah, Daughter of John Thurgood & Sarah his wife, Bap : Feb : 5th.

Frances, Daughter of Tho : Rosse and of Mary his Wiffe, was Bap : ye 17.

1706.

Elizebeth, Daughter of James Cary and of Elizebeth his Wiffe, was Bap^d Ap^{ll} ye 2^d.

Lyonell, ye son of James Batsford, church clerk, and of Ann his Wiffe, was Bap^t Ap^{ll} 23.

Isabell, Daughter of Will : Potter and of Elizabeth his Wiffe, was bapt. May 13.

John, ye Son of Daniell Ram and of Katherin his wiffe, was bap^t July ye 6, 1706.

Samuel, Son of Samuel Boutell & Susanna his wife, Baptiz'd August ye 5th, 1706.

Elizebeth, Daughter of Thomas Madwell and of Sarah his wiffe, was baptized ye 10 August, 1706.

Abigail, daughter of John & Elizabeth Ottaway, was Baptiz'd 8bre 30th, 1706.

Elizebeth, Daughter of Henery White & Ann his Wiffe, was bap^t S^{pt} ye 1, 1706.

Francess, Daughter of Edwd Windham & [*blank*] his wife, was Baptized 10^r y^e 15, 1706.

James, Son of James Helms & Mary his wife, was Baptiz'd 10^r y^e 19, 1706.

Mary, Daugh^t of Mr Tho : Binks, Atturny, bap. D^{br} y^e 27, 1706.

Richard, y^e sonn of Edward Strutt and of Mary his wiffe, was bap^d Jany ye 10, 170$\frac{5}{6}$.

Elizebeth, Daughter of William Wasket & Susan his Wiffe, was Bap. Feb : y^e 2^d, 170$\frac{5}{6}$.

Richard, son of John Stanes & Sarah his Wiffe, Bap : Feb : 5th, 170$\frac{5}{6}$.

Richard, son of Richard Francis and Sarah his Wiffe, Bap^t Feb^r 17, 170$\frac{5}{6}$.

Mãrgett, Daugh^r of John Knight & of Denniss his Wiffe, was bap^t Feb^r y^e 23, 170$\frac{5}{6}$.

Mary, Daughter of Samuel Glascock & Prudence his Wife, was Baptiz'd
  March y⁰ 12ᵗʰ, 170⁶⁄₇.

1707.

Robert, sonn of Robert Stanes and of Sarah his Wiffe, was baptizᵈ Apˡˡ
  yᵉ 4, 1707.
Sarah, Daughter of Joseph Brown and of Olive his Wiffe, was Baptiz'd yᵉ
  12 of May, 1707.
Robᵗ, son of Robᵗ Whitehead & of Elizebeth his Wiffe, was Bapᵗ yᵉ 16 of
  Augᵗᵗ, 1707.
John, son of John Havers, was bapᵗ yᵉ 10 of Oᵇʳ, 1707.
Georg, son of Tho : Pegg & of Martha his Wiffe, was bap. Oᵇʳ yᵉ 14,
  1707.
Mary, Daughter of William Russell & of Susan his Wiffe, was bapᵗ Nouᵇʳ
  7, 1707.
John, son of John Ottaway and of Elizebeth his Wiffe, was bapᵗ Decbʳ
  yᵉ 3, 1707.
Elizebeth, Daugᵗ of Edward Windham & of Elizabeth his Wiffe, was
  Bapᵗ Feb. yᵉ 20.
Mary, Daughᵗ of John Thurogood and of Sarah his Wiffe, was Bap.
  March 1.
Mary, Daughᵗ of Michell Perry and of Francis his Wiffe, was Bapᵗ
  March yᵉ 4.

1708.

Thomas, son of Nathanell Allen, was Bapᵗᵈ ye 11 Apˡˡ.
Easter, Daughter of William Searll & of Elizabeth his wiffe, was born yᵉ
  8 day & bapᵗᵈ yᵉ 12 of Apˡˡ, 1708.
Samuell, son of Samuell Glascok and of prudence his Wiffe, was Bapᵗ
  Apˡˡ yᵉ 14, 1708.
James, yᵉ son of James Cary & of Elizebeth his Wiffe, was bapt. yᵉ 26 of
  Apˡˡ, 1708.
Katerine, Daugᵗ of Daniell Ram, bap. yᵉ 27 May, 1708.
John, the Sonn of John Say & Hester his wife, was Baptised the 27 of
  May in yᵉ year of our Lord 1708.
James, yᵉ sonn of Henry White & of Ann his Wiff was Baptiᵈ yᵉ 15
  of Augᵗᵗ.
Abraham, yᵉ son of John Havers & of Mary his Wiffe, was Bapᵗ yᵉ 3ᵈ of
  Oᵇʳ, 1708.
William, son of Jonas Haince and of Elizebeth his wiffe, was Baptized
  29 Nōᵇʳ, 1708.
Hannah, yᵉ Daughter of Mʳ Tho : Binks and of Sarah his Wiffe, was
  Bap. 28 Dᵇʳ, 1708.
Katherine, Daughʳ of Thomas Ross and his Wiffe, was Bapᵗ yᵉ 2ᵈ of
  Jan : 1708.
St[e]phen, yᵉ son of Thomas Finch & of Marget his wiffe, was Bapᵗ yᵉ
  1ˢᵗ of March, 170⁸⁄₉.
Thoˢ, son of William Francis & of Mary his Wiffe, was Bapt. yᵉ 16 of
  March, 170⁸⁄₉.

Susanna, Daughter of John Ottaway & of Elizebeth his Wiffe, was Bapᵗ yᵉ 30 March, 1709.

Mary, Daughter of Rob: Clift & of Elizabeth his Wiffe, was Bapᵗ yᵉ 17 Apˡˡ, 1709.

Mary, yᵉ Daughter of James Helms and of Mary his Wiffe, was bapᵗ yᵉ 15 of May, 1709.

Elizebeth, Daugᵗ of William Clerk & of Dorithy his wiffe, was Bapᵗ June yᵉ 27, 1709.

Elizebeth, Daughter of James Hills & of Elizebeth his Wiffe, was baptᵈ July yᵉ 17.

Philip, son of Joseph Brown & of Olive his Wiffe, who was buried this same day that this Child was baptised, being July 29, 1709.

Richard, yᵉ son of William Stanes & of Mary his wiffe, was Bapᵗ yᵉ 4 of Sᴾᵗ, 1709.

John, yᵉ son of John Thurogood & of Sarah his Wiffe, was Bapᵗ yᵉ 11 of Sᴾᵗ, 1709.

Sarah, Daughter of Richard Ward & of Sarah his Wiffe, was Bapt. yᵉ 2ᵈ of Obʳ, 1709.

Elizebeth, Daughter of John Miller & Ann his Wiffe, bap. Obʳ yᵉ 9, a traviling man.

Thomas, son of Thomas Pegg & of Martha his Wiffe, was Bapᵗ yᵉ 9 of Nᵇʳ, 1709.

Mary, yᵉ Daughter of Mʳ Thomas Binks & of Sarah his Wiffe, was Bapᵗ yᵉ 23 Nᵇʳ, 1709.

William, son of William Crabb & of Elizebᵗ his wiffe, was bapᵗ yᵉ 16 of Dᵇʳ, 1709.

Elizebeth, Daughᵗ of Daniell Ramm & of Katherine his Wiffe, was Bapᵗ March 12, 17⁰⁹/₁₀.

Ann, daughter of James Batsford (church cleark), and of Ann his Wiffe, was Baptized on Easter day, yᵉ 9 of Aprill, 1710.

Mary, yᵉ Daughter of Edward Strutt & of Mary his wiffe, was born yᵉ 7ᵗʰ of May, & Bapᵗ yᵉ same day, 1710.

Alexander, son of Walther Buchanan and of Mary his Wiffe, was Bapᵗ yᵉ 12 of June, 1710.

Ann, the Davghter of John Havos and Mary his Wife, was Bapt. June 26ᵗʰ, 1710.

William, son of Sarah Cary, alias Jolly, was Bapᵗ yᵉ 16 July, 1710.

John, son of William Crampin and of Ann his Wiffe, was Bapᵗ yᵉ 18 July, 1710.

James, yᵉ son of John Wennell and of Elizebeth his Wiffe, was Bapᵗ July 23, 1710.

Prudence, Daughtʳ of Tho. Rosse and his Wiffe, was bap. ye 19 Sᴾᵗ, 1710.

John, yᵉ son of William Searll & of Elizebeth his Wiffe, was bap. Obʳ yᵉ 6, 1710.

Thomas, sonn of Thomas Sanford and of Elizebeth his Wiffe, was Baptᵈ yᵉ 26 Obʳ, 1710.

Thomas, son of Mr Thomas Binks & of Sarah his Wiffe, was Bapt. Nb^r
y^e 23, 1710.
Thomas & Robert, sons of Sam^{ll} Bowtell and Susan his Wiffe, was Bapt.
y^e 4 of D^{br}, 1710.
Ann, Daughter of Joseph Brown and of Ann his Wiffe, was Bap^t Jan. 16,
17$\frac{10}{11}$.
Ann, Daugh : of Henry White and of Ann his Wiffe, was Bap^t Jan. 29.
Robert, sonn of Robert Wrenn and of Ann his Wiffe, was Bap^t y^e 4 of
March, 17$\frac{10}{11}$.

1711.

Georg, sonn of William Shead and of Mary his Wiffe, was Bapt. y^e 2^d of
July, 1711.
John, sonn of Benjamine Ash & of Cordelia his wiffe, was Bap^t y^e 17
July, 1711.
Thomas, ye son of James Cary & of Elizebeth his Wiffe, was Bap^t y^e 24
of Augst, 1711.
Elizebeth, Daugh^r of Willi : King & of Susan his Wiffe, was Bap^t D^{br} y^e
4, 1711.
Georg, son of Mr Thos Binks & of Mary his wiffe, was Bap. D^{br} y^e 7,
1711.
John, y^e son of Joseph Brown & of Ann his Wiffe, was Bap. D^{br} 12.
William, son of Daniell Ramm & of Katherine his Wiffe, was Bap^t y^e 10
of Feb^r, 17$\frac{11}{12}$.
Joseph, son of Walther Buchanan & of Mary his Wiffe, was Bap^t Feb.
y^e 12, 17$\frac{11}{12}$.
John, sonn of William Crabb & of [blank] his wiffe, was Bap^t y^e 24
Feb. 17$\frac{11}{12}$.
William, son of William Clerk & of Dorithy his wife, was Bap^t Feb. y^e
26, 17$\frac{11}{12}$.
Ann, Daugh^r of Robert Wrenn & of Ann his Wiffe, was Bap^t Feb. y^e
28, 17$\frac{11}{12}$.
Elizebeth, Daughter of William Angier and of Elizebeth his wiffe, was
Bap^t y^e 23 March, 17$\frac{11}{12}$.

1712.

Rose, y^e Daughter of Richard Hagger & of Rose his Wiffe, was Bapt.
Ap^{ll} y^e 16, 1712.
John, y^e sonn of Thomas Wiseman and of Ann his Wiffe, was Bapt^d
Aprill y^e 23, 1712.
Thomas, sonn of John Saunders & of Abigall his Wiffe, was Bap^t Ap^{ll} y^e
30, 1712.
Sarah, Daughter of John Till and of Sarah his Wiffe, was Bap^t. ye 25
June, 1712.
Benjamine, son of John Say & of Hester his Wiffe, was Bap^d ye 17 of
Augst in ye year of Our Lord 1712.
Thomas, son of Thomas Sell & of Mary his Wiffe, was Bap^t ye 9 of S^{pt},
1712.
Sarah, Daughter of Mathias Hunt & of Elizebeth his Wiffe, Bap^t Ob^r y^e
12, 1712. Strangers.

Elizebeth, Daughter of John Ottaway & of Elizaᵇ his Wiffe, Bapᵗ Decebʳ
 yᵉ 1ˢᵗ.
Mary, Daughter of James Cary & of Elizabeth his Wiffe, was Bapᵗ Deᵇʳ
yᵉ 7ᵗʰ, 1712.
Benjamine, son of Benjamine Ash & of Cordelia his Wiffe, was Bapᵗ Dbʳ
yᵉ 9, 1712.
Sarah, Daughter of Mʳ Thomas Binks and of Sarah his Wiffe, was Baptiᵈ
Dbʳ yᵉ 30, 1712.
James, yᵉ son of Nathˡˡ Brewer and of Mary Pennington, Widdow, base
born, Bapᵗ Dbʳ 31, 1712.
William, yᵉ Son of Will: Shead & of Mary his Wiffe, Bapᵗ Feb. yᵉ 8,
17$\frac{12}{13}$.
Ann, Daughᵗ of Mʳ William Searll & of Elizebeth his Wiffe, was Bap.
March 9, 17$\frac{12}{13}$.
Mary, Daughter of Josiah Bryan and of Mary his Wiffe, was Bapᵗ March
25, 17$\frac{12}{13}$.

1713.

Dennis, Daughᵗ of Richard Ward & of Sarah his Wiffe, was Bapᵗ
Apˡˡ 19.
Rose, daughʳ of Walther Buchanan & of Mary his Wiffe, Bap. Apˡˡ yᵉ
20, 1713.
John, yᵉ sonn of Job Tucker and of Elizebeth his Wiffe, babᵗ Apˡˡ 27ᵗʰ,
1713.
Joseph, sonn of Samuell Glascok & of prudence his Wiffe, was Bapᵗ
May 12, 1713.
Elizebeth, Daugᵘʳ of James Allen and of Jane his Wiffe, Bapᵗ May yᵉ
17, 1713, this Allen said his habytation was at Ramsie, in Huntin-
tonshire.
William, sonn of William Munday & of Mary his Wiffe, was Bapᵗ June
28, 1713.
Thomas, sonn of William Francis & of Mary his Wiffe, was Bap. Aug.
12, 1713.
Sarah, Daughter of Henery White & of Ann his Wiffe, was Bap. Aug.
19, 1713.
Elizebeth, Daugʰ of Robᵗ Wrenn and of Ann his Wiffe, was Bapᵗ Aug.
yᵉ 26, 1713.
Nathaniell, the sonn of Nath. Allen & of Lydia his wiffe, was Bapᵗ Sᵖʳ
yᵉ 6ᵗʰ, 1713.
Susanna, Daugʳ of John Havers & of Mary his wiffe, was Bapᵗ Sᵖʳ yᵉ 8,
1713.
Martha, Daughʳ of Tho. Pegg & of Martha his Wiffe, was Bapᵗ Obʳ yᵉ 4,
1713.
Ann, Daugʳ of Richard Haggar & of Rose his Wiffe, was Bapᵗ Nobʳ 18,
1713.
Mary, Daughʳ of Ed. Attredg & of Susan his Wiffe, was Bapᵗ Obʳ yᵉ 2ᵈ,
1713.
Jacob, yᵉ sonn of Mʳ Thomas Binks & of Sarah his wiffe, was Bapᵗ Dbʳ
29, 1713.
John, son of John Till and of Sarah his wiffe, was Bapᵗ January yᵉ 5,
17$\frac{13}{14}$.

Joseph, son of Joseph Brown & of Ann his Wiffe, was Bap^t January y^e
5, 17$\frac{11}{14}$.

1714.

Mary, Daugh^r of Williä Clerk & of Dorithy his Wiff, was Bap. Aprill 11,
1714.

Timothy, son of Thiomothy (*sic*) Tode & of Sarah his Wiffe, was Bap. May
y^e 16, 1714.

Elizebeth, Daugh^r of Mr Thomas Sanford & of Elizabeth his Wiffe, was
Bapt. June 10, 1714.

Stafford, son of Richard Hays & of Ann his Wiffe, Bap. June 13,
1714.

John, sonn of Thomas Tabour & of Elizebeth his Wiffe, was Bap^t July y^e
4, 1714.

John, sonn of John Glascok & of Dorithy his wiffe, was Bap. Augt ye 1,
1714.

Richard, sonn of James Cary & of Elizabeth his Wiffe, Bap^t S^{pr} 5,
1714.

John, Sonn of ye Widow Lewis, who liveth in Scotland, was Bap: 10^{br}
25, 1714.

John, Sonn of Thomas and [*blank*] Borst, baptized January ye 30,
1714.

John, Sonn of Williä and Mary Munday, Baptized Jan: 31, 1714.

John, sonn of Edward and Susanna Attaridge, Baptized March 20, 1714.

1715.

Richard, Son of the Widow Hagger, Baptized Aprill 13, 1715.

Abraham, of Thomas and Mary Sell, Baptized June y^o , 1715.

Rebecca, Daugh: of Josiah and Mary Bryon, Bap. July 18, 1715.

William, Son of W^m and Mary King, Aug. 15.

John, of Jo^n and Mary Havers, Bap^d Augt 23, 1715.

Joseph, of Joseph and Ann Brown. Bapt^d Augst 30, 1715.

John, of Walter Niel and Lydia Allen, Bapti: Septem: 4th, 1715.

Ann White, privately Bap. Dec. 17, 1715.

Bartholomew, of Sam. and [*blank*] Glascock, Bap^d Dec. 28, 1715.

John, of John and Elizabeth Ottaway, Baptized Decem. 30, 1715.

Joseph, of Thomas and Olivè Wiseman, January ye 4th, 1715.

Straccy, of Jo^n and Sarah Till, Jan. 23th, 1715.

Dorathy, of John and Dorathy Glascock, Baptized ffeb : 6, 1715.

Ann, of Williä Stone, Ju^n, and Ann, Bap: ffeb: 6.

Edward, of Edward and Martha Georg, Bap: ffeb: 26.

Elizabeth, of Richard and Alice Wood, March 14, 1715.

1716.

John, of Jo^n and Sarah Monday, Ap. 17, 1716.

Rebecca, of Robert and Eliza: Cliff, May 25.

Ann, of Joseph and Ann Brown, June 30th.

Edmund, of Edward and Susan Attridg, July 29th.

Elizabeth, of John and Sarah Traveler,[1] Aug : 14th.
Elizabeth, of Benjamin and Cordelia Ash, Aug. 20th.
Thõ, of Thomas and Abigail Allen, Dec^{br} 2^d.
Elizabeth, of Jo^n and Sarah Till, Jan : 20th, 1716.
Mary, of Philip and Mary Burrel, Jan : 22.

1717.

William, of William and Mary Perry, Ap^l 2^d, 1717.
Mary, of Mr Thomas and Elizabeth Sandford, Ap^l 16, 1717.
Elizabeth, of Joseph and Ann Brown, June 10th.
Olive, of Thomas and Olive Wiseman, July 6.
Josiah, of Josiah and Mary Bryon, Octo^r 1st, 1717.
Mary, of Jo^n and Mary Havers, No^{br} 3^d, 1717.
Godfrey, of Mr Godfrey and Mrs Jane Jones, 10^{br} 1st. The said Godfrey
    was born the 12th of November.
John, of John and Mary Stapeler, Janua : 10, 1717.
Nathanael, of Nathanael and Eliz : Brewer, Ja : 19th.
Edmund, of Jo^n and Sarah Till, Janua : 23, 1717.
Abigail, of Thomas and Abigail Allen, ffeb : 10.
Mary, of W^m and Mary King, ffeb : 23, 1717.
Elizabeth, of Stephen and Mary Bridgman, March ye 7th, 1717.

Batized 1718.

June 28th. John, of William and Mary Shed.
July 21. Elizabeth, of John and Jane Bridges.
August 3^d. John, of Henry and Eliza : Sweeten.
    4th. Richard, of Richard and Alice Wood.
    31. Mary, of W^m and Mary Munday.
Sep^{br} 3. Benjamin, of Jo^n and Eliz : Attawey.
Octo : 26. Thomas, of Jo^n and Dorathy Glascock.
No : 10. Sarah, of Tho : and Olive Wiseman.
    20. John, of Jo^n and Elizabeth Lucas.
March 2^d. Mary, of Benjã : and Cordelia Ash.

Bapt^d. 1719.

April 18th. Mary, of W^m and Mary Perry.
    19. Jacob, of Isaac and Elizã : Saward.
        Mary, of Thos and Abigail Allen.
May 14. Jo^n, of John and Sarah Traveller.
    19. Pearson, Son of Jo^n and Sarah Till.
June 12. Mary, of Tho : and Martha Pegg.
Aug : 2^d, Emm, of Stephen and Mary Bridgman.
Baptized Sep : 20, 1719, Mary, of M^r Jo^n and Mary Clemence.
Nov^{br} 23. Joseph, of Joseph and Ann Brown.
    25. Samuel, of Jo^n and Eliza : Bridges.
Janu : 25. Mary, of Wm Stanes, Ju^r, and Ann.

[1] Travel in some other entries.

ffebru : 7.   Robert, of Robert and Eliz : Porter.
  19th.   Charles, of Nathanael and Eliz : Brewer.
  25.   Joseph, of W^m and Mary King.
March 2^d.   Jane, of Philip and Mary Burrel.

1720.

Ap^l 13th.   John and Amy, of Tho : and Elizabeth Taber.
  20.   Cave, of Cave Knight and Mary Bridges, base borne.
  25th.   John, of Jo^e and Jane Bridges.
May ye 8.   Joⁿ, of Joⁿ and Eliz : Hawkins, trav^r.
  10.   James, of James and Eliz : White, of Norten.
June 29.   John, of Joⁿ and Mary Michal.
Augst 12.   Thomas, of Thomas & Elizabeth Witham, of Blackmore.
  15th.   Mary, of James and Mary Chaplyn.
Sarah, the Daughter of William & Millecent Bayford, was baptiz'd
  August the 31th.
Anne, Daughter of Richard & Anne Bolt, was baptiz'd October the 1st.
Abigail, the Daughter of Thomas & Abigail Allen, was baptiz'd October
  ye 3^d.
Anne, the Daughter of Thomas & Olive Wiseman, was baptiz'd October
  ye 5th.
Thomas, the Son of Samuel & Anne Gillet, was baptiz'd October ye 14th.
William, the Son of John & Sarah Travel, was baptiz'd October ye 24th.
William, the Son of Richard & Alice Wood, was baptiz'd October
  the 30th.
Susanna, the Daughter of James & Elizabeth West, was baptiz'd Nov^r
  ye 23.
John, the Son of John & Sarah Paperill, was baptized Feb^{ry} ye 27th.
Stephen, the Son of Stephen & Mary Bridgman, was bapt. March 5th.
                                                    Godfrey Jones, Rector.

1721.

Anne, the Daughter of Henry & Elizabeth Sweeting, was baptiz'd
  April 30th.
Anne & Charles, the Children of Nathaniel & Elizabeth Brewer, were
  baptiz'd June the 21st.
James, the son of James & Mary Chaplyn, was baptiz'd June ye 26th.
Martha, the Daughter of Isaac & Elizabeth Saward, was bapt. August
  the 16th.
Thomas, the son of John & Elizabeth Bridges, was bapt. September
  ye 4th.
William, the son of John & Mary Mitchell, was bapt. September ye 7th.
Millecent, the Daughter of William & Millecent Bayford, was baptiz'd
  September the 12th.
Sarah, of William & Mary King, was baptiz'd September the 14th.
Joseph, of Joseph & Anne Brown, was baptiz'd October the 5th.
William, of William & Dorothy Clarke, was baptiz'd October ye 16th.
Robert, of William & Anne Stanes, was baptiz'd November ye 1st.
John, the Son of William & Anne Sadler, was baptiz'd Feb^{ry} ye 6th.

Trahearn, the Son of Trahearn & Mary Brown, was baptiz'd March the 2^d.
Alice, ye Daughter of Richard & Alice Wood, was baptiz'd March ye 18th.

Godfrey Jones, Rector.

Baptisms 1722.

Anne, ye Daughter of Barnaby & Mary Eates, was baptiz'd March ye 28.
Elizabeth, the Daughter of Henry & Mary Corney, was baptized April ye 25.
Thomas, of William & Clement Munday, was baptiz'd April ye 29th.
James, of John & Jane Bridges, was baptiz'd May ye 13th, Whitsunday.
James, of James & Mary Chaplin, was baptiz'd May ye 16th.
Elizabeth, of Robert & Elizabeth Porter, was baptiz'd May ye 20th.
Susanna, of Samuel & Anne Gillet, was baptiz'd July ye 31st.
James, of John & Sarah Travel, was baptiz'd August ye 1st.
Edward, of Edward & Elizabeth Gray, was baptiz'd October ye 14th.
Eleanor, of Stephen & Mary Bridgman, was baptiz'd November ye 12th.
Martha, of John & Mary Mitchell, was baptiz'd Jan^{ry} ye 2^d.
Benjamin, of Walter & Mary Buchannon, was baptiz'd Jan^{ry} ye 20th.

Godfrey Jones, Rector.

1723.

Anne, of Benjamin & Cordelia Ash, was baptiz'd April ye 17th.
Mary, of Thomas & Mary Cowper, was baptiz'd April ye 25.
Mary, of Joseph & Anne Brown, was baptiz'd June ye 3^d.
Sprainger, of Henry & Mary Corney, was baptiz'd August ye 8th.
Amy, of Samuel & Anne Gillet, was baptiz'd August ye 9th.
Mary, of Barnaby & Mary Eates, was baptiz'd September the first.
William, of William & Anne Sadler, was baptiz'd October the 15th.
Anne, of Isaac & Elizabeth Saward, was baptiz'd November the 3^d.
Mary, of William & Anne Staines, was baptiz'd Novr ye 5th.
Sarah, of Samuel & Sarah Glascock, was baptiz'd Novr ye 8th.
James, of James & Elizabeth Chaplin, was baptiz'd Jan^{r}y ye 5th.
Elizabeth, of William & Abigal Jasper, was baptiz'd Jan^{r}y ye 7th.
Lettice, of Philip & Mary Burrell, was baptiz'd Feb^{ry} 2^d.
Elizabeth, of William & Elizabeth Angier, was baptiz'd Feb^{ry} ye 9th.
Martha, of John & Elizabeth Ingram (a Traveler), was bapt: Feb^{ry} 16th.
Mary & Nathaniel, of Nathaniel & Elizabeth Brewer, were baptiz'd March the sixth.
Edward, of John & Elizabeth Bridges, was baptiz'd March ye 15th.
John, of Edward & Elizabeth Gray, was baptiz'd March ye 23^d.

1724.

Robert, of Richard & Alice Wood, was baptiz'd April ye 12th, 1724.
Elizabeth, of James & Elizabeth West, was baptiz'd May ye 1st.
Henry, of Henry & Elizabeth Sweeting, was baptiz'd June ye 16th.

62

Elizabeth, of Joseph & Anne Brown, was baptiz'd June ye 29th.
Richard, of Richard & Anne Houtchin, was baptiz'd July ye 17th.
Samuel, of William & Mary King, was baptiz'd August ye 30th.
Richard, of Joseph & Margaret Peate, was baptiz'd September ye 20th.
Richard, of Richard & Hannah Guy, was baptiz'd October ye 23^d.
Jane, of John & Jane Bridges, was baptiz'd Novr ye 1st.
William, of William & Anne Sadler, was baptiz'd December ye 16th.
Anne, of James & Martha Draper, was baptiz'd Jan^{ry} ye 27th.
Olive, of Thomas & Olive Wiseman, was baptiz'd February ye first.
Mary, of Henry & Mary Corney, was baptiz'd February ye 24th.

Godfrey Jones, Rector.

Baptisms 1725.

Elizabeth, of Isaac & Elizabeth Saward, was baptiz'd April 6th.
Elizabeth, of William & Anne Staines, was baptiz'd April the 14th.
Thomas, of Stephen & Mary Bridgman, was baptiz'd July the first.
John, of John & Anne Bettis, was baptiz'd August the fifteenth.
Thomas, the base born son of Mary Colins & George Wadley, the
    reputed Father, was baptiz'd October the 24th.
Elizabeth, of James & Elizabeth Chaplin, was baptiz'd November ye 21st.
Abigail, of William & Abigail Jasper, was baptiz'd November the 24th.
Richard, of John & Sarah Stanes, was baptiz'd December the first.
Anne, of Richard & Anne Houtchin, was baptiz'd December ye eighth.
Joseph, of Joseph & Anne Brown, was baptiz'd Jan^{ry} ye 17th.
Mary, of Henry & Mary Corney, was baptiz'd March the third.
Mary, of James & Elizabeth West, was baptiz'd March the ninth.
Samuel, of Samuel & Anne Gillet, was baptiz'd March the tenth.

Godfrey Jones, Rector.

1726.

Mary, of Edward & Elizabeth Gray, was baptiz'd March 28th.
Dorothy, of Isaac & Elizabeth Saward, was baptiz'd March 29th.
John, of William & Anne Stanes, was baptiz'd April y^o 6th.
John, the base born son of Sarah Curds & John Goldesburgh, the re-
    puted Father, was baptiz'd May the tenth & bury'd the eleveuth
    Day.
Elizabeth, of John & Elizabeth Bridges, was baptiz'd May the twenty-
    fourth.
Elizabeth, of Edward & Mary Fog, was baptiz'd May ye twenty-ninth.
George, of Richard & Alice Wood, was baptiz'd July the third.
Hannah, of Richard & Hannah Guy, was baptiz'd July the 31th.
Sarah, of Samuel & Anne Lucas, was baptiz'd August the 17th.
Mary, of Richard & Elizabeth Gouldesburgh, was baptiz'd August the
    25th.
Mary, of James & Lettice Clift, was baptiz'd October the 13th.
Abigail, of Thomas & Mary Cowper, was baptiz'd October the 17th.
Susanna, of John & Sarah Stanes, was baptiz'd Novr the 9th.
Septame (?), of John & Anne Mitchell, was baptiz'd Novr the 17th.

Mary, of Henry & Elizabeth Sweeting, was baptiz'd Jan'y the 7th.
Anna, of William & Anna Sadler, was baptiz'd March the 15th.

Godfrey Jones, Rector.

1727.

Sarah, of George & Elizabeth Buchannan, was baptiz'd May the 21st.
Anne, of Philip & Mary Burrel, was baptiz'd June the 18th.
Elizabeth, of Richard & Hannah Guy, was baptiz'd September the 10th.
John, of Richard & Anne Houtchin, was baptiz'd September the 17th.
James, of John & Anne Bettis, was baptiz'd September the 23d.
Alexander, of Joseph & Anne Brown, was baptiz'd October the 9th.
Anne, of James & Sarah Turner, was baptiz'd October the 9th.
John, of John & Sarah Stanes, was baptiz'd November the 15th.
Anne, of James & Lettice Clift, was baptiz'd Jan'y the 31st.
Sarah, of Isaac & Elizabeth Saward, was baptiz'd Feb'y the 21st.

1728.

John, of William & Anne Stains,
Thomas, of William & Mary Madewell, } were baptiz'd April the 17th.
James, of Edward & Mary Fogg, was baptiz'd May the 12th.
Cordelia, of Henry & Mary Corney, was baptiz'd May the 22d.
Anne, of John & Anne Mitchell, was baptiz'd June the 22d.
Mary, of William & Abigail Francis, jun', was baptiz'd July the 23d.
Elizabeth, of Edward & Elizabeth Gray, was baptiz'd Sept' ye 18th.
John, of John & Sarah Stanes, was baptiz'd Nov' the 17th.
Sarah, of James & Elizabeth Chaplin, was baptiz'd January the 5th.
Elizabeth, of William & Mary Chifens, was baptiz'd February the 2d.
Sarah, of Samuel & Anne Gillet, was baptiz'd February ye 27th.
James, of John & Anne Bettis, was baptiz'd March the 5th.

Godfrey Jones, Rector.

Baptisms 1729.

Anna-Maria, of William & Mary Nicholls, was baptiz'd April the 1st.
Victory, the son of Thomas & Mary Paveley, was baptiz'd April the 27th.
Edward, of Richard & Anne Houtchin, was baptiz'd May the 4th.
John, of Richard & Alice Wood, was baptiz'd June the 15th.
Olive, of Peter & Mary Spiller, was baptiz'd August the 6th.
Mary, of George & Elizabeth Buchannan, was baptiz'd August the 31st.
Francis, of William & Anne Sadler, was baptiz'd September the 4th.
Benjamin, of John & Elizabeth Bridges, was baptiz'd Sept' the 17th.
James, the son of Sr John Bull, Knight, & of Elizabeth his Lady, was
    baptiz'd the 21st of September.
William, of William & Sarah Harrison, was baptiz'd October the fifth.
Esther, of Joseph & Sarah Allin, was baptiz'd November the twenty-
    eighth.
Mary, of Joseph & Anne Browne, was baptiz'd December the twenty-
    first.

Anne, of John & Anne Bettis, was baptiz'd March the sixth.
Joseph, of Richard & Hannah Guy, was baptiz'd, March the eighth.
Anne, of Edward & Elizabeth Gray, was baptiz'd March the eighth.
Mary, of William & Mary Madewell, was baptiz'd March the Eleventh.
Anne, of Isaac & Elizabeth Saward, was baptiz'd March the twelfth.

Godfrey Jones, Rector.

1730.

Mary, of Stephen & Jane Finch, was baptiz'd June ye Seventeenth.
Elizabeth, of John & Anne Mitchell, was baptiz'd July ye tenth.
William, of Henry & Elizabeth Sweeting, was baptiz'd July ye nineteenth.
Phillis, of James & Lettice Clift, was baptiz'd July the twenty-sixth.
Maria, of Thomas & Mary Paveley, was baptiz'd October the fourteenth.
Susanna, of Richard & Anne Houtchin, was baptiz'd October the twenty-eighth.
Anne, of Samuel & Anne Lucas, was baptiz'd November the twentieth.
Anne, of George & Anne Stephens, was baptiz'd November the twenty-fourth.
Thomas, of Thomas & Anne Clarke, was baptiz'd December the thirteenth.
Richard, of William & Anne Stane, was baptiz'd December the 27th.
Jane, of Joseph & Jane Burrel, was baptiz'd January the tenth.
Thomas, of John & Grace Bourne, was baptiz'd March ye Seventh.
Elizabeth, of James & Elizabeth White (Travellers), was baptiz'd February ye seventeenth.
Sarah, of Thomas & Sarah Wennel, was baptiz'd March the fourteenth.

Godfrey Jones, Rector.

1731.

Susanna, of John & Elizabeth Bridges, was baptiz'd May the 13th.
John, of John & Mary Knight, was baptiz'd May the 30th.
Robert, of Robert and Elizabeth Staines, was baptiz'd Augst 29th.
John, of William & Mary King, was baptiz'd September the fifth.
Mary, of Peter & Mary Spiller, was baptiz'd September the twelfth.
Susannah, of Nathaniel & Elizabeth Brewer, was baptiz'd October the 3^d.
Susannah, of Isaac & Elizabeth Saward, was baptiz'd October the 15th.
Anne, of William & Sarah Harrison, & } were baptiz'd October the 29th.
Robert, of Christopher & Mary Moore, }
John, of James & Elizabeth Chaplin, was baptiz'd October the 31st.
John, of John & Olive Ramsay, was baptiz'd November the 3^d.
Francis, of Francis & Jane Laurence, was baptiz'd November the 17th.
Sarah, of William & Sarah Thurgood, was baptiz'd November the 25th.
Sarah, of John & Sarah Stane, was baptiz'd December the 1st.
Anne, of John & Anne Bettis, was baptiz'd December the 19th.
Mary, of Richard & Hannah Guy, was baptiz'd Jan^{ry} ye 12th.
Joseph, of Joseph & Sarah Allin, was baptiz'd Feb^{ry} the 12th.
John, of James & Lettice Clift, was baptiz'd Feb^{ry} the 23^d.
William, of John & Grace Bourne, was baptiz'd March the 12th.

Godfrey Jones, Rector.

k

Baptisms 1732.

Sarah, of Edward & Mary Fog, was baptiz'd March the 26th.
James, of John & Anne Mitchel, was baptiz'd April the 19th.
Susannah, of James & Sarah Turner, was baptiz'd June the 16th.
Anne, of George & Anne Stevens, was baptiz'd July the 5th.
Mary & William, of William & Mary Little, were baptiz'd July the 31st.
Anne, of Thomas & Anne Clarke, was baptiz'd September the 24th.
Mary, of Thomas & Sarah Wennel, was baptiz'd October the 1st.
Kitty, of Sr John Bull, Knight, & of Dame Elizabeth his Wife, was baptiz'd October the fifth.
Seppy, of John & Sarah Stane, was baptiz'd November the twenty-second.
Martha, of Edward & Elizabeth Gray, was baptiz'd November the twenty-sixth.
William, of William & Martha Sheed, was baptiz'd Jan'y the seventeenth.
Sarah, of Isaac & Elizabeth Saward, was baptiz'd Jan'y the twenty-fourth.
Thomas, the reputed son of Thomas Smith & Mary Bunnell, was baptiz'd January the twenty-eighth.
Sarah, of Richard & Mary Stane, was baptiz'd Feb'y ye thirteenth.

Godfrey Jones, Rector.

1733.

William, of William & Sarah Thurgood, was baptiz'd March the 26th.
Elizabeth, of Joseph & Jane Burrell, was baptiz'd May the 6th.
Grace, of John & Grace Bourne, was baptiz'd May the 14th.
Thomas, of Richard & Anne Houtchin, was baptiz'd June the 20th.
Elizabeth, of Richard & Alice Wood, was baptiz'd July the 11th.
Elizabeth, Daughter of William & Martha Jasper, was baptised Aug. 10th, 1733.
Anne, Daughter of Edward & Mary Fog, was baptised Aug. 26, 1733.
James, the son of William Harris & Sarah his Wife, was baptised Sepr 23, 1733.
Lionel King, the son of William King & Mary his Wife. [no date.]
George, the Son of John Beety & Ann his wife, was baptised Octobr 28, 1733.
Sarah, the Daughter of Stephen Finch & Jane his wife, was baptised Nov. 16, 1733.
Mary, the Daughter of Trahern Brown & Mary his Wife, was baptised Jan. 9th, 1733.
Anna Maria, Daughter of Peter & Mary Speller, was baptised Jan. 2d, 1733.
Susanna Finch, ye Daughter of George Finch & Susanna his Wife, was baptised Jan. 11, 1733.
Anne Bernard, alias Mole, was Baptised Jan. 14, 1733.
Richard, ye son of Richard & Mary Stane, was baptised Jan. 30, 1733-4.
William Lawrence, the son of Francis & Jane Lawrence, was Baptised Feb. 24, 173¾.

66

John _(sic)_
William, ye Son of William King & Mary his Wife, was Baptised Mar. 8,
   173⅔.
                                  Thomas Velley, Rector.

1734.

Elizabeth, Daughter of Robert Stane & Elizabeth his Wife, was baptised
   April 3^d, 1734.
Sarah, the Daughter of William & Sarah Thurgood, was baptised April 17,
   1734.
John, ye Son of John Thorogood & Mary his Wife, was baptised April 24,
   1734.
James Clift, Son of James Clift & Lettice his Wife, was baptised May 24,
   1734.
Ann, Daughter of William Shead & Elizabeth his Wife, was baptised
   June 1st, 1734.
William, Son of William Madewell & Mary his Wife, was baptised
   Aug. 18th, 1734.
William, Son of John Stane & Sarah his Wife, was baptised Sept^r [blank]
   1734.
Anne Searle, Daughter of Harry Searle & Anne his Wife, was baptised ✓
   Sep^tr 6th, 1734.
George, son of George Stephens & Ann his wife, was baptised Sep^tr 25th,
   1734.
Ann, Daughter of Samuel & Ann Gillet, was baptised Novr 7th, 1734.
Elizabeth, Daughter of Thomas & Ann Clark, was baptised Novr 19th.
Samuel Kent, the son of Samuel Kent & Ann his Wife, was baptised
   Nov^r [blank]
Joseph, the Son of Joseph Burrell & Mary his Wife, was baptised Mar.
   2^d, 1734.

1735.

George Dore, the Son of Mr Luke Dore & Ann his Wife, was baptised
   Apr : 6th, 1735.
Sarah, ye Daughter of Edward Fog & Mary his Wife, was baptised April
   6th, 1734.
Mary, ye Daughter of William Wasket & Mary his Wife, was baptised
   April 13th, 1735.
George, the son of Richard Stane & [blank] his Wife, was baptised April
   [blank] 1735.
William Thurgood, Adult aged 25 years, was baptised June 1st, 1735.
Susannah Munday, base born Child, was baptised June 18th, 1735.
Mary Thurgood, the Daughter of John Thurgood & Mary his Wife, was
   baptised June 18, 1735.
Robert Young, Son of Robert Young & Mary his Wife, was baptised
   July 1st, 1735.
Mary, the Daughter of James & Elizabeth Chapman his Wife, was bap-
   tised Aug. 18th, 1735.
Stephen & Anne, ye Son & Daughter of Stephen Finch & Jane his Wife,
   were baptised Octob^r 18th, 1735.

Ann, the daughter of Ann Brown, Widow, was baptised Dec' 24th, 1735.

Peter Speller, the Son of Peter Speller & Mary his Wife, was baptised Jan: 4th, 1735.

Austin Stane, the Son of Robert & Elizabeth Stane, was baptised Feb: 4th, 1735.

William Thurgood, the Son of William Thurgood & Sarah his wife, was baptised Feb: 13th, 1735.

Mary, the Daughter of John Stane & Sarah his wife, was baptised Mar: 10th, 1735.

Baptisms 1736.

Robert Searle, the Son of Harry Searle & Anne his Wife, was baptised Mar: 28th, 1736.

Joseph, the Son of Joseph Allen & Sarah his Wife, was baptised April [*blank*], 1736.

Mary, the Daughter of Richard Stane & Mary his wife, was baptised Apr: 7th, 1736.

Sarah, the Daughter of Will: & Mary Little his Wife, was baptised April 21, 1736.

James, the Son of James & Susannah Wennel his Wife, was baptised June 20th, 1736.

Magnus, the Son of Thomas Wennell & Mary his Wife, was baptised Sep^{cr} 12th, 1736.

Wi . . . . . . Bornes, the [*blank*] of John Bornes & [*blank*] his Wife, was baptised Sept^r [*blank*] 1736.

Mary Mitchel, the Daught: of John Mitchel & Anne his Wife, was baptised [*blank*] 1736.

Sarah, the Daughter of Samuel Kent & Elizabeth his Wife, was baptised Novr 21st, 1736.

Stane, the Son of Richard Houchen & Anne his Wife, was baptised Feb: 10th, 1736.

Robert, the Son of John Thorogood, Junr, & Mary his Wife, was baptised Feb: 25th, 1736.

Susannah, ye Daughter of [*blank*] Monson & his Wife, was baptised Mar: 6th, 1736.

Anne, ye Daughter of Richard Frances & Anne his Wife, was baptised March [*blank*] 1736.

Thomas Velley, Rector.

Baptisms 1737.

Richard White, alias Crabb, was baptised April [*blank*] 1737, ye base born Son of Ann Crabb.

Olive, the Daughter of Edward Fogg & Mary his Wife, was baptised May 15th, 1737.

Alice, the Daughter of Richard Stane & Mary his Wife, was baptised July 13th, 1737.

Mary, Daughter of Jos: Burrell & Jane his Wife, was baptised July 17th, 1737.

Margaret, the Daughter of Thomas Fox & [*blank*] his Wife, was baptised
Aug. 3, 1737.

John, the Son of Richard Guy & Hannah his Wife, was baptised Aug:
24, 1737.

Samuel, the Son of [*blank*] Dellower & [*blank*] his Wife, was baptised
Oct. 20th, 1737.

Philip, the Son of Will: Thorogood & Sarah his Wife, was baptised Oct.
12th, 1737.

Ann, Daughter of Thomas Wheeler & Mary his Wife, was baptised Novr
30th, 1737.

Anne, Daughter of Will : Littel & Mary his Wife, was baptised Decr 14th,
1737.

Katherine, Daughter of Robrt Stane & Elizabeth his Wife, was baptised
Jan7 [*blank*] 1737.

Mary, the Daughter of William Madewell & Mary his Wife, was baptised
Feb : 19th, 1737.

Frances Bornes, the Daughter of John & Grace his Wife, Baptised Mar.
12th, 1737.

Baptisms 1738.

Rawlins, the Son of Rawlins Herne & Elizabeth his Wife, was baptised
April 12th, 1738.

William, the Bastard Son of Samuel Nichols & Sarah his Servant, was
baptised Ap: 30, 1738.

Esther, the Daughter of Stephen Finch & Jane his Wife, was baptised
May 3d, 1738.

Anne, ye Daughter of Harry Searle & Ann his Wife, was baptised Aug.
6th, 1738.

Mary, the Daughter of William Shed & Mary his Wife, was baptised
Aug. 25th, 1738.

Sarah Stane, the Daughter of John Stane & Sarah his Wife, was baptised
Octobr 11th, 1738.

Ann, the Natural Daughter of Abigail Anger, of ye Parish, was baptised
Feb : 7th, 173⅞.

Thomas, ye Son of Richard & Ann Frances, was baptised Febr: 21st,
173⅞.

Tho' Velley, Rectr.

Baptisms 1739.

Rachel, the Daughter of Tho' Wennel & Sarah his Wife, was Baptised
Apr : 1st, 1739.

Sarah, the Daughter of Thomas Wheeler & Mary his Wife, was baptised
Apr: 18, 1739.

John, the Son of John Munday & Mary his Wife, was baptised May
28th, 1739.

Elizabeth, the Daughter of Peter Speller & Mary his Wife, was baptised
June 7th, 1739.

John, the Son of Will: Shead & Mary his Wife, baptis : June 24th,
1739.

Benjamin, Son of James Chaplin & Elizabeth his Wife, baptis'd July
1st, 1739.

Richard, Son of James Wennel & Susannah his Wife. baptiz : Oct. 3^d.
Henry, Son of Will : Thurgood & Sarah his Wife, baptised Oct. 11th.
Samuel, the Son of Samuel Monson & Alice his Wife, was baptised
 Feb. 8th, 1739-40.

Thos Velley, Rect^r.

Baptisms 1740.

Edward, the Son of Edward Fogg & Mary his Wife, was baptised Mar.
 28th, 1740.
John, Son of Joseph Burrell & Jane his Wife, was baptised Apr : 20,
 1740.
Sarah, the Daughter of John Nettleton & Anne his Wife, was baptised
 May 9th, 1740. She was born Oct. 4th, 1739.
Rebeccah, daughter of Rich : Guye & Hannah his Wife, was baptised
 July 2^d, 1740.
Elizabeth, Daughter of Step^n Finch & Jane his Wife, baptised Aug: 28,
 1740.
Ephraim, Son of John Knight, baptised Aug. 24, 1740.
Sheffeld, Son of Thos Warren & Mary his Wife, baptiz'd Oct. 10, 1740.
[blank] Daughter of William Madle & [blank] his Wife, baptiz : Oct. 12.
Ann, Daughter of [blank] Bret, baptized Jan : 4th, 1740.
Ann, Daughter of John Thurgood & Mary his Wife, baptized Feb : 2^d.

Thomas Velley, Rector, 1740.

Baptisms 1741 : Mar. 25.

Mary, Daughter of Francis Lawrence & Jane his Wife, baptized July 5,
 1741.
Elizabeth, Daughter of Peter Speller & [blank] his Wife, baptized Aug :
 2^d, 1741.
Sarah, Daughter of Thomas Fox & Frances his Wife, baptized Sep^{tr} 8,
 1741.
Philippa, Daughter of Thomas Warren & Mary his Wife, was baptised
 Decr 2^d, 1741.
William, Son of John Munday & Mary his wife, was baptised Decr 16,
 1741.
John, the Son of Thomas Wennel & Sarah his Wife, baptized Jan : 10th,
 1741.
William, the Son of Samuel Kent & Elizabeth his Wife, baptised Jan : 13,
 1741.

Thomas Velley, Rector, 1741.

Baptisms Mar. 25, 1742.

Elizabeth, Daughter of Samuel Nichols & Ann his Wife, was baptised
 May 9th, 1742.
Alexander, Son of Thomas Velley, Rect^r of this Parish, & Jane his Wife,
 was born May the 8th & baptised May 21, 1742.
[blank] Bettyes, son of John Bettyes & Ann his Wife, was baptised Aug :
 1st, 1742.

[*blank*] Lawrence, Son of Francis Lawrence & Jane his Wife, baptised Aug. [*blank*], 1742.

Joseph, Son of Bartholomew Oram & Mary his Wife, baptised Feb : 13, 1742.

Elizabeth, Daughter of Tho' Warren & Mary his Wife, bapt : Feb : 13, 1742.

here ends y° year 1742. T. Velley, Rector.

Baptisms 1743.

Sarah, Daughter of Sar : Howgate, priv : bap : Apr :   , 1743.

Thomas, Son of Thomas Velley, Rector of this Parish, & Jane his Wife, was born March 17ᵗʰ, 1742, & baptized April 6ᵗʰ, 1743.

Elizabeth, Daughter of Will : Shed & Mary his Wife, baptised June 13ᵗʰ, 1743.

Sarah, Daughter of Hen : Searle & Ann his wife, bapt : Jul : 8, 1743.

Henry John, Son of Capⁱⁿ Charles Hutchinson & Elizabeth his Wife, was baptised July 24ᵗʰ, 1743.

Elizabeth, Daughter of George Stephens & Ann his Wife, baptised Aug. 26, 1743.

Thomas, the Son of Thomas Alsop & Ann his Wife, baptised Oct. 9, 1743.

Margarett, Daughter of Will : Littel & Mary his Wife, baptised Decʳ 2ᵈ, 1743.

Ann, Daughter of Dan : Christy & Jane his Wife, baptised Jan. 4ᵗʰ, 1743.

James, Son of John Monday & Mary his Wife, baptised Feb. 29, 1743.

Ann & Mary, Daughters of Thomas Velley, Rectʳ of y° Parish, & Jane his Wife, were baptised privately Feb : 17ᵗʰ, & publickly Mar. 14ᵗʰ, 1744. Mem : y° said Ann & Mary were born Feb : 14, 1744 (*sic*).

Thomas Velley, Rectʳ, Mar. 24ᵗʰ, 1743.

Baptisms March 25, 1744.

Ann, Daughter of Will : Madle & Mary his Wife, was baptised Mar. 30ᵗʰ, 1744.

Johannes Antonius, Son of Antonius Dongar & Maria his Wife, baptised June 13, 1744.

Elizabeth, Daughter of Edwᵈ Daniel & Mary his Wife, baptised June 24, 1744.

Ann, Daughter of Will : Weal & Mary his Wife, bap. June 24, 1744.

Charles, Son of Charles Porter & Mary his Wife, bap. Decʳ 28, 1744.

Margaret, Daughter of Robert Con & Ann his wife, baptiz'd Mar : 24, 1744.

Tho' Velléy, Mar. 24, 1744.

Baptisms 1745.

William, Son of Joseph & Mary Hobbs, baptized May 11, 1745.

Sarah, Daughter of Thomas Bridges & Sarah his Wife, baptized May 28.

71

Sarah, Daughter of Mr John Boodle & Sarah his Wife, baptized June 16, 1745.

John & Abraham, Sons of Peter Speller & Mary his Wife, baptised June 16th.

Elizabeth, Daughter of John Bettys & Elizabeth his Wife, baptised June 28, 1745.

Thos, son of Thos Onion & Elizabeth his Wife, Bap: Aug: 11, 1745.

Robert, Base born Son of Mary Clift, bapt. Sep^{tr} 8th.

Margaret, Daughter of George Poole, Soldier, & Kath : his Wife, Bap. Sep. 13.

John, Son of J^n Baron & Ann his Wife, bapt. Jan : 6, 1745.

John, Natural Son of Mary Clift, baptiz : Jan. 15, 1745.

Thos, son of John & Mary Munday, bap. Jan. 15.

Cornel, Son of Will : & Mary Shed, bapt : Feb : 28, 1745.

Anne, Daughter of Stephen & Jane Finch, bapt. Mar. 8.

Thomas Velley, Rect^r, Mar. 24, 1745.

Baptisms Mar. 25, 1746.

George, Son of Charles & Mary Porter, baptised Apr : 15, 1746.

Joseph, Son of [*blank*] Lawrence & [*blank*] his Wife, baptised May 11th, 1746.

Mary, Daughter of Will : & Susan Bannister, baptis : June 13, 1746.

John, Son of Will : Weald & Sarah his Wife, baptised June 15, 1746.

Elizabeth, Daughter of John Woollins & Ann his Wife, baptised June 25, 1746.

Elizabeth, Daughter of Thos Bridges & Sarah his Wife, born (*sic*) July 22, 1746.

Richard Cary, Son of Richd Cary & Ann his Wife, baptised Novr 18th, 1746.

Richard, Son of Richd Daniel & [*blank*] his Wife, privately baptis'd Novr 30th, 1746.

John & Richard Bernard, Sons of John Boodle & Sarah his Wife, privately baptized Decr 1st, publickly Decr 28th, 1746.

Ann, Daughter of Thos Alsup & An his Wife, baptized Jan. 5th, 1746.

Richard, Son of Thos Unwin & Eliz : his Wife, baptiz'd Jan : 11th, 1746.

Mary, Daughter of Henry & Ann Searl his Wife, bap : Feb : 2^d, 1746.

Thos Velley, Rect^r, Mar. 24, 1746.

Baptisms Mar. 25th, 1747.

Mary, the Daughter of John & Abigail Travel, his Wife, bap. May 26, 1747.

Mary Pyke, Daughter of John & Ann his Wife, bap. 9, 1747.

Charlotta, Daughter of George & Dennis Stephens his Wife, baptised Oct. 20th, 1747.

Henry, Son of J^n Munday & Mary his Wife, bap. No : 18. 47.

James, Son of [*blank*] Meridith, baptis'd Novr 20th.

Ann, Daughter of J^n & Ann Woollins, bap. Jan. 29. 47.

Ann, Daughter of Rich^d & Ann Carey, bap. Jan. 29. 47.

Dorothy, Daughter of Thos & Eliz : Unwin, bap. Feb. 18. 47.

Thos Velley, Rector, Mar. 24, 1747.

Baptisms Mar. 25, 1748.

Richard, Son of Samuel & Mary Colmer, baptised May 6, 1748.

Thomas, Son of Thomas Velley, Rector of this Parish, & Jane his Wife, was born May 15th, 1748, privately baptised June the first, & publickly June 10th, 1748.

Martha, Daughter of William & Mary Madle, baptised June 22^{d}, 1748.

Mary, Daughter of Mr John Boodle & Sarah his Wife, baptised July 25th, 1748.

Richard, Son of Richd Daniel & Ann his wife, privately baptised Aug: 11th, publ: 21.

Jane, Daughter of Daniel Christy & Jane his Wife, baptiz'd Aug. 26, 1748.

Mary, Daughter of Joseph Brown & Ann his Wife, baptized Sep^{tr} 25, 1748.

John, Son of John Travel, Junr, & Abigail his Wife, baptized Octr 7, 1748.

Eliz: Daughter of Jn: Bettyes, Ju^{r}, & Ann his wife, bapt: Oct: 9, 1748.

Ann Rowley, Bastard of Ann Rowley, privately baptised Oct: 12, afterwards publick:

Thos Emerson Bridges, Son of Thos & Sarah his Wife, bap. Novr 28th, 1748.

Eliz: Daugh: of Isaac & [*blank*] Battle, bapt. Jan: 17.

Willm, Son of J^{n} Baron, bap. Jan 25th, 1748.

Willm, Son of Will: Weald, bap. Feb. 5, 1748.

Dorothy, daughter of John Lenham & Dorothy his wife, privately bap. Feb. 15, pub: Mar. 6th, 1748.

Richard, Son of Mr William Dore & Olive his Wife, bap: Mar. 10, 174$\frac{8}{9}$.

Mary, Daughter of J^{n} Munday, Ju^{r}, bap: Mar. 22th, 1748.

Thos Velley, Rect^{r}, Mar. 24th, 1748.

Baptisms Mar. 25, 1749.

Charles, Son of Daniel Crouchman & Susannah his Wife, baptized May 14.

Edward Parnell, Son of Ed: & Eliz: Matthews, Ap: 5.

James, Son of James Travel & Elizabeth his Wife, baptized May 24, 1749.

Ann, Daughter of Thos Arnold & Ann his Wife, baptized June 9, 1749.

James, Son of James Meredith & Olive his Wife, baptiz'd June 13, 1749.

Sarah, Daughter of John Woollins & Ann his Wife, baptized July 24th, 1749.

John, Son of John & Sarah Woolmer, priv^{ly} bap. Sep. 14.

Martha, Daughter of William Shead & Mary his Wife, baptized Octr 8, 1749.

Ann, Daughter of J^{no} Baron, bap. Oct. [*blank*] 1749.

John, Son of Mr John Lenham & Dorothy his Wife, baptised privately Feb. 12th, publickly March 13th, 1749.

Thomas, Son of Mr John Boodle & Sarah his Wife, baptised Feb. 27, 1749.

Olive, Daughter of Mr William Dore & Olive his Wife, baptised Mar. 7, 1749.

Tho' Velley, Rector, Mar. 24, 1749.

Baptisms March 25, 1750.

Sarah, Daughter of Daniel Christy & Jane his Wife, bap. Mar. 30, 1750.

· [*blank*] Son of John Travel & Abigail his Wife, bap. Ap : 6.

James Beasing, Son of James & Elizabeth his Wife, privately baptiz'd June 23 & received publickly in the Church, July 6, 1750.

John, Son of James Meredith, privately baptized July 6th.

John, Son of Will : Wood & Phillis his [Wife], bap. June 7th, 1750.

Anne Battle, Daughter of Isaac & Jane Battle, baptized Sep^{tr} 9, 1750.

Charles Porter, Son of Charles & Mary his Wife, baptized Aug. 10.

Octob^r 27. Stephen, Son of Rich^d & Mary Daniel, Bap^d.

Kitty Lenham, Daughter of John and Dorothy, priv^{ly} bap^d Jan^{ry} 17, 1750.

Rich^d, Son of John Woollens & Anne, was bap^d Jan^r 21.

Anne, D^r of Rich^d & Anne Carey, baptiz'd ffeb^{ry} 2nd.

Sarah, of Richard and Sarah Barnes, bap^d March 10.

Baptized.

William, ye son of William Potter and Elizebeth his Wiffe, was bapt. June 25, 95.

Charles, ye Son of William Potter and of Elizebeth his Wiffe, was bapt. [*no date given.*]

John, ye Son of William Potter and of Elizebeth his Wiffe, was bapt. March y^r 9, 1699.

Elizebeth, ye Daughter of Willi : Potter and of Elizebeth his Wiff, was bapt. Decem. 31, 1700.[1]

---

[1] The above four entries occur on a page of the Register of the year 1748.

Marriages.

Vortrage.

Mariages.

A° d. 1560.   Richard Walys & Katherine Penny were married 20 July.

    1561.   Edmond Chadweeke & Isabel Brand were married 21 deceb.

          William Hurt & Margaret Sell were married 15 Jañ.

          Georg Paine & Jone Huntingtō were married 25 Jañ.

    1562.   Robert Chaunsey & Phillip Nicols were marr̃ 1 June.

          Henry Ting & Joan Palm̃ were married 1 Sept.

    1564.   Willm̃ Horne & Joan Browne were marr̃ 30 Octob.

    1566.   Anthonie Barwicke & Margery Hughes were marr̃ 30 June.

    1569.   John Baker & Annys Fynch were marr̃ 28 Aprill.

          Richard Rogers & Grace Alsop were marr̃ [no date].

    1570.   Thomas Morice & Margaret Lynd were marr̃ 15 decēb.

    1574.   John Crab &   [blank]   were marr̃ 8°. Aug.

R. Eliz. 21.   1578.   Francis Alsop & Elizabeth Weav̊ were marr̃ 25 Maie.

          Willm̃ Harris & Mary Stam̃er were marr̃ 10 Jan.

          Henry Ting & Ellin Turuish were marr̃ 10 Febr.

22.   1579.   Willm̃ Bourne & Marie Morice, gent., were marr̃ 21 Jañ   R. Eliz. 22.

          Matthew Glascock & Joan Fynch were marr̃ 8 Febr.

    1580.   John Palm̃ & Anne Calis were marr̃ 12 Aprill.

          John Weldon & Catherine Angier were marr̃ 28 Sept.

          John Turuish & Ales Milford were marr̃ 1 Nouemb.

          John Soule & Anne Lagden were marr̃ 15 Nouemb.

23.   1581.   Henry Tailo̊ was married [blank] of Aug.

          Jeffrey Alsop & Grace Fynch were marr̃ [blank] of Octob.

24.   1582.   Tho. Wyat & Grace Deringtō were marr̃ 20 Maie.

25.   Robart Bourne & Katherine Medley were marr̃ 11 Decēb.

27.   1585.   Robart Breme & Joan Morrell were mar̃ 19 Sept. R. Eliz. 27.

28.   1586.   Henry Barnard & Thomasin Lambe were mar̃ 5 Maie, R. El : 28.

          Edward Turno̊, gent., & Mrⁱˢ Anne Morice were marr̃ 1 Noũeb.

77

R. Eliz. 29.   1587.   Tho. Hodskin & Dorethy Greene were marr̄ 15 Maie.
Tho. Rogers & Marie Isbroke were marr̄ 7 June.
30.   1588.   Barthomew Deringtō & Elizabeth Lathom were marr̄
19 Maie.
Robart Powel & Barbary Wright were mar̄ 2 June.
Tho. King & Margett Fynch were mar̄ 28 Aug.
Thomas Turuish & Joan Dennis were mar̄ 15 Sept.
31.   Edw. Banistʳ & Rose Babtharstō were mar̄ 1 Decēb.
1589.   Ric. Hutley & Eliz. Barnard were mar̄ 29 June.
32.   1590.   Peter Deringtō & Jone Forstʳ were mar̄ 16 Aug.
Tho. Ting & Eliz : Stane were mar̄ 27 Sept.
33.   1591.   Nicolas Westwood & Grace Turuish were mar̄ 13
June.
34.   1592.   Edm. Willand & Jone Burre were mar̄ 28 June.
Eliz. 34.
Willm̄ Wignall & Eliz. Hathwaie were mar̄ 18 Octob.
John Palm̄ & Mariā White were mar̄ 3 Febr.
35.   1593.   James Woodcock & Mary Barnard were mar̄ 25 Aβll.
Georg Pechie & Mary Angier were mar̄ 8 July.
John Ramsey & Elizabeth Burton were mar̄ 19 July.
John Morice, gent., & Catherine Poynes, gent., were
mar̄ 24 Octob.
36.   Richard Gualter & Ales Turuish were mar̄ 14 Deceb.
R. Eliz. 36.
1594.   Georg Goodwin, Clerk, & Eliz. Morice were mar̄ 19
Maie.
37.   1595.   Christopher Ty & Ales Langley were maried 15 June.
Eliz. 37.
Georg Parmeter & Eliz. Alsop, wid., were mar̄ 16 June.
38.   Georg Wrath, gent., & Margaret Medley were mar̄ 15
Deceb̄.
1596.   James Penymā & Annis Wilcock were mar̄ 19 Sept.
Tho. Cakebread & Martha Abell were maried eodē
momētō.
39.   1597.   Andrew Wamsley & Dorathy Burton were mar̄ 21
Sept.
40.   1598.   Willm̄ Bett & Susan Swinow were marr̄ 5 June.
Eliz. 40.
Eliz. 41.   1599.   Williā Tabor, D. of Diuinitie & Archd. of Essex, and
Elizabeth Morice, gent., were maried 10° April,
& Eliz. Reg. 41°.
Thomas Sawkin & Elizabeth Brainwood were maried
1° Octobʳ.
John Barrett & Ellin Pechie were maried 8° Octobr.
George Butler & Anne Jones were maried 15 Noueb̄ :
Eliz. 42.   1600.   Richard Ditton & Katherine Thornℓ were maried 14
Septeb̄.
Willm̄ Batsford & Annis Mallery were maried 5
Octobr.
George Babbs & Phillis Nowell were maried 27°
Octob.
Eliz. 43.   1601.   Thomas Tydy & Eliz. Parmeter, widow, maried 20
Januar̄.

Eliz. 43. 1601. Henry Estick & Mary Dowsett were maried 24
August.
Richard Felpes & Catherine Rowland were maried
21° Septemb.
El. 44°. 1602. Willm̃ Bennett & Annis Derington were maried
on All Saintes Daie.
Jacobi R.1°. 1603. John Crabb & Mary Sweeting were maried 9° May,
1603. Ja : R. 1°.
George Haselwood & Elizabeth Small were maried
1° Noueb.
Ja : 2°. 1604. Thomas West & Susan Read, widow, maried 27°
June, 1604. Jac : 2°.
1604. Geffrey Nicolson & Frances Browne maried 28 Maie,
eodē anno.
Henry Smith & Joane Gary maried 29 July. A°
eodē.
John Spalding & Annis Colford maried 25 Sept.
A° eodē.
Ja : 3°. 1605. Nicolas Parker & Sara Graue, widow, maried 24°
June.
James Derington & Elizabeth Campion were maried
2° Julij.
Richard Bradbent & Mary Weldon were maried 12
Aug.
Ja : 4. 1606. Thomas Bennet & Jane Holibred maried 30° Julij,
1606. Jacob : 4°.
Willm̃ Barnard, of High Roding, & Martha Willis, of
Keldon, maried 7° Octob., 1606.
Thomas Foote & Jone Hockley maried 24 Noueb̃ʳ.
Ja : 4. 1606. John Browne & Annis Elderton maried 3° Febʳ.
Ja : 5. 1607. Edward Maior & Mary Derington mař 27 Jan.
Ja : 6. 1608. Michael White & Margaret Hills maried 16 May,
1608. Ja : 6.
John Crab & Anne Glascock maried 2° January.
Ja : 7°. 1609. Thomas Wilsmore & Joane Chervill maried 17 Aprill.
John Reading & Anne Nelson maried 2° July.
Roger Sewell & Anne Leger maried 9 Octob.
Josias Mason & Mary Browne maried 26 Octob.
Ja : 8. 1610. Willm̃ Tiler & Anne Scampion maried 9° Apl, 1610.
Robart Crab & Margeret Waller maried 28 Maij.
Willm̃ Dowly & Mary Burre were maried 27 July,
1610.
John Small & Mary Estick maried 12 July.
Thomas Sharpe, of Writtle, & Tabitha Watson, of
Shering, mař 13 Julij.
Thomas Wittam and Jane Collyn were maried 10
Septemb.
Thomas Champnis & Ellyn Barrett, widow, maried
8° Octob.
Ja : 9°. 1611. Thomas Derington & Mary Goodding 18° June
maried.
Willm̃ Best & Joñe Derington, widow, were maried
24 June.

Ja : 9°. 1611. Auery Lacy & Jane Derington were maried y ͤ last of Noueb͛.

Ja : 10. 1612. Edward Harrys & Zephora Tunbridg maried the 1° Sept.

Ja : 11°. 1613. James Brainwood & Alice Fensam maried 10 of Maij.

George Greene & Joan Santon maried 14° Sept.

Willm̄ Collis & Mary Raynold were maried 21 Sept.

Tho. Willm̄s & Mildred Wilson maried 19 Octob͛.

Edward Barefote & Easter Sweting maried 20 Octob.

Ja : 12. 1614. Edward Pecock & Eliz: Weldon maried 26 Aprill.

Willm̄ Hardman & Martha Deringtō maried 5 of May.

Samuel Raynoldes & Margaret Warn̄, Widow, of Writtle, maried 26 June.

John Stoddard & Debora Tariar maried 29° Sept.

Henry Garrett & Alice Richardson maried 28 Octob͛.

Bartholomew Chapm̄ā & Margery Charuill, widow, maried 14 Octob͛.

Tho. Platt & Annis Baker, maid, maried the 24 of Noueb͛.

Ja : 13. 1617. Samuell Scampiō & Mary Peachy ware maried ii September.

Henry Lorrance & Lidia Smale ware maried 6 October.

Thomas Munsel and Mary Galloway maryed 20 October.

Jac : 17. An. 1619. John Barefoot, inhabitant in Blackmoor, and Ellen Harris, servant in Chepen Ongar, were maryed March 30.

Edward Pool, an inhabitant of Dagnam, & Joan Cowper, servant in Cheping Ongar, were maryed y ͤ 19 of October.

John Duckfield, shoemaker, and Grace Smal, of Cheping Ongar, y ͤ daughter of Giles Smal, deceased, were maried October 28.

Jac. 18. Anno dom : Theophilus Derington, of Romford, son vnto
1620. Richard Derington, of Cheping Ongar, and Sarah Beard, daughter of Thomas Beard, of Cheping Ongar, were maryed y ͤ 25 of April.

William Plat, of Shelloe, & Margaret Cuts, a maiden, Maryed ffebr : 22.

Jac : 19. An : dom : Henry Mallery, a tayler, & ffrances Vayl, a mayden,
1621. were maryed y ͤ 21 day of May.

Thomas Graves, minister of Cheping Ongar, and Anne Bowyer, servant vnto y ͤ right honorable y ͤ Earle of Kildar, maryed y ͤ 29 day of May, 1621.

Jasper Smyth, a smith, and Elizabeth Anjer, daughter of Thomas Anjer, were maryed y ͤ 18 day of June, 1621.

So

Jac: 19. An: dom: Barnaby Peacock and Margaret Stanes, both of
1621. Cheping Ongar, were maryed ye 26 of June,
1621, in ye parish Church of St Peters, in
Thames Street, in London.

Thomas Prentice, husbandman, was lawfully
maryed to Mary Hammerstone, widow, of y^e
same parish of Cheping Ongar, in Essex,
were maryed Novemb: 30 An: dom: 1621,
wthin y^e royal Castle of y^e tower of London,
called Saint Peters ad vincula, bands being
taken, and no impediement to y^e contrary.
Will$\bar{m}$ Hubbock, ye yonger, being y^e minister
that maryed them.

Jac. 20. An: dom: John Wulpit, singleman, of Cheping Ongar, in
1622. Essex, and Mary Crab, widow, of y^e same
parish, were solemnely maryed at St Andrewes Church, in y^e Wardrobe, in London,
by Thomas Jackso^n, Clericus et Magistrum
in Artibus, being then vnder Mr Edward
Whithorn, minister of ye parish, they were
maryed according to the Canons and
lawes established in ye Church of England
on Easter Munday, the 22 day of April,
1622.

Thomas Prentice, Cowper, and Singleman, and
Mary Starky, both of Cheping Ongar, were
maryed ye third day of September.

ffrancis Alsop, ye elder. ⎫
Edward Harris. ⎬ Churchwardens.
                ⎭

Thomas Graves, Pastor of Cheping Ongar.

Jac. 20. An: dom: Thomas Scholley, singleman, of Prittlewell, and
1622. Mary Saxie, ye daughter of John Saxie, of
Cheping Ongar, were maryed ye first day of
October.

Thomas Horrard, ye son of Giles Horrard, of
Cheping Ongar and Annis Hynes were maryed
ye twenty-first day of October.

John Nicholson, Shoemaker, and Elizabeth
Turnes, were maryed in ye parish Church of
ffyfield the third day of July, an: Dom:
1622, as witnesseth Edward ffosbury, Curate
there.

Charles Blomer, barbar surgean, and Anne Big,
daughter in law vnto Jeffray Brainwood, of o^r
parish, were maryed at Cheping Ongar y^e 19th
of January.

Jac. 22. An: dom: Richard Thornton, of Brentwood, in South Weald
1624. parish, and Jone Bennet, y^e daughter of Will$\bar{m}$
Bennet, of Cheping Ongar, were maryed at
Chep: Ongar, Septemb. 6.

Jonathan Pope, a yong man, and Mary Grave,
daughter of widow parker, of Cheping Ongar,
were maryed Octob^r 18th.

Anno dom: 1625.

George Bash, of y^{e} parish of Belchamp Roothing, in Essex, yeoman, & Mary Ingold were maryed May 12th, 1625.

Anno regni regis Caroli 1°.

Jacob Archer and Margaret King, daughter of John King, of our parish, were maryed ye 14th day of June.

John Sammon & Anne Horrard, ye daught^{r} of Giles Horrard, were maryed Novemb. 22.

Anno Domini 1626. anno regni regis Caroli 2°.

Willm̃, ye son of Willm̃ Bilt, of Cheping Ongar, and Mary, ye daughter of Henrie Lilburn, of Murton, were maryed October 18th, 1626.

Anno Domini 1627, anno regni regis Caroli 3°.

Willm̃ Betty and Susannah Clark, ye daughter of John Clark, of this parish, were maryed March 27th.

Daniel Stepping, of St Giles parish without Cripple-gate in London, and Sarah Miller, the daughter of Giles Miller, of o^{r} town of Ongar, maryed Aprill 25th.

George Wright, son of George Wright, of Shelly, and Rebecca Svtton, maryed May 14th.

Thomas Wennel & Mary Elkin were maryed May 27th day.

Anno Domini 1629, annoq, regni regis Caroli 5°.

Thomas Anjer, ye son of Thomas Anjer, & Mary Trapps, a maidservant, maryed Apr. 7th.

Thomas Hewes, of Castle Heningham, and Dennis White, of Cheping Ongar, were maryed June 16 day.

James Batsford, son of Willm̃ Batsford, & Jone King, a maid servant, both of o^{r} parish, were maryed June 29th day.

Anno Domini 1630. annoq, regni regis Caroli 6°.

Gregory Wallis and Mary Babs were maryed Aprill 13 day.

Philip Bacon and Amy Stokes were maryed October 18 day.

Anno Domini 1631. annoq, regni regis Caroli 7°.

James Hurrell, of Old Saling, in ye county of Essex, gent., and Mary Samuel, widow, were maryed June 2 day.

Anno Domini 1632. annoq, regni regis. Caroli 8°.

John Brown & Margaret Miller, daught^{r} of Giles Miller, were maryed May 1 day.

David Owen, singleman, & Rebecca Cleaveland, maryed May 21.

Giles Batsford, son of Willm̃ Batsford, and Phyllis Babs, maid servant eleven yeares to Tho: Graves, pastour of Cheapen Ongar, maryed Octob^{r} 2 day.

Anno Domini 1634. annoq, regni regis Caroli 10.

James Stone and Elizabeth Lacy, daughter of Avery Lacy, maryed May 1.

John Niccolson and ffortune Chake were maryed Dec. 16.

John Keel, widower, and Mary Squire, widow, were maryed Jan 27th.

Anno Domini 1635. annoq, regni regis Caroli 11°.

John Vmphrye, viduatus, & Mary Prentice, vidua, maryed August 10th.

William Reeves & Frances Gibson, February 1.

George White & Mary Exeter, " 2.

Anno Dom. 1636.   William Cole, of Abbis, & Jone Wood, de eadem,
   anno regis   were marryed July 4th.
   Caroli 12°.   Nath : Bilt & Mary Courtnole marryed No-
                     vemb. 1.
Anno Dom. 1637.   Richard Woolvett & Joane Platt, May 2, 1637.
   anno regis 13°.   George Babbs & Elizabeth Lorkyn, August 24.
                     Thomas Overill & Elizabeth Taylor, October 10th.
                     John Owen & Elizabeth Jasper,   „   16th.
        Edward Alexander & vidua Garrett, of ffobbing, marryed at
           or parish Feb. 20th.
        Joseph Holt & Martha White, March 5th.

Anno Dom : 1638.
        Christopher Preston & Lydia Small, June 10th.
        James Derrington & Anne Cleveland marryed July [n. d.].
        Avery Waylett & Anne Gosling, September 4th.

Anno 1640.
        Thomas Tiday & Elizabeth Luther, 13th of Aprill.
        Richard Throwgood civis Lond : & Elisabeth Richoll,
           May 6th.
        John Warner and Mary Kinge married June 4th.
        John Munke & Martha Spranger, Septemb. 21th.
        Thomas Browne and Sarah Whetston, Septem. 28th.

Año domnⁱ, 1641.
        Henry Borā and Clemence Westwood, April 26th.
        William Hogge & Elisabeth Younge, June 24th.
        ffrances Lane, civis Lond., & Alice Sorrell, July 22th.
        Wm [blank], of Hornchurch, and Anne Bush, „ 28th.
        John Tayler & Sarah Crooke, August 31.
        Joñ Abell & Grace Cordall, Septemb. 14.
        Laurence Morton & Katharine Grainge, Septemb. 29th.
        Edward Neale & Elisabeth Poole, Octob. 18.
        Mr Hill, Citizen of London, and Anne Kinge, daughter of
           John Kinge, married Decemb. 13th.

Anno Dom : 1642.
        John Rogers, of Hatfield, & Elisabeth Cottyn, of Belcham
           Roothinge, March 29th.
        Henry Addams & Elisabeth Wolvet May 19th.
        Isaac Wells & [blank] August 2d.

Anno 1643.
        John Nayler & Jane Lacy, Ap : 20th.
        Thomas Tanner & Joane Champnes, of Navestock, married
           Octob. 2d.
        John Duke and [blank] October 21th.
        Wm Cakebread & Mary Wallis, Novembr 7th.

        (No entries between 1643 and 1655.)

An : Dom. 1655.

Maryed William Stane and Susan Godson one Easter Tusday the yeare above written.
James Clift and Rebeccah Staines maried Sept. 3, 1655.

(No entries between 1655 and 1658.)

Henry Beans & Elizabeth Tabor maried January 5th, 1658.
Francis Warner and Sarai his Wife married Nouember the Seuen-teenth in ye yeare of or Lord One Thousand Six hundred and fifty Eight.

January the 16th, 1659.

Marryed the day and yeare abovesaid Mr Thomas Allexander and Mrs Margarete Neale, Widdo, att Chippinge Ongar.
Maryed Thomas Aynger and Sarah Meller the ffirst day of October, Anno domynie 1660.
Maryed John Chopping & Eliz : Odwell, both single psons, the 10 day of October, Anno 1660.
John Dyer, of Standford Ryvr, and Susan Rose, of this pish, ware maryed the 24th day of December, Anno 1660.

An : Dom : 1662.

Maryed Robert Stane & Frances King, Jan. 22.

Maryed Phillipp Garriott, of Stapleford Tany, & Elizabeth Shutlewood, of the same, ye 7 day of May, An : dom : 1663.
Maryed Thomas Foord, of London, shōmaker, and Jane White, of Chip : Onger, Aug. ye 17th, 1663.
James Jenkin, of London, Haberdasher, maried to Mary Neale, daughter of John Neale, of Shelley, Esq, on the ffeast day of St Bar-tholomew.
Married William Hardie and Margerett Barker, Septr ye 28th.
Married Robert Milles and Ann Younge the same 28th of Septr, 1663.

Annoq 1664.

Jacob ffoster & Rose Glascocke married July 25th.
Robert Boram & Emme Benton, Nouember 1.
William Clarke and Clemence Tabor, Novem : 3.
Henery Traps & Jane Wood, Nouem : 17th.
James Crooke, Rector.
John Burrill, James Smiggersgill, Churchwardens.

Married 1666.

Wm Thayer & Mary Burrill, Aprill 18th.
Wm ffrancis & Susaña Tabor, June 4th.
Lawrence Pickerine & Winifred Platt, September 26th.
James Crooke, Rector.
William Tabor, John Burrill, Churchwardens.
84

Married 1667.

George Stanes & Katherine Chopping, May 30.
John Sweetapple & Mary Aker, December 26th.
James King & Elizabeth Reynolds, ffebru : 3d.

James Crooke, Rector.
William Tabor, William Thurgood, Churchwardens.

Married 1668.

Nathan Tomlinson & Lydia Hockley, May 11th.
Samuel Bones & Mary Ingold, June 22th.

Married 1669.

Robert Goodell & Mary Turner, October 5th.
Robert Hinton & Mary Overill, October 7th.

James Crooke, Rector.
William Thurgood & William Stains, Churchwardens.

Married 1670.

ffrancis Cutler & Katherine Wilkin, January 12th, 1670.

Married 1672.

John Lucke and Rebecka Chake Married ye 16 of October.

Married 1674.

November 22th.   James Scambler & Mary Smith.

Married 1676.

George Haines and Sarah Inhivor were Married May 30, 1676.

1677.

George Pegge and Rebeckah Lillbourne were Marryed Septem. 24,
1677.
James Kinge and Rebeckah Wibert were married Octob. 23, 1677.

Thomas Odwell and Elizabeth Stañley were married Feb. 2d, 16⅞.
Daniell West and Sarah Cole were married June 1, 1680.
Thomas Norrington and Sarah Wott were married Novembr 9th, 1680.

Henery Bridge & Johana Parkes were married Septr 21th, 1682.
William Porter and Jeane Lacy weare married Jan. 15th, 1683.

Married March 15th, 168⅚.   Auery Lacie & Doritie Whitehead.
[march] 25th, 86.   Sam. Whitehead & Tho : Babs'es Widdow.

85

Aug. 24th, 86. Daniell Chapman & Sr Witt: Apletun's Coock maid was Maried.
May 17th, 1687. Married Tho : Beard & the Widd. Parkes.
October 18th 1687. Married Robert White & Elizabeth Hills.
July 9th, 1688. Married Sam. King & Ann Waylett, Widdow.
Octo. ye 23. Married Thomas Cooper and Abigale Clift.
. . . . 30. Married att Griensted Georg Phips.
May the 17, 1689. Married Jeames Batsford and Anne Bibbe.

(No entries between these dates.)

Maried 1693. William Priket and y^e Widdow Baron, Jan. 29.
James Trapps and Ann Allen were maried at High Ongar, March y^e 15, 169$\frac{3}{4}$.
Samuel Glascock and Prudence Saunders ware married at High Onger, March y^e 26, 1695.
Henery Lewsly and Ann Legget, both of Malden, Sep. 29, 95.
William Munday and Rebecca Bibbe, O^{br} 24.
Robert Clift and Mary Geff was maried July [*blank*] 1696.
Robert Stanes and Sarah Almond ware married at Dudinghurst Novem : 3^d, 1696.
Thomas Sell & Mary Green were maried ye 22 of December, 1697.

Thomas Parrish and Mary Dew ware maried ye 8 of June, 1699.
John Wennell and Elizebeth Bastick ware maried ye 18 day of Octob^r, 1700.
Thomas Miller and Mary Merrills ware maried ye 19 June, 1701.
Aron Kettlewell and Martha Turner ware married ye 2 of O^{br}, 1702.
Edward Windham and Elizebeth Robjon ware mar : March ye 16.
John Wood & Susan Godfry ware married June 22 [? 1703].
Witt Russell & Susan Stanes ware married the 9 of December, 1703.
William Waskett and Susan Benton, December 5, 1704.
Daniell Ramm and Katherine Carie, Ob^r ye 8, 1705.
Thomas Horsnaile and Marget Prentice, Augt 16, 1706.
Georg Dane and Ann Embeson, May ye 4th, 1707.
Rob. Howard & Elizebeth Woodhouse, July ye 22.
Married 1708. Thomas Bannister, of Shelley, and Margery Turner, of this parrish, June ye 3^d.
Richard Ward, of Little Laver, and Sarah Knight, No^{br} ye 5. [? 1708.]

Mr Hugh Nicolds, of Witham, and Mrs Mary Dountin, of this parrish, ware married ye 30 of Aprill, 1710.
William King & Susan Whitehead ware married ye 30 of X^{br}, 1710.
William Angier & Elizebeth Crow weare married y^e 2 of May, 1711.
Ed : Sheadd and Mary Hockly, widdow, are married y^e 30 Ob^r, 1711.
John Madle & Katherine Knight, both of Buchamp Roothing, ware married y^e 28 of X^{br}, 1711.
John Saunders, widdower, and Abigall Guy, his servant, Feb : y^e 8, 17$\frac{11}{12}$.
Edward Monk, of Hennam, y^e . . . & Sarah Bridges, Ap^{ll} y^e 29, 1712.
William Munday and Mary Stepens ware married O^{br} y^e 5, 1712.

Thomas Bass & Sarah Ballard ware married May y^e 25, 1713.

John Chambers & Mary Havers June y^e 12, 1713.

Robert Twinn & Rebecka Porter ware married July y^e 5, 1713, both of Burham parrish.

Thomas [*blank*] and Katheren Dellon ware married D^{br} 22, 1713.

Christopher Salmon & Ann Renolds ware married Aug. ye 20, 1714.

Robert Rogers & Mary Bunn, both of Maulden, ware maried ye 20 of Sp^t, 1714.

John Monday and Sarah Sell, both of this Parish, married April 27th, 1715.

Philip Burrel, of ffryoning, Singleman, and Mary Peters, of this Parish, Singlewoman, married Decem: 27, 1715.

Thomas Allen and Abigail Saunders, Wid., September 2^d, 1716.

Mr Thomas Waggstaff, of St Margarets, Westminster, Singleman, and Mrs Sarah Siday, of this Parish, Singlewoman, Janua : 8th, 17$\frac{16}{17}$.

John Bridges and Jane May, both of this Parish, June 10, 1717.

Henry Sweeten, of High Ongar, and Elizabeth Bush, of this Parish, Octo : 13th, 1717.

Edward Sandford and Mary Humphrey, both of Quenden in Essex, and Single Persons, No^{br} 25th, 1717.

John Lucas, Junr, and Elizabeth Clarke, Janu : 7, 1717.

James Sawkins, Batch^r, and Ruth Gowers, Spin^r, of Kelwedon, were married ffebrua : 11, 1717.

James ffinch, of Brentwood, and Mary Thorn, of Rumford, were married Octo : 20, 1718.

George Peg, Widower, aged 70, and ffrances Bones, Widow, were married ffeb : 4th, 1718.

Williā Crab, Wid^r, and Mary Jonson, Singlewo : of Bobinger, were married May 24th, 1719.

Mr Barton Booth, of ye Parish of St Gyles in the fields, Middlesex, wid : and Mrs Hester Santlow, of ye Parish of St Paul Covent Garden, Single : but in ye same County, were Married at Chipping Ongar Church, August ye 3^d, 1719.

Joseph Ward, of Eppin, and Susan Wilsher, of this town, were Married Octo : 14th, 1719.

John Coe, of Ingatestone, Singleman, and Mary Dowthy, of this Parish, Singlewoman, were Married Octo : 25, 1719.

James Chaplin and Mary Parish, both of this Parish, were Married Janua : 10th, 1719.

John Tovey, of St Andrews Parish in London, Singleman, & Frances Faulker, of Stanford Rivers, Widdow, were marry'd the 18th of October, 1720.

John Brown, of Rumford, & Mary Irons, of Blackmore, were married November the Ninth, 1721.

Samuel Wilson, of Dagenham (a Presbyterian Teacher) & Mary Spranger, of this Parish, were marry'd December ye 12th, 1721.

James Nash, of Bobbingworth, & Mary Belcher, of this parish, were marry'd November ye 11th, 1722.

Richard Guy, of South Weald, & Hannah Warmsley, of this Parish, were marry'd December the 30th, 1723.

Richard Cole, of Stanford Rivers, & Mary White, of this Parish, were marry'd May the tenth, 1724.

John Stringer & Martha Stoakes were marry'd October y^e 31st, 1724.

James Cowland & Martha Howard were marry'd November y^e 3^d, 1724.

John Bettis & Anne Brainwood were marry'd Jan^{ry} y^e 24th,
James Clift & Lettice Peters were marry'd February the third, $\Big\}$ 1724.

Henery Thorowgood & Rebecca Warmesley were marry'd September the fourteenth, 1725.

George Finch & Susanna Day were marry'd February the Eighth, 1725-6.

The Reverend Mr Thomas Evans, Rector of Clungonas als Clungonford, in the County of Salop, & Mrs Olive Sadler, of this Parish, were married April ye 21st, 1726.

John Setch & Rose Marcold, both of Blackmore, were married November the 14th, 1726.

William Rust, of Norton, & Susan Crow, of Stonedon, were married November the 18th, 1726.

Edward Hampshire & Margaret Osborn, both of Blackmore, were marry'd December the 15th, 1726.

Richard Norris, of High Ongar, & Elizabeth Fowler, of Blackmore, were marry'd December the 21st, 1726.

John Perry & Elizabeth Woodland, of the Parish of Cheshunt, in the County of Hartford, were marry'd the 25th of June, 1728.

The Reverend Mr Thomas Sampson, Rector of Hadleigh, widdower, & Mrs Elizabeth Hill, widdow, were maryed the 17th of July, 1728.

William Young, of South Hanvil, & Catherine Davies, of Navestock, were marry'd October the 4th, 1728.

How Leonard & Johanna Wakelin, of High Easton, were marry'd November the 11th, 1728.

John Ramsey, of Kelvedon Hatch, & Olive Bridges, of this Parish, were marry'd November the 18th, 1728.

John Davies, of Moreton, & Anne King, of Blackmore, were marry'd December the 26th, 1728.

Joseph Clarke & Mary Philips, both of Kelvedon, were marry'd September the third, 1729.

John Potts, of Kelvedon, & Sarah Martin, of Stanford Rivers, were marry'd September the 18th, 1729.

Benjamin Luck & Mary Little, both of Abbats Rooding, were marry'd Decr ye 2^d, 1729.

Joseph Burrell, of Fryarning, & Jane Greene, of this parish, were marry'd February the 8th, 1729.

Thomas Clarke, of Rumford, & Anne George, of this Parish, were marry'd October the 18th, 1730.

George Reynolds, of Shelley, & Abigail Francis, of this Parish, widdow, were marry'd December the 27th, 1730.

William Jasper, of Chipping Ongar, & Martha Smeth, of High Ongar, were married February the second, 1730.

William Thurgood & Sarah Thorogood, both of this Parish, were marry'd March the thirtieth, 1731.

Richard Eve & Esther Lee, both of the Parish of Eythrop, were marry'd April the 30th, 1732.

John Vinton, widdower, & Abigail Stoakes, singlewoman, both of the Parish of Harlow, were marry'd September ye 3^d, 1732.

John Laybank, of Wanstead, & Anne Greene, of Barking, were marry'd September the 28th, 1732.

James Paveley, jun[r], of High Ongar, & Elizabeth Umwell, of Stapleford Tany, both single persons, were married November the 27th, 1732.

Thomas Wheeler, of Ansty, in the County of Hartford, & Mary Thorogood, of this parish, were marry'd April the 17th, 1733.

David Burton, of this parish, & Mary Nicholls, of Willingale Doe, were married July the 15th, 1733.

Abraham Perry, of the Parish of Roxwell in Essex, & Susan Clay, of this Parish, were married Octob[r] 25th, 1733.

James Wennell & Susan Reynolds, both of this Parish, were married Nov[r] 5th, 1733.

Thomas Velley, Rector.

Harry Searle, of this Parish, Batchelour, & Anne Wrenn, of the same Parish, spinster, were married Dec[r] 13th, 1733.

Bannister Yates, of this Parish, Batchelour, & Mary Stapeler, of the same Parish, Single Woman, were married Sept[r] 30th, 1734.

Thomas Morrell, of the Parish of Writtle in y[e] County of Essex, Husbandman, & Ann Petitt, of the Parish of Blackmore, in Com : Pred : Widow, were married in this Parish Church, Octo[br] 1[mt], 1734.

John Price, of the Parish of Shenfield in the County of Essex, & Mary Green, of this Parish, were married November 4th, 1734.

Andrew Young, soldier quartered in this Town, & Eleanor Starecroft, in y[e] same Town, were married Dec[r] 2[d], 1734.

Benjamen Larking, of the parish of Kelvedon in the County of Essex, Batcheler, & Sarah Stracey, of the same Parish, Spinster, were married in Chipping Ongar Church, Dec[r] 30th, 1735.

Vic : Green, of this Parish, Singleman, & Olive Wrenn, Spinster, of y[e] same Parish, were married Oct[br] 9th, 1736.

William Westwood & Sarah Bathrip, of the parish of Blackmore, were married in this Church of Chip : Ongar, Jan[ry] 4th, 1736.

John Turner & Ann [blank], of the Parish of Blackmore, were married in Chip : Ongar Church, Feb : 8th, 1736.

Henry Roffey & Ann Biggs, spinster, of this Parish, were married Sept[r] 27th, 1737.

John Munday, of High Ongar, & Mary Tarling, of ys Parish, Spinster, were married Oct[br] 2[d], 1738.

(No entries between 1738 and 1742.)

Samuel Wall, single man, & Sarah Nailor, both of this Parish, were married Oct : [blank], 1742.

William Gardiner, of y[e] Parish of Mashbury, & Elizabeth Perry, of this Parish, were married Oct : 26, 1742.

Daniel Christy, of Bishop Stortford, & Jane Stokes, of this Parish, were married Oct. 28, 1742.

Married Tho[s] Willey to Jane Twene, Oct. 21, 1744.

Rich. Cary & Ann Wren, Married Aug. 3[d], 1745.

Thomas Barter & Sarah Barber, Mar : Aug. 5, 1745.

George Reynolds & Sarah Harrison, Mar. Jan. 20, 1745.

George Stevens & Dennis Groves, Married at Chip : Ongar, Aug. 4th, 1746.

Thomas Chamberlin, of [*blank*], & Sarah Buchannan, of this Parish, single woman, were married June [*blank*], 1748.

Henry Fane, Esq', a Widower, of the Parish of S' James, Westminster, & Miss Charlotte Luther, of Chip : Ongar, Spinster, a Minor, were married August 13th, 1748.

William Wood, of the Parish of Abbas Roothing, & Phillis Cllift (*sic*), of Chip : Ongar, Spinster, were married June 18, 1749.

Burials.

Burialls.

Aᵒ. d. 1558. Willm̄ Hūtington, 3ᵒ Deceb̄.
Brigit Chidwick, 14 Deceb̄.
John Wels, 21ᵒ Deceb̄.
Robert Sedgwick, 7ᵒ Jan.
John Field, 12ᵒ Febr.
Margaret Polly, 19ᵒ Feb :
Joane Būningtō, 25ᵒ Feb.
Edmund Willond was bur̄ 2ᵒ March.
Ric. Barnes, 3ᵒ March.
Aᵒ.d. 1559. John Alsop was buried 10 Octob.
Ellin Lee was buried 29 Decemb.
1560. Joan Blyten was buried 26 July.
Tho : Polley was buried 15 Aug.
Margaret Willand, Daughtᵉ of Edm : Willand, was bur. 21
Aug.
1561. Avelin Willand was bur. 13 Januar̄.
Joan Fox was bur. 7 June.
1562. John Butchᵉ was buried 20 Octob.
Edmund Chadwick was buried 24 Noueb̄.
Jone Brainwood was buried 24 Sept.
Anne Turff, wif of Rob. Turff, was bur. 5 Febr.
1564. Joan Abbatt was bur. 4 June.
George Fosten was buried 9 July.
Willm̄ Edmunds was bur. 18 Aug.
Jeffrey Butler was buried 9 Octo.
1565. Joan Ducket was bur̄ 27 Jan̄.
Mary Thomas was bur̄ 28 Sept.

1568. Moses Bennet was bur̄ 28 Maie.
Tho : Ward was bur̄ 2 Noueb̄.
Joan Adams was buried 14 Noueb̄.
Ric. Tagell was buried 6 Deceb̄.
Georg Ingr̄a was buried 17 Deceb̄.
John White was bur̄ 15 Januar̄.

1571. Willm̄ Turnish buried 25 July.
Eliz : Turnish bur̄ 17 Octob.

93

1572. John Turnish bur. 4 June.
Joan Branwood buried 13 Febr.
John Cole was bur. 12 Maie.
Alice Binder bur. 19 Octob.
1573. Joan Martin bur. 10 Febr.
Joan, y⁰ wife of   Martyn, bur. 13 March.
1574. Thomas, a Strang', Surgeõ of Londõ, ⎫
         buried 28 July. |
      Tho. Leonford bur. 17 Aug. |
      Alice Griffin bur. 20 Aug. |
      Anne Brew' bur. 31 Aug.   Died of
      Jone Painter was bur. 15 Sept.   ⎬ the
      Joan Adams buried 2 Octob.   Plague.
      Edm. Adams bur. 19 Octo. |
      Margery Hughes bur. 24 Octob. |
      Ales. Adams bur. 1 Noueb. |
      Tho. Abbott bur. 14 March.   ⎭
1575. Henry Morice, sonne of Ja. Morice, Esq'., buried 26
         Sept.
1576. Joan Alsop, wife of Jeffrey Alsop, was bur. 29 Aug.
      Tho. Pomfrett bur. 1 Sept.
      Willm̃ Ansell was bur. 17 Sept.
      Jane Ducket, wife of Rob. Ducket, buꞃ 28 Sept.
      Robart Ducket was bur. 29 Octob.
      Georg Pane was buꞃ 13 Decemb.
R. Eliz. 19. 1577. Eliz: Betts, wife of Jeffrey Betts, bur. 23 June.
      Robart Turfl was bur. 29 Aug.   R. Eliz. 19.
20. 1578. John Alsop, sonne of Jo: Alsop, was bur. 20 Aꝑll.
      John Questel, sonne of Jo. Questel, was bur. 27 May.
      Joan Ting, wife of Henry Ting, was bur. 16 Sept.
21.   Elizabeth Harrison, wife to W. Harrisõ, buried 18 Octob.
      Martin Foster was buꞃ last of Noueb.
      Alice Weldon, wife of Jo : Weldon, bur. 30 Deceb.
1579. Francis Hubbard was buried 7 Aprill.
1579. Willm̃ Sanders was bur. 24 Aug.
1580. John Denys was bur. 26 July.
22.   Ja : Questell, Daught' of Jo : Q. was bur. [blank] Aug.
23.   Bennet Pole bur. 6 Febr.
24. 1581. Robert Fynch was bur. 16 Jañ.   Eliz. 24.
          [blank] Stapletõ was buꞃ 14 Febr.
25. 1582. Richard, sonne of Tho. Clerke, buꞃ 20 Febr.   Eliz. 25.
1583. Robart Crab, sonne of Jo: Crab, was buꞃ 18 June.
      Mary Turnish was buꞃ 22 Aug.
26. 1584. Water Willm̃s was buꞃ 23 Aug.   El. 26.
      Jo. Saling was buꞃ 12 Sept.
27.   Mary Weldon was buꞃ 14 Januaꞃ.
      Elizabeth Tasker was buꞃ 7 Febr.
1585. Margaret Midletõ was buꞃ 31 March.
      Grace Fynch, widow, was buꞃ 12 July.
      Henry Wailet buꞃ 25 July.
      Eliz. Hallingworth bur. 17 Aug.
      Richard Cheston was buꞃ 26 Octob.
28. 1586. Ed. Hurle was buꞃ 12 June.

28. 1586. Alice Small bur. 22 June.
    1587. Anne Palm̄ bur. 3 Deceb.
30.   Richard Grene bur. 3 March.
          Allice Hellā bur. 9 March.
    1588. Henry Ting was bur. 6 June.
          Eliz. Weldon bur. 5 Noueb̄.
31.   John, sonne of Hugh Ince, bur. 21 Febr.
    1589. A sonne of Barth : Deringtŏs vnbapt. bur. 10 Maye.
          Jo. Webst' was bur. 26 May.
    1591. Stephen Fynch bur. 4 Aprill.
          Jo. Browne bur. 27 Sept.
33.   Grace Fynch was bur. 12 Noueb̄.
34.   Andrew Kent bur. 21 Noueb̄.
    1592. Tho : Deringtŏ, sonne of Pet' D., bur. 11 Aβll.
35.   Jeffrey Alsop bur. 25 Noueb̄. Eliz. 35.
          A child of Willm̄ Barnards vnbaptised was bur. [blank] Jan.
          Joan Crow was bur 14 March.
    1593. Margaret, wife of pore clarke, bur 28 Maie.
          John Turnish was bur. 19 June.
          Mary Bourne, wife of M' W. Bourne, was bur. 26 Aug.
          Moth' Martin was bur. 10 Octob.
36.   John Olif̄ was bur. 28 Noueb̄. R. Eliz. 36.
    1594. Jeffrey Alsop was burietl 30 Maie.
          John Questell was bur. 14 Sept.
37.   Tho : Adams was buried 30 Deceb̄.
          Elizabeth Meade was bur. 5 Aprill.
          Ellin Kent, wid., was bur. 11 Aprill.
          Moth' Adams was bur. 19 Aprill.
          Eliz. Deringtŏ, Daught' of Barth : bur. 28 Octo.
38.   Henry Ting, sonne of Tho : Ting, was bur. 2 Deceb̄.
    1596. John Harrys was bur. 2° Febr : R. Eliz. 39.
39.   James Morice, Esq', Atturney of y° Q : Maᵗⁱᵉˢ Court of
            Wardes, was buried 6° Febr. Died 2° Febr.
    1597. Elizabeth Ting, wife of Tho : Ting, was bur. 17 June.
          A boy called Stane was bur. 2° July.
          Georg Parmeto' was bur. 17 July.
          John Sugdin was bur. 21 July.
          Tho : Small was bur. 23 July.
          Annys Alsop was bur. 8° Octob.
          Jo. Barefoote was bur. 10 Noueb̄.
40.   Moth' Ansell was bur. 18 March. R. El. 40.
    1598. Moth' Clerke was bur. 23 Aprill.
          Moth' Jones was buried 6 Maye.
          John Cole was bur. 30 Maie.
          Joane King was bur. 2° Aug.
          Brigitt Stane, wife of Jo. Stane, was bur. 3° Aug.
          Avery Jones was bur. 3 Octob.
41.   Joane Hockley, widowe, was buried 17 Januar.
          Elizabeth, wife of Bartlemew Derringtŏ, was buried 12°
            Martij.
    1599. Marie Pechie, Daught' of George Pechie, was buried 29°
            Martij.
          Richard Barrett was buried 9° Septemb.

95

42. 1599. Margaret Batemā, infant, was bur. 14° Januar.
Phenenna Forman, infant, was buried eodē die.
Marie Batemā, infant, was bur. 17° Januar.
1600. Thomas, sonne of Tho : Anzer, was bur. 23 May.
Francis Anger, an old man sʳ, was buried 1° Junij A° pd.
43. Martha Hale, infant, was buried 18 Deceb.
Zachary, sonne of Za. Batemā, was buried 26 Jan.
1601. Bennet, wife of Richard Willett, was buried 12ᵗʰ Aprill,
1601.
Mary, Daughtʳ of Tho. Anzer, butchʳ, bur. 2° Junij.
Edward, sonne of John Crab, buried 18 June.
Catherine, Daughtʳ of Ric. Willet, buried 23 August.
[*blank*], wife of John Crab, buried 5 July.
44. 1602. Hugh Abbott was buried the vᵗʰ of August, 1602. Eliz. 44.
Francis Esterley, habberdashʳ, was buried 16° Septeb.
45. William Lauender, Sawier, was buried 22° Jaſl.
1603. Tho. Grave, sonne of W. Grave, was buried 19° July A°
Ja. R. 1°. 1° Jacobi Regis 1603.
Abigall Weldon, Daughtʳ of Jo. Weldon, buried 3° Octobr.
Elizabeth Morrice, widow, late wife of James Morrice, Esqʳ,
bur. 29 Septemb.
Elizabeth, Daughtʳ of John Browne, buried 14 Januarij.
Marie, wife of the said John Browne, buried 15° Januarij.
Willm̄ Graue, gloū, buried the 17° Januarij.
Anne, Daughtʳ of John Browne, bur. 1° Febr.
1604. Edward Tunbridge, gardiñ, bur. 25 Maij, A° D. 1604 &
Ja. 2°. Ja. R. 2°.
Zachary, sonne of Zacharie Batemā, buried 21 Januarij.
George, sonne of Willm̄ Fynch, buried 12° Febr.
1605. A daughter of John Browne's vnbaptiẑ, buried 23 Noueb.
Ja : 3°. 1605.
Bartholomew Derrington, bricklaier, buried 25° Noueb.
Anne, wife of John Browne, buried 2 December.
Francis Johnson, gloū, buried 8 Deceber.
Willm̄ Anscll, an old mā, buried 23° Jañ.
Cornelius, Sonne of Giles Small, buried 24 Januarie.
1606. Matthew, sonne of John Browne, buried 7 June, 1606.
Ja : 4. Alice, the wife of John Crab, Junior, buried 19 Sept.
Mothʳ Crow buried 30 October.
Susan, wife of Tho. Dunmowe, buried 20 Febr.
1607. Thomas, sonne of John Weldon, buried 24 of Nouēber.
Ja : 5°. A° 5° Jac.
Anne, daughter of Hugh Ince, pastor of this Church, died
23 Martij & buried 24 A° 5° Ja. R.
1608. John, sonne of John Browne, laborer, buried 29 Martij.
Ja. 6. Tho. Greene, a shomaker, drowned, was buried 17 June.
Laurence, base borne of Ales Clerk, buried 5 Aug.
Andrew, sonne of Willm̄ Fynch, buried 26 of Septeb̄.
1609. Mary, daughtʳ of John Scampion, buried 24 June, 1609.
Ja. 7. Ja. 7.
Henry, sonne of Tho. Prentise, murthered, was buried 9
Aprill.
John Barrett, Coop, buried 13 July.

1609. Jeffrey Alsop, sonne of Fr. Alsop, was bur. 28 Feb.
1610. Tho:, sonne of Rob. Tydy, bur. 2° May, A° 1610.
Ja. 8. Richard Clerk, a blind mã, was buried 8° July, 1610.
Elizabeth, wife of Tho. Prentise, buried 22 July.
Elizabeth, wife of Tho. Beard, buried 25 July.
Samuel, sonne of John Scampion, buried 3° Aug.
Prudence, wife of Willm̃ Fynch, was bur. 18° Octobʳ.
Willm̃ Lauender buried August 20.
Roger Saywell was buried 25 Octob.
John Stane buried 26 Novēbʳ.
John Peacock buried 27 Noueb.
Marie, daughtʳ of Tho. Prentise, buried 3° Januarij.
Giles, sonne of Rich. Lankford, buried 22 Decebʳ.
1611. John Alsop, an old mã, was buried 28° Aβll, 1611.
Ja. 9°. Willm̃ Duddesborow buried eodē die.
Willm̃ Bett was buried 19 June.
Solomon, sonne of Robʳᵗ Crab, buried 9° Sept.
1612. Widow Miller, an old womã, buried the 8° of Aprill, A°
Ja. 10.   1612. R. Ja. 10.
Williã Nicols buried 14 Aprill.
Mary, daughtʳ of Rich. Hills, of Rumford, buried 12 Maie.
Beniamin, sonne of And. Wamsley, buried 17 June.
George Haryson was buried 30 Aug.
Edward Elderton buried 18 Sept.
Thomas Brainwood buried 30 Jan.
1613. Dennis, Wife of Jo. Browne, buried 6 Aprill, 1613.
Ja. 11. John, sonne of Willm̃ Howbroke, buried 22 Maij.
John, sonne of Tho. Foote, buried 4 of August.
Luce, wife of Tho. Stracy, buried 21 Sept.
Mother Sugdin was buried 20 Noueb.
Willm̃, sonne of Henry Coke, of London, Ciᵖ, buried 4° of
Febr.
1614. A daughter, vnbapt., of Willm̃ Small was buried 20 Aprill,
Ja. 12.   1614. Ja. 12.
Edward, sonne of Tho. Lankfield, buried 24 of Aprill.
Thomas, sonne of Tho. Stracy, buried 14 of August.
Jeremy, sonne of Jo. Scãpion, buried 16 Sept.
Sara, wife of Tho. Platt, buried 28 Octob.
Old mothʳ Branwood buried 27 Noueb.
Thomas, sonne of Willm̃ Best, buried 7 Noueb.
Willm̃, sonne of Steuen Euerist, of London, buried 26
Deceb.
Old mother Alsop was buried 22° Januarij.
1615. Mary, daughter of Ja. Brainwood, buried 13 Maij, 1615.
Ja. 13°. Robert, sonne of John Weldon & Katherine his Wife,
buried 4° Sept.
Mary, Wife of Barthol. Chapman, buried 23 Sept.
Willm̃, sonne of Francis Cravin & Mary his wife, bur. 2°
Noueb.
John, sonne of John [blank], buried 24 Noueb.
Dorothy, daughtʳ of John King, buried 1° Martij.
1616. John Pettit buried the 30 of March, 1616.
Ja. 14. Mothʳ Evered, an old widow, buried the 20 of Aug.

1616.   Tho., sonne of Willm̄ Batsford, buried 12 of May.
        Mothr Lauander, an old pore widow, buried 22 Noueb'.
1617.   John Dickinson, whelewright, buried vlt° Martij, 1617.
Ja. 15. Sara, daughtr of Phillip Ew̄ard, buried 5° June.
        Mary, daughtr of Barthol. Deringtō, buried 23 June.
        Anne Story, a stranger, buried 28 June.
        Mr Henry Ince, pastor of Chippin Vnger, was buried the 24
            of October, 1617.
        Martha, daughter of Edward Mare, buryed November 4 day.
        John, son of John Lees, buryed the 24 of January.
1618.   John Campion, a poor old man, buryed 24 of Aug.
Jac. 16. Mary, daughter of Joshua Haggar, buryed 4 of ffebruary.
An: 1619. Phillip Mallery, a poor inhabitant of our parish, buryed
Jac. 17.   April 4.
        Jone Bancks, an old widow woman, buryed June 10.
        Thomas Chambers, an inhabitant of Willingale Doe, dying
            in Cheping Ongar, was buryed there June 20.
        Old Giles Smal, yᵉ sexton, buryed July 7. he was church
            cleark many years.
An. 1620. Willm̄, son of Willm̄ Smal, buryed yᵉ 20 of May.
Jac. 18. Anne, yᵉ wife of Mr Abel Waynsworth, buryed June 13.
        Margaret, yᵉ wife of John Anjer, buryed August 16.
        Martha, daughter of George Hasley, buryed October 3.
        Jone, yᵉ Wife of Walter Corbet, buryed Novemb. 4.
        John . Crab, an ancient inhabitant of yᵉ parish, buryed
            Novemb'r 16.
        Thomas, yᵉ sonne of John King, buryed yᵉ 1 day of
            December.
        Robert, ye sonne of John Gryffyn, buryed Decemb'r 17.
        Thomas Bush, a pobre man, buryed yᵉ same day.
        Mary, yᵉ daughter of Willm̄ Batsford, buryed January 13.
        Elizabeth Pomfret, an ancient widow, was buryed yᵉ 30 of
            January.
        Jone, yᵉ wife of Thomas ffoot, was buryed yᵉ 15 of March.
                        Thomas Graves, pastor of yᵉ parish.
                        The mark X of ffrancis Alsop, Nicholas
                        Sparkes, Church- wardens.
An. 1621. Thomas Turnes, an inhabitant of yᵉ parish, buryed yᵉ 1 day
Jac. 19.   of May.
        John Ingoal, another inhabitant in yᵉ parish, buryed yᵉ 8 day
            of June.
        Anne Abbot, alias Anne Hewes, an old poor widow, buryed
            yᵉ 5 day of July.
        Thomas Laurence, a stranger, was buryed yᵉ 5 day of
            October.
An. Dom : 1622. Mary Prentis, an infant, yᵉ daughtr of Tho : Prentis,
regni Jac. 20.   husbandm̄a, buryed July 21.
            Jone, yᵉ wife of old Jeffray Read, yᵉ Curriour, buryed
                Septemb'r 28.
        John, yᵉ son of John Gryffyn and Love his wife, buryed yᵉ
            21 of October.
        James Smyth, a youth, Willm̄ Stayns prentice, was buryed
            yᵉ 5 of Novemb'r.

1622. Thomas Ailet, eldest son & heir vnto Vmfry Ailet, of ffyfield, buryed Novemb^r 6.

ffrancis Renalds, son of Thomas Renalds, of Blackmore, prentice to Tho. Beard, buryed 16 November.

William Crab, an infant, ye son of Robert Crab, barber, buryed ye 1 day of Decemb^r.

John Wels, whale bone body maker, a poor man, buryed ye 16 of December.

Anne Boste, an infant, ye daughter of John Boste, a vintn^r, of Londõ, buryed Decemb^r 28.

Robert Batsford, a child, ye sonne of Willm̃ Batsford, buryed ye 17th of January.

Elizabeth Polly, ye only child of M^{ris} Mary Polly, widow, buryed ye 6 of ffebruary.

An : Dom. 1623, James Derington, blacksmith, son of Richard Dering-
regni Jac. 21.   ton, buryed ye first of Aprill.

John Read, son of Jeffray Read, ye Currio^r, buryed ye 4th of Aprill.

George Horrard, ye son of Giles Horrard, buryed ye eleventh day of Aprill.

Anne Crab, a poor widow, buryed ye 18 of June, 1623.

John Broun, Cobler, a poor old man, buryed ye 25 day of October, 1623.

ffrances Mallery, an infant, ye daughter of Henrie Mallery, buryed Novemb^r 10.

John Saxie, scrivener, was buryed the third day of December, 1623.

Agnes White, a yong maid, ye daughter in law of Nicolas Spark, buryed 23 Decemb^r.

Elizabeth Batsford, a child, ye daughter of Willm̃ Batsford, buryed ye 11th of January.

Elizabeth Keel, an infant, daughter of John Keel, buryed Jan : 18th.

Elizabeth, ye wife of ffrancis Alsop, glover, buryed ye eleventh of ffebruary.

Anno domini Henrie Wels, a journeyman shomaker, buryed ye 14th day
1624,   of May, 1624.
anno regni   Steven Shipton, ye sonne of John Shipton, of Cheping
regis Jacobi Ongar, buryed ye 10th of July.
22.   Robert ffynch, ye eldest sonne of Willm̃ ffynch, of High Ongar, buryed the 25 day of August, in Cheping Ongar Church.

Samuel, ye sonne of Willm̃ Small, was buryed ye 31 day of August, 1624.

Anne, a child drowned in a tub of water, ye daughter of John Niccolson & Elizabeth his wife, buryed Septemb^r 23, 1624.

Prudence ffynch, ye daughter of Willm̃ ffynch, of High Ongar, buryed ye Third day of October, 1624. ·

John Davis, a poor man, was buryed October 30th.

Michael White, son of Michael White, buryed Octob^r 31.

Margaret, ye daughter of John Roberts, buryed Novemb^r 5.

John White, ye son of Michael White, buryed Novemb^r 11th.

1624. Richard Bilt, ye son of Willm̄ Bilt, Buryed Novemb^r 13th.
Andrew White, ye son of Michael White, buryed Novemb^r 21.
Elizabeth, the wife of Thomas Tydie, buryed Decemb^r 10th.
Thomasyn, ye wife of John Keel, buryed December 22.
Willm̄ Peacock, an infant, ye son of Barnabe Peacock,
buryed Jan. 9th.
Anne Bareford, widow, an ancient gentlewoman, sometyme
ye wife of Mr John Bareford, of Lamborn hall in Essex,
buryed the 18th of January.
Esther, ye daughter of Nicolas Spark, buryed ffebr. 25.
John Smyth, a poor journeyman shoemaker, was [*blank*] 21.
Thomas Horrard, a poor man, ye son of Giles Horrard,
buryed March 22.
Anno Domini 1625, Annoq̄, ffrancis Alsop, glover, an ancient Pa-
regni Regis Jacobi 23.   rishioner, buryed March 25.
Anno Domini 1625, Emma ffynch, ye daughter of Willm̄ ffynch of High
anno regni   Ongar, buryed April 20th.
regis Caroli   John Langfyeld, a child, ye son of Richard Lang-
primo.   fyeld, buryed Aprill 22.
Hugh Willans, ye son of Edmund Willans, buryed
Septemb^r 2.
Jone Lacy, widow, sometyme ye wife of Willm̄ Lacy, of
Stansted, buryed Septemb^r 18th.
Richard Samuel,   ⎱ both inhabitants of o^r parish,
Bartholomew Chapman, ⎰   buryed Octob^r 26.
Thomas Sedgewick, a poor man, buryed Novemb^r 15th.
Jone Chapman, ye daughter of Bartlemew Chapman,
Deceased, buryed 25 of Novemb^r.
Abraham Offyn, butcher, buryed December 9th.
By me Thomas Graves, pastour of Cheping
Ongar in Essex.
by me Auery Lacy, ⎱ Church Wardens.
John Parker, ⎰
Anno Domini 1625.   Thomas Anjer, an ancient man, brother to John
annoq̄, regni   Weldons wife, buryed the 5 of January.
Caroli   John Jiggins, a falconer, lying & dying at Thomas
regis 1°.   Champnis house, was buryed Jan : 11th.
John Weldon, an ancient inhabitant in o^r Town, buryed
the fift day of ffebruary.
Elizabeth, ye wife of Henrie Scampion, Carpenter, buryed
March 4th.
Samuell Weldon, ye son of John Weldon, lately deceased,
buryed March 13th.
John Archer, butcher, an ancient man, buryed March the
16th day.
Anno Domini 1626.   Sarah Parker, an ancient godly widow, buryed
annoq̄, regni regis   Aprill 20th, 1626.
Caroli 2°.   James Penyman, an ancient inhabitant of this
parish, buryed April 23.
Anne Gryffin, ye daughter of Willm̄ Gryffyn, buryed April 29th.
Elizabeth, the wife of Edward Peacock, was buryed the
first day of May.
John, the son of Edward Peacock, buryed May 8.

1626. Mary, the wife of Jo : Archer, of Epping, buryed May 9th.
Edward Peacock, shopkeep, buryed May 10th.
Willm̃, son of Edward Peacock, deceased, buryed May 13.
Thomas, son of Edward Peacock, deceased, May 17th.
Elizabeth, Daughter of Richard Langfyeld, wth her child
vnchristened, buryed May 17th.
Margaret Castle, dwelling wth Thomas Champnis, buryed
May 18.
Steven, son of Edward Peacock, deceased, buryed May
20th.
Anne, ye wife of John Gryffin, Cutler, buryed May 28.
Jone Harris, widow, an ancient woman, buryed Aug. 15th.
Martha, the wife of old Richard Derington, buryed Septem-
ber 11th.
Marian, ye wife of old John Palinge, was buryed October
14th.
Dorothy, ye daughter of Nicolas Sparks, buryed Octob^r
30th.
Thomas Saxie, a yong man, buryed March 4th, 1626.
Anno Domini 1627. Mary Samuel, the daughter of Richard Samuel,
annoq̃ regis 3°   deceased, buryed June 5.
Caroli.   Jone Mallery, an ancient poore widow, buryed
the 11th of September.
Anno Domini 1628. John Herrington, an ancient yoman, buryed
annoq̃ regni regis April 21.
4to Caroli.   Walter Crab, the sonne of Robt Crab, was buryed
April 22.
Thomas Champnis, an husbandman, was buryed May 25.
John Barret, ye son-in-law of Thomas Champnis, buryed ye 1
day of August.
Willm̃ Mathewes, the son of Bennet Mathewes, a child, buryed
Aug. 7th.
Mary ffynch, the daughter of Willm̃ ffynch ye yonger, of
High Ongar, buryed August ye 8 day.
Margaret White, daughter of Michael White, was buryed
Septemb^r 10 day.
Peter Mathewes, ye son of Benedict Mathewes, was buryed
Octob^r ye first day.
John Peacock, ye son of Barnabas Peacock, was buryed
Octob^r 7th day.
Jane, ye wife of Avery Lacy, was buryed the 18th day of
ffebr.
Nicolas Sparke, Shoemaker, was buryed ffebr. 27th, 1628.
Anno Domini 1629. Elizabeth, ye wife of George Hasley, was buryed
annoq̃ regni regis March 28.
Caroli 5°.   Mary, ye wife of Anthonie Harwood, was buryed
April 14th day.
Mary, ye daughter of. Anthony Harwood, was buryed
April 18th.
Richard Blaxe, servant vnto John Andrewes, buryed May
31.
Mathew Lacy, ye sonne of Avery Lacy, was buryed June 4th
day.

1629. John Parker, singleman, and by trade a whitetayer, was
    buryed 2 of Septemb[r].

Thomas Shipton, y[e] son of John Shipton, was buryed y[e] 31
    day of October.

• Thomasyn Spark, widow, y[e] wife of Nicolas Spark, deceased,
    was buryed Novemb[r] 20th.

John Spark, a singleman, a yong man, y[e] son of Nicolas
    Spark, deceased, was buryed Decemb[r] 20th.

John Yong, Gentleman and singleman, was buryed Decemb[r]
    21 day.

John Parnbe, y[e] son of Richard Parnbe, was buryed ffebr. 17th.

Anno Domini 1630. Mary, wife of John Andrewes, sometyme y[e] wife
annoq regni regis   of Robt. Polley, was buryed March 26 day.
Caroli 6°.   Joseph Spark, the son of Nicolas Spark, deceased,
                     was buryed June 2 day.

Mary Barker, y[e] daughter of Robt. Barker, was buryed
    July 13th day.

Katherine, y[e] wife of ffrancis Derington, glover, was buryed
    August y[e] third day.

Elizabeth, y[e] wife of Jeffray Brainwood, laborer, was buryed
    Aug. 24th.

Thomas Beard, Shoemaker, and an headburrough of O[r]
    Town, buryed Septemb : 20.

Jacob Parsons, a child, y[e] son of Rafe Parsons, was buryed
    Septemb : 21.

Matthew, an infant, left alive in y[e] shambles on High Ongar
    faire day at night, lived a moneth, & was buryed y[e]
    Octob[r] 10th.

Mary Mayer, y[e] daught[r] of Edward Mayer, buryed Novemb[r]
    27th.

John Parnbe, an infant son of Richard Parnbe, was buryed
    Decemb[r] 3 day.

Richard Derington, an ancient parishioner, was buryed Jan :
    1 day.

Grace Hewes, an old wench, was buryed Jan : 18 day.

Prudence Barbar, daughter of James Barbar, Buryed ye 22
    day of ffebruary.

Mercie, ye wife of Samuel Osborn, Shopkeeβ, buryed
    March 22.

            Per me Thomam Graves, Rectorem Ecclesiæ de
            Cheapen Ongar in Essexiæ.

            Jacob Archer,   } Churchwardens.
            Simon Burrell, }

Anno Domini 1631. Elizabeth Penyman, ye daughter of James Peny-
annoq regni regis   man, deceased, buryed June 1.
Caroli 7°.   Margaret Small, daught[r] of Willm Small, was
                    buryed ye 7th of June.

John Niccolson, son of John Niccolson, buryed July 24th.

Sara Mayer, y[e] daughter of Edward Mayer, buryed Sept :
    4 day.

Anno Domini, 1632. Margaret, wife of Henrie Archer, & sometyme
annoq regni regis   wife of John Slane, was buryed Aprill 3
Caroli 8°.   day.

1632. Richard Langfyeld, son of Richard Langfyeld, was buryed
    Aprill 5 day.
John Small, a poor inhabitant, was buryed Aprill 17th.
John Roberts, a poor inhabitant, was buryed May 6 day.
John Palmer, a poor aged man, was buryed June 30 day.
Jeffray Clark, son of John Clark, buryed Sept. 20 day.
Thomas Tidie, an aged man, was buryed October 17th day.
Thomas Beard, ye son of John Beard, was buryed Novemb:
    19th.
Rebecca, wife of Mr Josua Wilson, minister of God's word,
    was buryed Novembr 30th day.

Anno Domini, 1633. Margaret Small, daughter of Willm Small, buryed
annoq regni regis   Aprill 30th.
Caroli 9°.   Edmund Willans, a poor man, buryed May 7th
    day.
John Niccolson, son of John Niccolson, buryed June 18th.
Elizabeth Read, daughter of Willm Read, buryed June 22.
Katherin Weldon, widow, sometyme ye wife of John Weldon,
    buryed July 16.
Mary, ye wife of Edward Mayer, was buryed November 8
    day.
Anne, ye wife of John Sedgewick, was buryed Novembr
    17th.
Robt. King, an infant, son of Robt. King, buryed Jan:
    14th.
Margaret Sweeting, a poor ancient widow, buryed Jan: 15th.
Mary Derington, ye daughter of James Derington, deceased,
    buryed Jan: 28.
Jasper Smyth, a smyth, was buryed ye 4th day of ffebruary.
Thomas Renalds, a child, ye son of Thomas Renalds, was
    buryed ffebr. day 21.

Anno Domini 1634. Robert, son of Robert Stane, was buryed Aprill
annoq regni regis   1 day.
Caroli 10.   Elizabeth, daughter of ffrancis Archer, buryed
    April 15 day.
Elizabeth Derington, a child, daughter of John Derington,
    buryed May 6.
Jone Harwood, daughter of Giles Harwood, was buryed
    May 12th.
Alice Plat, daughter of Thomas Plat, was buryed May 23.
Elizabeth, the wife of John Nicolson, buryed June 12th.
Marjory Chapman, an ancient poor widow, was buryed ye
    4th of September.
Jone, ye wife of Willm Best, glover, was buryed the 25 day
    of October, 1634.
Alice, ye wife of Willm Wood, was buryed the second day of
    December.
Thomas Prentise, an ancient inhabitant, was buryed the
    third day of December.
Robt. Stane, an infant son of Robt. Stane, was buryed
    March 12 day.
Alice Saxie, an ancient poor widow, was buryed March 13
    day.

Anno Domini 1635. John Read, an ancient poor man, buryed Aprill
annoq regni regis   19th day.
    Caroli 11°.   John Burrell, a child, son of Simon Burrell, was
                        buryed the 25 day of May.
              Thomas Graves, Parson of Cheping Ongar, buryed June xth.
              Jane, the daughter of Mr James Darvile, Julye 20th.
              An infant of Thom. Reynolds, Septemb. 21.
              Mary, the wife of ffrances Archer, October 2.
              Elizabeth, of John Nicolls, December 27th.
              Frances, of Robert Childs, Februarye 7th.
              Robert Tyday,   „   13th.
              Daniell, of Mr James Sedgwick „   26th.
    Anno Dom : 1636. John Lorkyn, Aprill 12th.
annoq Caroli Regis John Niccolls buryed June 23.
        12°.   ffather Tomson buryed Julye 10th.
                    Sary, the daughter of Richard Kinge & Anne,
                      buryed October 22.
              Henry Elkin buryed Octob. 31.
              Samson, [son] of Samson Sheffield, of Navestock, gent.,
                buryed Decemb. 22.
              Thomas Reynolds, Jan. 22th.

    Anno Dom : 1637. Regis 13°.

              David, of Mr Hardred, of London, was buryed Aprill 18th.
              William, of Simon Burrell [April] 27.
              William Small the yonger buryed June last.
              William Finch thelder, of High Ongar, buryed in o^r parish,
                June 16, 1637.
              An infant of Thomas Tabor buryed December 28th.
              Robert, of Edward and Alice Parker, buryed February 3.
              Richard, of Richard and Anne Kinge,   „   15th.
              Anne, of Anthony & Elisabeth Harwood, March 15.

    Anno 1638. March [*sic*].

              Mrs Jane Pallavicine, 27th Aprill.
              Lydia, Grandchild of Wm Small, buryed May [*blank*].
              Frances Smith buryed May 27th, 1638.
              Thomas Angier buryed June 4th.
              Elisabeth, wife of Wm Read, June 22th.
              Thomas Sparks buryed July 31th.
              Rebekah, the wife of William Hogge, August 6.
              Alice Platt, widdow, August 9th.
              Mary, daughter of Christopher Beard, buryed August 15th.
              Thomas Wennell buryed August 21th.
              Infans Thomæ Chaplayn   „   27th.
              vid' Samuell buryed September 9th.
              Infans Jacobi Batsford   „   10th.
              John, [son] of Philip Poole „   12th.
              Henry Crab, Novemb. 21th.
              The wife of John Clarke, 23th.
              vidua Pennyman   „   27th.

Anno Dom : 1639.

Isaac White buryed March 31.
Anne Harwood buryed May 25th.
ffrances Peacock, a nurse child, July 11th.
John Whetstone, July 20th.
George Pennyman, August 15th.
Mrs Allice Younge, Septemb. 6th.
Twoo children of a Pedler called Thomas ffootman, whereof
    one baptized, the other still borne [Sept] xth.
Elisabeth . . . . . . 19th.
Mary . . . . 3th.
William Bettye buryed November 11th.
Thomas Champnes, January 17th.
A nurslinge of Goodman Johnsons, of High Ongar, ffebruary
    [blank].
Anne, daughter of Mr Ewin, Londinen : ffebruary 8th.
Andrew Grainge buryed March 8th.

1640. The wife of [blank] Burton, May 10th.
Lydia, of Xtopher & Lydia Preston, Novemb. 15th.
John, of Robert Staines   ,,   16th.
George, of George Babbs, Jan. 16th.
John, of Thomas ffootman, ffeb. 12th.
Ann Raynbeard, ffeb. 14th.
Richard Kinge buryed March 11th.
Robert Stanes, March 12th.
John Clarke, March 22th.

Anno Domini 1641.

Sarah Crookes [March] 27th.
The wife of Simon Burrell, Aprill 19th.
Mrs Elisabeth, Wife of James Sedgwick, gent., was buried
    the seaventh of May, 1641.
Elisabeth Thomson, June xth.
Richard Lankfield, Julye 25th.
Ellin, of John Anger [no date].
Williã Hart, of Navestock, Septemb. first.
Captaine Mathew Wills   ,,   28th.
Nicholaus Babbs buryed Decemb. 14th.
Widdow Archer buried January 11th.
Robert, sonne of Robert Whyte, Jan : [blank].
Dan: of Philip Poole, ffeb. 27th.
Mary, wife of George Pennyman, buryed March 13th.
Thomas Turke buryed March [blank].

Anno Dom : 1642.

William Bilt buryed May 24th.
Rebekah, of Gamaliell Burton, 29th.
Andrew Stoddart, August 16th.
The Wife of Richard Granger, 21th.
George Pennyman, Septemb. 16th.
Infans Wm Tabor   ,,   26.
Anne Batsford, December 7th.

Anno 1643.

Robert, of Wm Read, Aprill 3^d.
John Keale buryed   „   20th.
Elisabeth Read, May 26th.
Obadiah Derrington, June 2^d.
George Hazel   „   26th.
Ellin, of John Angier, buryed Septemb. 8th.
Elisabeth, of Xtopher Glascock, October 26th.
Margarett, of Xtopher Glascock   „   30th.

(No entries between 1643 and 1648.)

Nono May, 1648. Horacio Pallavicine, Esquire, was buried.

(No entries between 1648 and 1659.)

1659.

Buryed Sarah, wife of Wm Smale, September the 19th, 1659.
Buryed John Owen, alias Williams, the seuenth of December, 1659.
Buryed Joseph Lanckfeild, sonne of Joseph, the fifteenth of December.

1660.

Buryed ffrancis, sonne of Wm Reynolds, of Wenington, Aprill ye 4th, 1660.
Buryed a ffemale Child of Will: and Mary Acres, Aprill ye 25th.
Buryed George Babs, of this towne, May the 14th day, Anno 1660.
Buryed William Smale, the sixteenth day of October, 1660.
Buryed Mr Collins, the 31th day of October, Anno Doⁱ: 1660.
Buryed Marey, da: of James & Eliz: Branwood, Nouember the 14th.
Buryed Priscilla, Daughter of Mr Dawes, of London, wine Coop, No: 19th.
Buryed David, sonne of Richard Tyler, the 28th of Nouember.
Buryed the widdowe Smale, the Eight day of December.

An: Dom. 1661. Buried.

Francess, the wife of Henry Mallery, March 26.
Thomas King, March 28.
Thomas Plat, June 4th.
Edward, the sonne of Timothy Mayer, June 6.
Jacob, the sonne of Jacob Archer, May 20.
Elizabeth, the daught. of [*blank*], Aug. 8.
Mrs Ann King, Widdow, August 14.
William, the sonne of William Godfry, October 23.
Anne, the wife of Robert Young, Gent., Octob. 30.
William, the sonne of [*blank*] Feild, and his wife Novr 3.
A female child of Thomas Babs and his wife, Dec. 7.

106

William, the sonne of Edward Ward and his wife, Dec. 12.
Rose, the wife of George Pepper, Feb. 21.
Alice, the wife of Nicholas Crab, March 3.

1662. Buryed.

Mary, the Daughter of Thomas Babs and his wife, May 20.
William, the sonne of Will Spranger and his wife, May 22.
William Aker, May 23.
A male child of William Smith and his wife, July [*blank*].
Robert Young, Gent., Septr. 4.
Daniell Lucas, Septr. 26.
Francess, the Daughter of John Bridges and his wife, Octo. 17.
A female child of William Not and his wife, Octob. 20.
Joan, the wife of Edmund Kendall, Novr 14.
Edward Alexander, Dec. 2.
Rebĕka, da : of Will. Stane, Dec. 9.
John, sonne of George Piper, Jan. 21.
A male child of John Carter, Feb. 26.

An. Dom : 1663.

Ralph Persons Buryed Sept. 4.
Mary, the daughter of Wm Parks, Nov. 3.
A male child of Georg Writt, Dec : [*blank*].
A female child of Wm Tabor, ffeb : [*blank*].

Anõ 1664.

Jane, ye wife of John Naylor, March 25.
John, of Josias & An Beard, May 1.
A female child of a Traueller, May 19.
Katherine Langfeild, widow, August 15th.
Mr Thomas Gouldesburgh, Gent., September 9th.
John Beard, January 13th.
A male Child of Thomas & Marget Crofts, ffebr. 2th.
ffortune Nichols, Widow, ffebruary 3^d.
Widow Alsop, March 10th.

1665. Buried.

Christopher Whetstone, March 26th.
Samuel, of Samuel Whitehead, Aprill 15.
Edward Browne, Aprill 17th.
Mrs Anne Ewer, widow, June 6th.
Anne Platt, September 10th.
Mrs Meggs, wth her child, 7^{ber} 26th.
[*blank*] Pickerine & her child, 8^{ber} 6.
Sarah Grubb & her child, 8^{ber} 8.
Widow Parsons, 8^{ber} 13.

Sarah Waylet, 8ber 22th.
George Pickerine 8ber 27th.
John Nichols, 9ber 3.
Charles Lucas, 9ber 3.
[*blank*] Thurgood, 9ber 5.
Mary Waylet, 9ber 7th.
[*blank*] Perryer, 10ber 12th.
Mrs Stoakes, Widow, 10ber 28.
Añe of Thomas & Marget Crofts, January 23.
Robert King, March 19th.

1666.

John Gwin, Aprill 20th.
Mary Warner, August 2d.
Elizabeth Pickerine, ffeb. 1.
John, of Wm & Joaña Smith, ffeb. 5.

Buried. 1667.

Widow Lucas, Aprill [*torn away*].
A female Child of John Chopping [*date torn away*].
Simon Erwin, May 29.
John, of Wm & Katherine Tabor, June 6th.
Wm, of Thomas & Mary Babs, June 17.
Wm Brewer, Sept. 16.
John Hancocke, Octber 3th.
Widow Salmon, Oct. 4th.
Mary, wife of James King, Oct. 28.
John, of Edward & Mary Phips, Nov. 3d.
Mr Hils, Nov. 27th.
Mr Bringhurst, December 11th.
Williä, of Henry White, Decber 8th.
Timothy Mayor, March 8th.
Elizabeth, of John & Abigail Boram, March 10.

Buried. 1668.

Robert Stains, March 30th.
Widow Owen, Aprill 5th.
Henery Slight, Aprill 16.
John Baynham, Gent., May 6th (?).
Jasper Smith, June 24th.
Israel Lucas, July 16th.
Robert, of Robert & Katherine Stains, September 2d.
Anne, of Thomas & Sarah Anger, September 25th.
Katherine, of James and Elizabeth Branwood, Nov. 2th
James, of James & Rebecca Cliffe, November 27th.
Elizabeth, wife of James Branwood, January 10th.

James Crooke, Rector.
William Thurgood, } Church Wardens.
William Stains,

Buried. 1669.

John Wilkin, March 31ᵗʰ.
William Waylett, August 9ᵗʰ.
John Bridges, August 23.
Mⁿ Sarah Spranger, Octo: 3ᵈ.
Mⁿ Graves, October 12ᵗʰ.
Mary King, No: 25ᵗʰ.
[*blank*], of Edward & Mary Phips, De: 14.
Widow Babs, ffeb: 8ᵗʰ.
Añe, of Thomas & Margaret Crofts, ffeb: 15ᵗʰ.
William, of Thomas & Mary Babs, March 14ᵗʰ.
Mary, wife of Edward Ward, March 17ᵗʰ.

1670.

Widow Anger, May 3ᵈ.
Katherine, wife of George Stains, July 9ᵗʰ.
Elizabeth, of James & Elizabeth King, July 10ᵗʰ.
Katherine, of George & Katherine Stains, July 19ᵗʰ.
William Anger, August 22ᵗʰ.
James, of Edward Ward, August 25ᵗʰ.
John Naylor, September [*blank*].
Agnes, of William & Elizabeth Thurgood, September 25ᵗʰ.
Richard Chopping, October 5ᵗʰ.
George ffrancis, October 10ᵗʰ.
Hannah, Daughter of Wᵐ & Hannah Lacey, Octobʳ 23ᵗʰ, 70.
Henry Malery, Noueɓ 7ᵗʰ.
Jane, of Thomas & Jane ffoard, ffeab: 23ᵗʰ, 1670.
Elizabeth, wife of Wᵐ Allexander, ffeab: 24ᵗʰ, 70.

(No entries for 1671.)

Buried August the nineth, 1672, Mʳ William Alexander, Gent.
Mˢ Susan Bowns. Buried the third of January, 1672.

1673. Buried.

Peter Fuellin, a Stranger, December [*blank*].
Thomas Bazen, drownd and buried February 17 in Christian burial in Chipping Onger.

Buriall of the dead 1674.

John Tabor buried September 18, 1674.
Ann, daug: of Georg & Mary Stoaks, buried Decem. 15, 1674.

1675.

Mˢ Hancock buried June 27, 1675.
Philip Batsford, September 29ᵗʰ, 1675.
Mʳ Thomas Bounds, October 19ᵗʰ, 1675.

Anne, daughter of Mr Benjamin Stebbin and Abigail his wife, was buried Apr. 30, 1676.

Mr Thomas Rednell was buried May 8th, 1676.

Margaret, wife of Mr Mathew Browne, was buried June 21, 1676.

[*blank*], Son of Michael Turner, and Martha his wife, was buried July 18, 1676.

Mathew, Son of Mathew Browne and Margaret his wife, was buried Septem. 21ⁿ, 1676.

Mary, wife of Thomas Babbs, was buried Octob : 4th, 1676.

John Hancocke was buried the 10th, 1676.

Elizabeth, daughter of Edward Peacock, was buried Oct. 16, 1676.

Joan Ramsey was buried Octob : 18th, 1676.

Sarah, wife of John Lucas, was buried Novem : 22, 1676.

Thomas Holt was buryed Decem. 9th, 1676.

Joan, wife of Philip Traherne, was buried Decem : 29, 1676.

William, son of William Tabor and Catherine his wife, was buried Jan : 21, 167⅚.

John Harris was buried Feb : 1, 167⅚.

1677.

Anne, wife of George Wright, was buried Apr. 18, 1677.

Elizabeth Harris, wid :, was buried July 9th, 1677.

Priscilla Tyler, widd :, was buried July 16, 1677.

Mary Anger, widd :, was buried Aug. 30, 1677.

Rowland, son of Philip Trayherne and Sarah his wife, was buried Octob : 11, 1677.

James Batsford was buried Jan : 16, 1677.

Mr John Wood, of High Easter, was buried Feb : 27, 167⅞.

William Tabor was buried March 1, 1677.

Elizabeth, daughter of Will. Whitehead, was buried Jan : (*sic*) 17, 1677.

John Brasier was buried March the seventh, 1677.

1678.

Sarah, daughter of Will : Munday, was buried Aprill 15, 1678.

Daniell, son of Daniell Chapman, was buried May 30, 1678.

Sarah, Daughter of John Young, was buried July 20, 1678.

Richard Sarrutt was buried July 19, 1678.

Samuell, Son of Samuell Eve, was buried July 27, 1678.

Sarah, Daughter of George Peg, was buried in woollen, Septem. 9, 1678, as appeared by Certificate.

Luce Dan, a Strang^r, was buried in woollen, according to the late act, Septem. 23, 1678, as appeared by Certificate.

Samuell King, son of James King, was buried in woollen, according to the late act (as appeared by certificate, Nov. . . . 1678).

Jacob Archer was buried in woollen, according to the late act, Decem : 13, 1678, as appeared by Certificate.

Elizabeth Mallcott was buried in woollen according to the late act, Jan. 6, $167\frac{8}{9}$, as appeared by certificate.

Mr William Godfrey was buried in woollen, according to the late act, Feb 5th. $167\frac{8}{9}$, as appeared by affidavit.

Thomas Anger was buried in woollen, according to the late act, Feb. 27, $167\frac{8}{9}$, as appeared by affidavit.

Mr Joseph King was buried Feb. 28, 1678, according to the late act [of] ꝑliament for burying in woollen, as appeared by affadavit.

1679.

Thomas White was buried March 31, for which no certificate was brought.

Thomas Anger, Junr, was buried Apr. 8th, 1679, according to the late act of ꝑliament for burying in woollen, as appeared by Certificate.

Thomas Larkin was buried Apr. 13, 1679, according to the late act of ꝑliament for burying in woollen, as appeared by certificate.

Samuel Kenton was buryed Apr. 13, 1679, according to the late act for burying in woollen, as appeared by certificate.

Elizabeth Bouchee, of [the] parish of St Giles in the feildes, was buried Apr. 26, 1679, according to the late act of ꝑliament for burying in wollen, as appeared by affidavit received May 1.

James Braynard was buried June 20, 1679, according to the late act of ꝑliament for burying in Woollen, as appeared by affidavit received June 24.

Thomas Whitehead, Son of Will. Whitehead, was buried Aug. the 8, 1679, according to the act of ꝑliament for burying in woollen, as appeared by affidavit received Aug. 15th.

Samuell, son of Daniell Chapman, was buried Sept. 7th, according to the act of ꝑliament for burying in woollen, as appeared by affidavit received.

John, son of John Rofe, was buried Sept. 22, according to the act of ꝑliament for burying in Woollen, as appeared by affidavit rec: Sept. 25.

Francis Woodfine was buried Sept. 22, according to the act of ꝑliament for burying in woollen, as appeared by affidavit rec: Sept. 27.

Elizabeth Munday was buried Sept. 13, 1679, according to the act of ꝑliament for burying in woollen, as appeared by affidavit rec: Sept. 14.

Elizabeth, daughter of John Wells, was buried Octob: 26, 1679, according to the late act of ꝑliament for burying in woollen, as appeared by affidavit received Novem: 5.

Dorothy, wife of Samuell Whitehead, was buried Decem: 17, 1679, according to the late act of ꝑliament for burying in woollen, as appeared by affidavit re: Decem: 22.

William Lacy was buried Decem: 28, 1679, according to the late act of ꝑliament for burying in woollen, as appeared by certificate re: Jan: 2, $16\frac{79}{80}$.

Edward ffipps was buried March 2^{d}, $16\frac{79}{80}$, according to the late act of ꝑliament for burying in woollen, as appeared by Certificate brought March 7.

1680.

Anne, Daughter of Jn° Waylett, Buried May 24, 1680.
Jn° Enever buried June 21.
William Price Buried July 25, 1680.
Sarah Holte Buried August 3, 1680.
Will: Cackbread Buried August 9th, 1680.
Mary Cary, Daughter of Richard Cary & Eliz: his wife, Buried Novembr 8th, 1680.
Will: Parks, Son of Will: Parks & Joannah his wife, Buried Novembr ye 12, 1680, & affidavit made accordingly.
Joshuah Beard Buried Decembr ye 4th, 1680, & affidavit made according to a late Act intituled an Act for burying in woolling.
Humphrey Hastler Buried January 17, 1680, and affidavit made accordingly.
Preston Norden, son of Weston & Eliz: his wife, Buried Jan: 18, 1680. Affidavit made accordingly.
Martha, wife of Michael Turner, buried February 23, 1680, and affidavit made accordingly.
Anna, wife of Will: Munday, buried March 6, 1680, and affidavit made accordingly.
Mary, daughter of Sam̄ll Kempton, buried March 18, 1680, and affidavit made accordingly.
Widdow Mayor buried March 24, 1680, and affidavit made accordingly.

Buried. 1681.

Widdow Cackbread buried Aprill ye 3rd, 1681, and affidavit made accordingly.
John Parks, son of Witt Parks & Johannah his wife, Buried May ye second, & affidavit made accordingly.
Eliz: Chopping, Daughter of John Chopping and Eliz: his wife, buried July 21, 1681, and affidavit made accordingly.
Rich: Wells, ffaither of John Wells, was Buried August ye 24th, 1681.
Frances, Wife of Peter Shefford, was Buried Septr 1st, 1681.
Sarah, Wife of Samll Kempton, Buried Septr 26, 1681.
Wm, Sonn of Wm Staines & Sussan his wife, Buried October ye 19th, 1681.
John, sonn of John Rowden and Ann his wife, Buried October 25, 1681.
Daniell, sonn of Daniell Browne, Buried March the 15th, 1681.
Edward, son of Edward Hills & Elizabeth his Wife, Buried March 19th, 1681.

Buried 1682.

Elizabeth, Daughter of Wm Munday, Buried Aprill 9th, 1682.
Abraham, Son of Abraham Griffinhoffe & Martha his wife, Buried Apll 18, 1682.
Katherine, Daughter of Mary Williamson, Widd., buried June 7th, 1682.
William Holbrooke was Buried the 3d of January, 1682.

Mary, the Daughter of Michall Turner and Mary his Wife, was Buried the 22th day of ffebr, 1682.
Elizabeth, Daughter of Tho: Leuerett & Mary his Wife, was Buried March 11th, 1682.

1683.

Mary Haynes, widdow, was burried Dece: 30th, 1683.
Tho: Sell was burrid Dece: 30th, 1683.
Elliner Wease, widdow, was burried Jan: 11th, 1683.
William Tabor was burried Sept. 4th, 1683.
Jeane Peacocke, ye wife of Edward Peacocke, was burried Jan. 12th, 1683.
John Stains, ye son of William Stains & Susan his wife, was buried ye 26 day of Feb: 1683-4.

1684.

John Burling was Buried ye 13 of Aprill, 1684.
[April] 18th. Buried Mary Munday's Daughter.
Aprill, 27, 1684. Buried Sarah Waylett, Daughter of Wm Waylett, & of M . . . his Wife.
Buried 4th of Decm̄, 1684, Jeames King.
Joan Waylett Buried Jañ 23th.
Buried Danniell Allsup, March 3th, 168⅘.
14th, Buried Elizabeth Allsup, Daughter of Daniell & Elizabeth his wife.

1685.

Aprill 10th. Buried Hannah Whitehead, the Wife of Samuell Whitehead.
May 6th. Buried George Wennell, iunior, 1685.
The 19. Buried Will: Sparks, Sexton of this p̄rsh.
June 7th. Buried Joseph King, ye son of Joseph King & Anne his wife.
July 20th, 1685. Buried Ann King, daughter of Joseph & of Ann his wife.
July 27th, 1685. Buried Elizabeth Stane, daughter of George & Katherine his wife.
Aug. 24th, 1685. Buried Me Scampion.
Mr Charles Capell, sonn of Gammaliell Capell, Esq̄, of Rucketts in Abbas Rooting, Dyed att ye Crowne in this Towne on ye 7 day of August, 1685.
Decem: 9th, 1685. Buried Abigal, the wife [of] Mr Beniamin Stebbing.
Jan. 1th, 168⅘. Buried Margrett, wife of Mr Jacob Archer, Draper in this prsh.
March 1th. Buried Sarah, da: of Abigale & Beniamin Stebbing.

1686.

June 1th, 1686. Buried Elizabeth, da: of Elizabeth & Will: Whitehead.
June 11th. Buried Tho: Anger ye Junior, Butcher.
The 13. William, ye Sonn of Elizabeth & Simond Rowse.

The 21. Mary, y⁰ Da : of Sarah & Joseph Pegrum.
July 14ᵗʰ. Jane, yᵉ Wife of Danniell Chapman.
George, Sonn of George Haynes, Junior, July 23ᵗʰ.
Aug. 26ᵗʰ. Buried Mⁱ Mary Spranger, 1686.
The 27ᵗʰ. Buried Lidiah, Da : of Ann & Jeame [sic] Branwood.
Sep. 12ᵗʰ, 1686. Buried Auery Lacie att The Brick house.
Octo : 3ᵗʰ, 1686. Buried Robert Neue, Rector of Dunton, & att this time
    Curate of this place.
Decꝫ 9ᵗʰ. Burried John Waylett, Junior.
Buried 21ᵗʰ. Mⁱ Margrett Allexander.
ffebu : 19ᵗʰ, 168⅚. Buried Katherine Cutler, fformmerly Wilkinn.

1687.

Aprˡˡ 12ᵗʰ, 1687. Buried John Thurgood, the Sonn of ffrancis Thurgood,
    of this p̄rsh.
Aprˡˡ 13ᵗʰ. Buried Tho. Blewett.
15ᵗʰ. Buried Mathew Miller.
20ᵗʰ. Buried Elizabeth Turner, a Grand Child of Mʳ Gouldsburgh.
May 1ᵗʰ. Buried George Stoakes, Senior.
May 13ᵗʰ. Buried Ann Fryer, a servant to Mʳ Chaplinn att yᵉ Castell.
May 22ᵗʰ. Buried Hannah, da. of Will : Porter & of Jane his wife.
    23ᵗʰ. Buried yᵉ Widd. White, wife of old George White yᵉ Black-
smith.
The same day Buried a Male Child of Jeames Branwood's.
June 21ᵗʰ, 1687. Buried Judie, daughter of yᵉ widow Allsup.
Sep. 4ᵗʰ. Burried Griffee, a Bastard Child of yᵉ widd : Waylctts.
No : 21ᵗʰ. Buried Jeffery Thurgood, Senior.

1688.

June 8ᵗʰ, 1688. Buryed a Male Child of Tho : Emsonns.
June 27ᵗʰ. Buried John, Sonn of Dennis & John Knight.
July 18ᵗʰ. Died in this p̄rsh Mary Wright, late wife of Abraham Wright
    of Parsley Hall, in High Ongar prsh.
Aug : 5ᵗʰ, 1688. Buried Elizabeth, wife of Saꝫ Eue & formerly wife of
    John Tabor.
    yᵉ 17. Buried Bogle, a sonn of Mʳ Turner's.
Sep. 6ᵗʰ. Buried Jeames, sonn of Jeames Cornell yᵉ Black Smith.
The 14ᵗʰ. Buried Olliue, da : of ffrances Sadler.
The 20ᵗʰ. Buried Elizabeth, the da. of George Oye.
Octo : the 18. Buried a ffemale Child of yᵉ same Man's.
No : yᵉ 19. Died in this prsh, Martha, da. of John Merrills.
Decꝫᵇᵉʳ yᵉ 9, 1688. Buried Will :, sonn of Will : Porter.
The 23. Buried Henry, sonn of Nathaneꝶ Allinn.
The 27. Buried Danniel Morse, Post man in this Towne.
Jannuary yᵉ 10, 168⅞. Buried Robert Platt.
February 15ᵗʰ. Buryed Elizabeth, da. of Thomas Leueret.
Dyed in this parish, the wife of Mʳ Hales, & buryed att High Onger
    ffeb : 20ᵗʰ.
March 3ᵗʰ. Buryed Rebecca, yᵉ da. of Weston Norden.

114

May 9th, 1689. Buried Ann, sister of Jeames Cornell.
The 29 Quoque. Buried Elias Key, who died att John Meade's.
August 15, 1689. Buried Richard, Sonn of John Sanders, Junior.
The 19. Buryed Samuel, Sonn of Joseph King.
Septem : 15th. Buryed a daughter of Mr Nicholas Alexanders, Citizen.
Jan. 8th, 1689-90. Buryed Mrs Simon Rouse.
Jan. 19. Buryed Susanna Stanes, Senior, at ye Lion.
Jan. 20, 1689-90. Buried the widdow Wallice.
Jaĥ 22th. Buryed ffrancis Sadler, a Child.
March 2. Buryed Mary Pegrum.
March 21. Buryed Mr Griffinhoofe's Mother.

1690.

April 7th, 90. Buried Steward Porter.
April 29th. Buried Daniel Chapman.
July 18th. Buryed a Daughter of Rebecca Bidges, alias Barrell.
April 30th. Buryed a male child of William Stanes, Junior.
Sep. 14th. Buryed Simon Rouse, junior.
    27th. Mr Clarke, Minister, died in this parish.
Octo. 6. Buryed John Lucas, Edd. Phipps his apprentice.
Novem. 27. Buryed James, Son of Joseph King.
Nouem. 30. Buryed a daughter of Tho : ffinches the baker.
Decem. 22th. Buryed the wife of Thomas ffinch.
    23th. Buryed John Whitehead.
Jan. 15th, 1690-91. Buryed George Guy, Junior.
ffeb : 5. Buryed John, the Sonn of Joseph King.
March 24. Buried Joseph, son of Joseph King.

1691.

March 27th, 1691. Buried Sarah Haynes.
Apr̃ll 12th. Buried Henry Benson.
    13th. Buryed Susanna Cary.
    17th. Buried Jonas Lacy.
    26th. Buried Mr George Stoakes.
May 2th. Buried Anne, da. of Richard Turner, Esqr.
    4th. Buryed James, son of John Mead.
    10th. Buryed Old Mr Chapman.
June 4th. Buryed a Male Child of Joseph Pegrams.
July 5th. Buryed Elizabeth, Daught^r of George Haynes.
    15th. Buryed Thomas, Son of George Stoakes his widdow.
August 1th. Buryed the Widdow Aker.
Sep. 3th, 1691. Buryed William Vdid, a Stranger that died at the Kings
    head : rec^d an affidavitt accordingly.
Sep. 4th. Buryed a female Child of John Sadler's, Junior.
Octob^r 20th. Buryed a Stranger, a Corke woman, that dyed suddenly
    in Mr Richard Staneses wagon, rec^d affidavit.
Novemb^r 5. Buryed Richard, a Child of Sarah Foster's.
Jaĥ 3, 1691-2. Buryed Old Edward Peacock.

Apr¹ 17, 1692. Buryed Elizabeth Sell.
July 14, 1692. Buryed Old Richard the Sawyer, yᵗ dyed at yᵉ brickt house.
July 17. Buryed Nathan Thomlinson.
Novembᵣ 4. Buryed a Souldier that dyed at the bull.
December yᵉ 21. Buried Richard, sonn of Mᵣ Richard Turner, dyed at London, and brought hear to be buried.
Buried 1692, Janneary yᵉ 9. Edward Wills.
Januʸ yᵉ 18. Ellen Wennell.
Feb : 12. John Mead, Glover.
March yᵉ 1. Elizabeth, daughter of William Munday and of Sarah his wiffe.
March yᵉ 6. Mᵣ Abram Griffenhoof.
March yᵉ 15. Buried a male Child of John Saunders.
March yᵉ 17. Buried a male Child of Thomas Parrishis.

1693. Burialls.

Aprill 17, the widdow King.
Ap¹ yᵉ 28. Love, the daughter of Hennery & Grace Whitte.
May yᵉ 18, a male Child of Joseph Pegrums & of Sarah his wiffe.
May yᵉ 23, a Travelling man, yᵗ dyed in Mᵣ Norden's barn.
July yᵉ 7. Jacob, yᵉ Son of Charls & Mary Havers.
July yᵉ 10. Philip, yᵉ sonn off William & Sarah Munday.
Novembᵣ yᵉ 5. Georg Guy.
Novembᵣ yᵉ 11. Mᵣ John Godfrey dyed at London, and brought hear to be buried.
Decembᵣ yᵉ 10. Susanna King, wiffe of William King, at yᵉ Bull.
Decembᵣ 25. Jeffery, the sonn of Jeffery Till, was Buried.
Thomas Bacon was Buried Decembᵣ yᵉ 29.

1694.

Susaña, the Daughter of William King, was Buried March yᵉ 27, 1694.
John, the Sonn of William and Jane Porter, was Buried Aprill yᵉ 19, 1694.
William Skinner was Buried August yᵉ 26, 1694.
William King, of yᵉ Bull, was Buried Sept. 25, 1694.
John Rice was Buried Nove : 22, 1694.
William, yᵉ Sonn off Thomas Leveritt, was Buried Decembᵣ yᵉ 11, 1694.
Elizebeth, daughter of Robert Clifft, Decem. 14.
Thomas Smith, John Thurogood's apprentice, Decem. 19.
John, the Sonn of Weston and Elizebeth Norden, was Buried Jan. yᵉ 11, 1694.
Frances, yᵉ Sonn of William Frances, was Buried Jan. yᵉ 21, 1694.
Old Goodwiffe Haines Buried February yᵉ 11, 1694.
Nathanill Racheld Buried ffebruary yᵉ 15, 1694.

Sarah, the Wiffe of William Searl, appotecarie, buried at High Onger, March 16, 169$\frac{4}{5}$.

March y^e 28, 95, y^n taken a list of yo^s who ware burried in y^e Parrish since No : y^e 5, 1693, & sent y^e same list to Epp :

1695.

Sarah, the Wiffe of William Munday, was Buried Aprill 12, 1695.
John Angier Buried Apr. 18.
William, y^e sonn of William Bridges, was Buried Apr. 29, 94 [sic].
John, sonn of Thomas Madwell, buried June ye 13, 95.
Mary Tabour alias Rumbold was Buried June ye 27.
Samuell, the sonn of Jeffery Till, Buried September ye 2^d, 95.
Mary, the Daughter of Joseph Pegrum, was buried Septem : 10th.
Robert, the Sonn of Mr Thomas Higgs, was buried Sept : 11th, 95.
William Enever was Buried October ye 17, 95.
Mary, the Wiffe of Edwd Phipps, was Buried Ob^r 25.
Ann, the Wiffe of Robert Clift, was buried Ob^r 27.
Rowland St John, Lieu : in Cap^n Charls Chrocheroods Company, belongin to the honorable Collonell Farrintons Riggement of foot, was Buried Decem : ye 8, 95.
James, ye sonn of John Knight and of Dennis his Wiffe, was Buried Janearie ye 8, 95.

1696.

Winnefred Platt, widdow, Buried March 27, 96.
Richard, the son of Richard Stanes, was buried May the 13.
Mary, the Daughter of Mr Thomas Higgs and of Mary his Wiffe, was buried May ye 16.
Thomas, ye Sonn of Thomas Madewell, was Buried May ye 20.
Mr William Spranger was Buried July 29.
Frances, ye Sonn of Frances and Ann Sadler, buried the 10 day of August.
Mathew, Daughter of Thomas Madewell, was buried ye 26 of August.
Katherine, ye Daughter of Edward Woodhouse, was Buried Ob^r ye 4.
Elizebeth, ye Wiffe of Weston Norden, was Buried Ob^r ye 12.
The widdow Chapman was Buried Ob^r ye 12.
John, ye son of Joseph Pegram, was buried Novem : ye 2^d.
The Widdow Tomlinson was buried ye 19 of November.
Mary, ye Wiffe of William Peacock, was buried No^r 26.
Goodman Hains w^s bur. Jan. 2^d.
Sarah, ye Daughter of Philipp Trayhern, was Buried Jan. 5.
Sarah, ye Daughter of Joseph Brown, Jan. 23.
Robert Stanes was Buried Jan. 31.
Frances, sonn of Frances Sadler, was Buried Feb. 14.

1697.

Mis Sprangier was Buried ye 7 of Aprill, 1697.
Robiat Gladden Buried Aprill ye 14.
Mr Essex Atwood died hear, buried at South Weall.

Samuell, yᵉ Sonn of Samuell Glascock, was Buried Ap. 26.
William Stanes was Buried yᵉ 27 of Aprill.
Henery, yᵉ Sonn of Willi Searl, was Buried May 16.
Samuell Brazier was bur. 17. yᵉ Wiffe of Sam. Brazier was Bur. 25.
Sarah, yᵉ Wiffe of yᵉ abovesᵈ Samuell Brazier, was Buried (*sic*).
Robert White was buried yᵉ 3 of Obʳ, he was fourscore & six years old,
    he left 24 great grandchildren behinde him.
William, the Sonn of Philipp Treyhern, was Buried October 19.
Ed. Woodhouse wˢ buried yᵉ 21 of Janeary.
Elizebcth, the Daughter of William Searll, was Buried yᵉ 20 of March.

1698.

Em Thurogood, Widdow, was buried yᵉ 27 May.
Margere Lacy, Widdow, was buried yᵉ 25 of August.
Old Richard Stanes was Buried November 25, and Richard Stanes his
    Sonn was Buried Decemᵇʳ 3ᵈ.
Robert, the sonn of Robert Stanes, was buried yᵉ 22 Decembʳ.
The Widdow Beard buried the 28 of December.
Martha, Daughtʳ of Richard Cary, was Buried yᵉ 5 Jan.
Richard, Sonn of Mʳ Thomas Higgs, was Buried yᵉ 24 of Janeary.
Mary, the Wiffe of Thomas Parrish, was Buried Feb. 29 (? 19).
William Munday was Buried Feb. 22.
Thomas Peacock was Buried yᵉ 9 of March.
Rowland, yᵉ son of Philip Treyhern, Buried March 19.

1699.

William Whitehead was Buried yᵉ 3ᵈ of May.
John Booyd (?), a Scochman, by Accedent was drowned in yᵉ brick hous
    mote, was buried yᵉ 9 of June, 1699.
John Young's darter was Buried yᵉ 19 of June.
Widdow Hills Buried yᵉ 18 of August, 1699.
Henery, yᵉ Sonn of Thomas Finch, was Buried yᵉ 22 Sept.
A begger woman that dyed at Tho. Souths buried yᵉ 4 of Decembʳ.

Buried 1700.

Jenny Smith was buried yᵉ 15 of June.
Michell Turner was buried yᵉ 19 of July.
George Haines was buried August 13.
Jonathan Hockley's Wiffe, Obʳ 23.
Samⁿ Bowtell's Wiffe, Noᵐᵇ 12.
Goody Roberds, No: 20.
Old Willi Roberds, No: 28.
Tho: Williams Child, Dec. 8.
Olive Fog, Dec. 11.
Joseph Bredges, Jan. 23.
Tho: Tabour's Child, Jan. 25.
Rebecka Wood, March 9.

1701.

James Penington's Child was Buried Aprill y⁶ 9.
Mary, Wiffe of Robert Clift, was Buried Aprill y⁶ 11.
Ann, y⁶ Wiffe of Josiah Beard, was Buried y⁶ 5 of May.
John Wilkinson was Buried y⁶ 27 of May.
Elizebeth, Daugh¹ of Tho: Leverit, was Buried y⁶ 13 of July.
Prudence, Daughter of John Saunders, Buried Aug^{st} 10.
Philip Godfrey, Oct. y⁶ 22.
John, y⁶ son of John Thurogood, Buried Decem^r y⁶ 11.
Ann King, Widdow, y⁶ 14 Dec.
William Bridges, De : 28.
William Thurogood, Jan. 30.
William Porter, Feb. 4.
Joseph, y⁶ son of Joseph Brown & Olive his Wiffe, was Bur : Feb. 26.

1702.

March 26.   Joseph King.
    y⁶ 26.   Mary Stanes.
    y⁶ 31.   Elizebeth Malcot.
Ap^r y⁶ 6.   John Godfrey.
May y⁶ 9.   Widd : Cooper.
Lionel Adams, July y⁶ 19.
Widdow Stane, June y⁶ 11th.
Widdow Angier, July y⁶ 24.
Thomas Frances, July 30.
Mary, y⁶ Daughter of William Lacy, Sept. y⁶ 9.
Sam^{ll} Gillet, Nov^b 9.
Ann, Wiffe of William Haince, Nov^b 15.
Mary Thurogood, widdow, buried Decemb^r y⁶ 7, 1702.
Thomas, son of Rob¹ Stanes [no date].
James Pennington, Jan. 20.
Benjamine Burton, March 1st.
Ann Skinner, March 3^d.
Mary, Wiffe of Edw : Strutt, March 12.
John Godfry, March 21.

1703.

William Tricket, Aprill 28.
Mary, Daughter of Ed : Windham [no date].
James, son of John Wennell, May 25.
Mary, Daughter of Mary Pennington, widdow, June 8.
John, son of John Enever, was buried y⁶ last of June.
Richard, son of John Stanes, was buried y⁶ 16 July.
Joseph, son of Joseph Brown, was Buried y⁶ 19 of Ob^r, 1703.
John Sweetapple was Buried y⁶ 7 of Novemb^r, 1703.
Robert, y⁶ son of Thomas Glascock, was Buried Novemb^r 26.
Mary Haines was Buried Feb. y⁶ 9, 1703.
Mr Thomas Goldsberg was Buried y⁶ 10 February, 1703.

1704.

Ann, Daughter of Thomas Parrish, was Buried May ye 2^d.
Richard, sonn of John Woolly & off Dothety [*sic*] his Wiffe, Inholder of Ingerstone, was buried ye 4 of May, 1704.
Philip, ye son of Joseph Brown & of Olive his Wiffe, was buried May 23.
Jonathan Hokly was Buried ye first of June.
Katerine, ye Daughter of William Stanes, was Buried ye 9 of July, 1704.
John Turoogood, a Cooper, was Buried ye 22 of July.
Elizebeth, Daughter of Richard Stanes, carrier, was Buried y^e 4 of August.
Thomas, son of Thomas Tabor, Shoomaker, was Buried y^e 21 of Augst.
John, ye sonn of John Say & of Easter his Wiffe, was Buried y^e 15 of S^{pt}. A Salesman.
Ye Widdow Wennell, N^{br} 6, 1704.
Elizebeth, y^e Wiffe of Nicolas Horsnaill, was buried y^e 16 March, 170$\frac{4}{5}$.
Thomas, the Son of Thomas Glascock and of Ann his Wife, was Buried y^e 18 of March, 170$\frac{4}{5}$.

1705.

Sarah, y^e Wiffe of Edward Phipps, was buried Ap^r 20.
John, the son of Henery White, was Buried y^e 9 of Aprill.
William Smith was buried y^e 13 of May. he was 103 years old.
A child of Thomas Ross was buried y^e 19 May.
John, y^e son of John Harris, was buried y^e 7 of June.
Judith, the Daughter of James Batsford and of Ann his Wiffe, was Buried ye 15 of June, being 2 y^{rs} 3 q^{rs} old.
John Jones was buryed ye 5th of July. Officer of excisse.
James Munday was buryed y^e 18 of July, 1705.
John Wolly was buried y^e 19 of S^{pt}.
Burried Ob^r y^e 14, Samiell Bones.
Dorethy Thurogood was Buried y^e 8th of January.
Thomas Harris was Buried y^e 10th of January.
William, y^e son of Wather Buchanan, was buried y^e 7th of Febru., 170$\frac{4}{5}$.
Mary, y^e Daughter of Thomas Stanes, was buried y^e 8 of Feb^y, 170$\frac{4}{5}$.
Garnett, y^e sonn of Samuell Clerk, was Burried Feb. y^e 24.

1706.

Sarah, Wiffe of John Lucas, was buried y^e 31 of March.
Josiah Beard was buried Ap^{ll} 12.
James Cornell was buried Ap^{ll} 17.
Joseph, son of Widdow Fogg, was buried y^e 15 August, 1706.
Tho: Westwood & Mary Ellett, children frō Lond, were bury'd August [*n. d.*].
Mary, wife of Willm Lacy, Bury'd 8^{br} 10, 1706.
Elizabeth, daughter of James & Eliz: Cary, bury'd y^e 22^d of 8^{br}, 1706.
Thomas Glascock was Buried Decemb^r y^e 29, 1706.
The Widdow Pouter, of Belsham Roothing, was buried y^e 14 of Feb^r, 170$\frac{6}{7}$.
M^r. Phillip Traherne was buryed y^e 13th of March, 170$\frac{6}{7}$.

1707.

Y^e Widdow Sweetapple was Buried y^e 16 May, 1707.
Richard, son of Richard Francis, was Buried July y^e 28, 1707.
Sarah, y^e Daughter of Joseph Brown, Bur. y^e 4th Aug^t.
Sarah, the Wiffe of John Sanders, Bur. y^e [*blank*] Sp^t, 1707.
Ann Glascock, Widdow, Burr. y^e 5th of Ob^r.
Eliza :, Daugh. of Willi. Wasket, Bur. Ob^r ye 14.
Elize^{bh}, Daughter of Tho. Madwell, was buried Ob^r ye 19.
Charls, son of John Havers, was buried Ob^r ye 20.
John, ye son of John Havers, was buried Ob^r ye 24.
William Potter buried Nm^{br} ye 9.
Sam^{ll}, son of Thos Finch, was buried ye 13 of No^{br}.
Rob^{rt}, sonn of Robert Whitehead, was buried ye 27 No^{br}, 1707.
Elizebeth, ye Daughter of William Clerk and of Dorithy his Wiffe, was
    buried Dec^{br} ye 12, 1707.
Marget, ye Daughter of John Knight, was buried ye 16 D^{br}, 1707.
Ann, Daugh : of John Leigh, was buried ye 20 Feb., 1707.
John, son of John Ottaway, was buried ye 24 Jan., 1707.

1708.

Samuell, son of Samuel Bowtell, was buried ye 22 of Ap^l, 1708.
Marget, Daugh^r of Thomas Horsnaile, was buried ye 24 Ap^{ll}, 1708.
Thomas Richardson, a Shoemaker, & John Knight, the son of John
    Knight, were burid ye 4 of May.
Ann Enever, Widdow, was buried ye 3^d of June, 1708.
Edward Windham was Buried ye 4 of July, 1708.
Elizebeth Thurogood, widdow, midwiffe, a Shopkeeper, was Buried ye 7
    Ob^r, 1708.
Ann Angier, Widdow, was Buried ye 28 Ob^r, 1708.
Katherine Ross, an infant, was Buried Jan. ye 6, 1708.
Thomas Cooper, butcher, was buried ye 20 Jan. 1708-9.
Elizebeth White, widdow, was buried Jany ye 24, 1708-9, aged 107 years.

1709.

Nicolas Horsnaill was buried ye 3^d of Ap^{ll}, 1709.
William Lacy was buried ye 8 of May, 1709.
Jesse, ye sonn of Francis Sadler, was buried ye 31 May.
Mary, Daughter of Mr Tho. Binks, dec^d hear, and was buried at Weall,
    ye 3^d of June, 1709.
Richard Francis was Burried ye 28 June, 1709.
Elizebeth, an infant, Daughter of Will : Clerk, was buried ye 6 July.
Sarah, ye Wiffe of Mr Binion, offeicer of excise in ye parrish, was Buried
    ye 7 of July, 1709.
Olive, ye Wiffe of Joseph Brown, was Buried ye 29 July, 1709.
Francis Sadler was buried 22 Augst.
Elizabeth, a Child of Benj : Burton, buried ye 22 Sp^t.
Susan, Daugh : of Tho : Tabour, was buried y^e 14 Ob^r, 1709.
Rowland, son of Francis Sadler, was Buried Nb^r y^e 30, 1709.

Philip, son of Francis Sadler, was Buried y^e 8 of D^{br}, 1709.
Thomas, son of Tho : Sell, D^{br} 16.
Thomas, sonn of Thomas Tucker, a Citizen of London, was buried Mch.
    19, 17$\frac{09}{10}$.

1710.

Mary Woodhouse was Buried Ap^{ll} 20.
M^{ts} Mary Pooll Buried at Bovenger, Ap^{ll} 22.
Elizebeth, wiffe of Mr Vauks, of Lond^n, was buried y^e 17 of July.
Elizebeth, y^e Wiffe of Thomas Tabor, was Buried y^e 12 of Augst, 1710.
John, son of Sarah Cary, alias Jolly, was buried y^e 9 of Ob^r, 1710.
John Goodwin was buried Ob^r y^e 26, 1710.
Jane Porter was buried N^{br} y^o 12, 1710.
Thomas, an Infant of Sam^{ll} Boutell, was buried y^e 10 D^{br}.
Mrs Nem Bridgman was Bur^d D^{br} y^e 16.
Tho: Bridgman, husband of y^e abovewritten Nem Bridgman, Bur^d
    D^{br} 20.
Rich :, son of John Stanes, was Bur^d Jan. 17, 17$\frac{10}{11}$.
Elizebeth Fogg was Buried Jan. y^e 21.

1711.

Ann Stebbing, y^e widdow of Mr Benj. Stebbing, late schoolmaster of this
    par., was buried y^e 21 of Ap^{ll}, 1711.
Elizabeth, y^e Daugh^t of William Crampon, was buried y^e 16 Augst,
    1711.
Ann, y^e Wiffe of Joseph King, was Buried y^e 4 of N^{br}, 1711.
Susan, y^e Wiffe of William King, was Buried Jan. y^e 18, 17$\frac{11}{12}$.

1712.

John, y^e sonn of Benjamine Ash & of Cordelia his Wiffe, was Buried
    March y^e 29, 1712.
Samuell Finch was Buried Aprill y^e 13th, 1712.
Elizebeth (*sic*) Woollard, Citizen of London, was buried Ap^{ll} y^e 20, 1712.
Danniell Ramm was Buried y^e 28 of June, 1712.
Ann, Daughter of James Batsford and of Ann his Wiffe, was Buried Sp^t
    ye 20, 1712.
Mary Brickly was Buried Decem. y^o 7, 1712.
Georg Tabour, Butcher, was Buried Decem : ye 10, 1712.
Mary Howard, beggar, was Buried D^{br} ye 31, 1712.
Elizebeth, ye wiffe of Mr John Skinner, was buried March 4.

1713.

Joseph, son of Joseph Brown, was Buried Ap^{ll} ye 12, 1713.
Joseph, sonn of Samuell Glascock, was Buried May ye 14, 1713.
Prudence, ye Wiffe of Sam^{ll} Glascock, was Buried May y^o 24, 1713.
Richard Stanes was Buried June 16th, 1713.

Elizebeth, a Child of Willi : Angeir, was Buried July 15, 1713.
M' Francis Sadler was Buried July 17, 1713.
Nathanell Allen was Buried Aug. 19.
John Knight was Bur^d Sp^t y^e 20, 1713.
Jeffery Till was Bur^d Ob^r y^e 14.
Sarah Spicer was buried D^br y^e 18, 1713.
The Widdow Sell was Bur^d D^br 27.
Joseph, son of Joseph Brown, was Buried Jan. y^e 7, 17$\frac{13}{14}$.
Willi, y^e son of Kather : Ram, Feb. y^e 14.

1714.

Rebecca, Wiffe of Georg Pegg, Ap^ll y^e 8, 1714.
Catharine Foster was Buried May y^e 7.
Thomas Bowtell was buried May 10, 1714.
June y^e 4. John Choppin bur. 77 years old.
Nath : Allen buried June y^e 4.
Nicolas Allexander, Gen^tt, buried Aug. 5.
Sarah, Wiffe of Richard Ward, bur^d Aug. 29.
Ann, ye Wiffe of Robert Wrenn, Sp^t 19.
Sarah, ye Wiffe of Will : Willans, Sp^t 24.
Thomas, sonn of Thomas Bridgman & of Damaris his wiffe, was buried
      Ob^r ye 7, 1714.
James Batsford, my Church Clarke, was buried No : 14, 1714.
Elizabeth, wife of Tho : fford, was buried Nov : 14, 1714.
Thomas Bridgman, Sen :, No^br 16.
Widow Monday, Nov : 20, 1714.
Saml Bowtel's wife, No : 20.
Tho : Wiseman's wife Nov : 24, 1714.
Robert, son of Saml Bowtel, Dec. 10th, 1714.
Elizabeth King, Wid :, Decem : 23, 1714.
John, son of Thomas Tabor, Dec : 26.
Mary Hasplam (sic), Dec^br 27th died, 1714.
Ann, daughter of Joseph Brown, Jan : 6, 1714.
Richard Hagger, Janvary ye 9th, 1714.
Thomas fford, sen :, Janu : ye 29th, 1714.
Richard Gunson, ffeb : 21, 1714, a Stranger.
Richard Bridgman, March 7, 1714.
Honest Williã Russell, March 11th, 1714.
Poore Jo : [blank] his Apprentice, March 22, 1714.
Sarah White, an Infant, March 23, 1714.

1715.

John Wiseman, a Stranger, May 27th, 1715.
Mary Say, an Infant, Augt 14, 1715.
Wm Clarke, a childe, Augt 21.
Joseph Brown, an Infant, Sept^er 27th, 1715.
[blank] Tabor, an Infant, Octo^br 1st, 1715.
Ann White, an Infant, Dec^br 20, 1715.
Elizabeth Whitehead, Wid : 10^br 21, 1715.
123

Bartholomew Glascock, Jan : 2^d, 1715.
Georg Stanes, Janua : 23, 1715.
Henry White, Jun : ffeb : 13, 1715.
Elizabeth Wood, an Inf^t, March 22th, 1715.

1716.

Elizabeth Davies, May ye 6, 1716.
Madã : Gouldesburgh, May 17, 1716.
Mary Shed, June 16, 1716.
Jo^n Tabor, Augst 30th, 1716.
Ann Whitehead, Sept^{er} 13, 1716.
Edward Phypps, Se : Dec. 3^d, 1716.
Tho : Allen, an Infant, Jan. 3, 1716.
Jonas Hance, Janua : 8th, 1716.
Eliza : Ash, an Infant, ffebru : 20th.
Mr Leigh, March 10th, 1716.
Elizabeth Traveler, an Infant, March 22th.

1717.

Elizabeth Skinner, May 31, 1717.
Mary Havers, an Infant, July 22th.
Mr Babbs, Nov^{br} 5th, 1717.
M^m Jones, January ye 9, 1717.
Edmund Till, Janua : 26, 1717.
Nathaneel Brewer, ffeb : 5, 1717.
Joseph Phillips, ffeb : 26, 1717.

Buried 1718.

April	7th.	Abigail Allen, an Infant.
May y^e	7th.	Wm Perrey, an Infant.
June	30.	Georg Shed, an Infant.
Aug.	22.	Henry Gyn.
Septem :	7.	Mary Munday.
Dec^{br}	10.	Katharine Stanes, wid :
Jan :	3.	Thomas Emberson.
„	22.	Damaris Pavit, wid :
ffeb :	13.	Robert Whitehead.
„	23.	Samuel Whitehead.

1719.

March [blank].		Susan Ottaway.
May	1st.	James Smyth.
June	4.	Josiah Bryon.
July	8.	John Lucas, Junr.
July	. . .	Olive Wiseman, an Infant.
Aug :	4.	Mr John Skinner.

Aug: 12. Joⁿ ffinch, of Ingatestone.
„ 28. Eliza : Brown, an Infant.
Sep. 4. Elizabeth Glascock.
Noᵇʳ 12. Mʳ Tho : Campe.
Decem. 11. Mʳ John Barrel.
Janua : 1ᵐ. Joseph Brown, an Infᵗ.
„ 22ᵗʰ. Mⁿ Ann Alexander.
„ 25. William ffrancis, Se :
Febru : 26. Charles Brewer, an Infᵗ.
March 9ᵗʰ. Mary Stanes, Infᵗ.

1720.

March 29ᵗʰ. Charles Havers, Se :
April 20. Mⁿ Sandford, wid :
„ 24. Joⁿ and Amy Tabor, Infᵗˢ.
May 2ᵈ. Samuel Bridges, an Inᵗ.
June 8. John Lucas, Se :
July 17. Cave Knight, an Infᵗ.
Augˢᵗ 30. Frances Peg.
Septʳ 10. Mary Chaplin, Infant.
The Reverend Mʳ John Camp, Rector of this Parish, was bury'd the
22ᵈ of September.
Mʳ David Chaillet (a Frenchman) was bury'd December yᵉ 7ᵗʰ.
Mary Pegg (an Infant) was bury'd March yᵉ 5ᵗʰ.

Godfrey Jones, Rector.

1721.

Mary Bonham was bury'd March the 30ᵗʰ.
Mary Clements was bury'd April the 12ᵗʰ.
Martha Madewell was bury'd June yᵉ 23ᵈ.
James Chaplin, an Infant, was bury'd June yᵉ 30ᵗʰ.
John Skinner was bury'd October the 20ᵗʰ.
Sarah Stanes was bury'd November yᵉ 8ᵗʰ.
Joseph Brown (an Infant) was bury'd November yᵉ 23.
Susan Francis was bury'd Febʳʸ 15ᵗʰ.
Jane Potter bury'd March yᵉ 17ᵗʰ.

G. Jones.

Burials 1722.

Thomas Spicer was bury'd March yᵉ 25ᵗʰ.
James Chaplin (an Infant) was bury'd May 18ᵗʰ.
Thomas Tabor was bury'd June yᵉ 21ᵗ.
Elizabeth Porter was bury'd July yᵉ 24ᵗʰ.
Elizabeth Porter (her child, an Infant) was bury'd July yᵉ 28ᵗʰ.
Mary Chaplin was bury'd October yᵉ 7ᵗʰ.
Mʳ Richard Bull (an Infant) was bury'd October yᵉ 16ᵗʰ.
William Staines was bury'd October yᵉ 25ᵗʰ.
Henry White was bury'd November yᵉ 13ᵗʰ.
Anne Brainwood was bury'd November yᵉ 18ᵗʰ.

Mary Chivers was bury'd November ye 27th.
Jane Benton was bury'd December ye 2^d.
John Lucas was bury'd Feb^{ry} ye 8th.
William Mitchell (an Infant) was bury'd March ye 20th.
James Bridges (an Infant) was bury'd March ye 22^d.

Godfrey Jones, Rector.

1723.

Mary Havers (an Infant) was bury'd March 30th.
Elizabeth King was bury'd April ye 3^d.
Mary Perry was bury'd May ye 21st.
Mr Charles Gouldesburgh was bury'd May ye 31st.
William Munday was bury'd June ye 16th.
Nathaniel Allin was bury'd July ye 21st.
Mary Brown (an Infant) was bury'd July ye 28th.
Anne Emberson was bury'd August the 3^d.
Richard Hills was bury'd September ye 10th.
Elizabeth Fogg (an Infant) was bury'd October ye 2^d.
Mary Eates (an Infant) was bury'd October ye 5th.
William Sadler (an Infant) was bury'd October ye 29th.
Mrs Charles Fowler was bury'd November ye 5th.
Henery Tedder (an Infant) was bury'd November 27th.
Anne Ash (an Infant) was bury'd November ye 28th.
Mary Staines (an Infant) was bury'd January the 8th.
James Brainwood was bury'd March ye 15th.

Godfrey Jones, Rector.

1724.

Mary Havers was bury'd June ye 11th.
Mrs Anne Fowler was bury'd August ye 1st.
Margarett Forbett (an Infant and a stranger) was bury'd September
ye 16th.
Richard Turner, Esq., was bury'd Jan^{ry} ye 23^d.
William Cornell was bury'd February ye 18th.
Thomas Parish was bury'd March ye 16th.

Godfrey Jones, Rector.

Burials 1725.

Elizabeth Chopping was bury'd May the twelfth.
Elizabeth Brown (an Infant) was bury'd August the 26th.
Olive Wiseman (an Infant) was bury'd September the 29th.
Abigail Jasper (an Infant) was bury'd December the first.
John Attaway was bury'd December the 9th.
John Eates was bury'd Feb^{ry} ye 6th.

Godfrey Jones, Rector.

1726.

Martha Thorogood (a Dissenter) was bury'd April the 4th.
Martha Curds was bury'd May the 30th.
Joseph King was bury'd July the 3[d].
Anne Philips (a Dissenter) was bury'd August the 26th.
Elizabeth Hance was bury'd October the 18th.
Mary Leigh was bury'd November the 2[d].
Joseph Brown (an Infant) was bury'd November the 20th.
Elizabeth Bridges was bury'd November the 27.
Mary Eates was bury'd December the 12th.

Godfrey Jones, Rector.

1727.

John Stanes (an Infant) was bury'd April the 3[d].
Elizabeth Stanes (an Infant) was bury'd April the 9th.
M[r] Thomas Bull (an Infant) was bury'd May the 11th. } S[r] John Bull's children & Twins.
M[r] Turner Bull (an Infant) was bury'd May the 18th. }
William Whasket was bury'd June the 10th.
Mary Peacock was bury'd June the 18th.
Dennis Collins was bury'd August the 6th.
James Cary, jun[r]., was bury'd September the 12th.
Richard Stanes (an Infant) was bury'd November the 12th.
Mary Choppine was bury'd November the 19th.
Robert White was bury'd December the 6th.
The Reverend M[r] John Hill, Rector of High Laver, was bury'd December the 20th.
John Stanes (an Infant) was bury'd December the 24.
M[r] William Sayer was bury'd January the first.
Henry Whitteridge (an Infant) was bury'd March the 17th.

Godfrey Jones, Rector.

1728.

Sarah Saward (an Infant) was bury'd April the 2[d].
Anne Burrell (an Infant) was bury'd April the 14th.
George Wood (an Infant) was bury'd May the 9th.
Alexander Brown (an Infant) was bury'd May the 13th.
Jane Angier was bury'd May the 19th.
John Cramphorne was bury'd May the 26th.
James Bettis (an Infant) was bury'd May the 31st.
Mary Clift was bury'd August the 23[d].
Anne Saward (an Infant) was bury'd August the 30th.
Anne Harrison (an Infant) was bury'd October the 5th.
Mary Ballard was bury'd January the 7th.
Sarah Till was bury'd February the 11th.

Godfrey Jones, Rector.

Burials 1729.

Mary Sell was bury'd April the seventh.
Captain Henry Alexander was bury'd April the tenth.
Margaret Finch was bury'd April the eleventh.
Thomas Besouth was bury'd April the twenty-third.
Gabel (a Traveller) was bury'd April the thirtieth.
Sarah Glascock was bury'd May the second.
George Pegg was bury'd May the fifth.
John Lucas was bury'd June the twenty-first.
Elizabeth Thorogood was bury'd August the tenth.
William Francis, jun', was bury'd September the fourth.
Benjamin Ash was bury'd September the twelfth.
John Wiseman was bury'd September the twenty-first.
Jesse Cooper was bury'd September the twenty-fourth.
Sarah Wrenn was bury'd October the twenty-third.
Mrs Johanna Alexander was bury'd November the first.
Abigail Jasper was bury'd November the sixteenth.
Elizabeth Brainwood was bury'd November the twentieth.
Mary Chifens was bury'd December the twenty-first.
Mary Lloyd (a Stranger) was bury'd December the twenty-seventh.
George Rock was bury'd January the thirteenth.
Joseph Browne was bury'd Jan^{ry} the twenty-third.
Thomas Francis was bury'd February the fifth.
John Stane (an Infant) was bury'd March the first.

Godfrey Jones, Rector.

1730.

Anne Bettis (an Infant) was bury'd March the twenty-eighth, 1730.
Elizabeth Attaway was bury'd April the first.
Robert Porter was bury'd April the twenty-seventh.
Elizabeth and Anne Saward were bury'd May the first.
Dorothy Saward was bury'd May the thirteenth.
Anne Read was bury'd June the third.
Charles Gouldesburgh was bury'd June the twentieth.
John Stane (an Infant) was bury'd July the fourteenth.
Victory Paveley (an Infant) was bury'd July the twentieth.
Sarah Bridges was bury'd July the twenty-first.
Robert Wrenn was bury'd November the twelfth.
Ann Stephens (an Infant) was bury'd December the eighth.
Sarah Evans (a wayfaring Person) was bury'd December the eighteenth.
Sarah Gillet (an Infant) was bury'd December the eighteenth.
Elizabeth Guy (an Infant) was bury'd December the twentieth.
Mary Brown (an Infant) was bury'd February the fourteenth.
Elizabeth Cornell was bury'd March the fourth.
Elizabeth White, of Brentwood, was bury'd January the nineteenth.
Alice Carter was bury'd March the eighteenth.

Godfrey Jones, Rector.

1731.

Richard Stane (an Infant) was bury'd March ye twenty-fifth.
Sarah Potter was bury'd April the first.
Mr James Bull (an Infant) was bury'd May ye 1st.
Nathaniel Brewer was bury'd May the 15th.
William Sadler, jun^r, was bury'd May ye 21st.
John Sheed was bury'd May the 31st.
Johanna Smith was bury'd June the 25th.
Benjamin Ash was bury'd July the 2^d.
Lettice Burrel was bury'd October the 12th.
Henry Sweeting was bury'd October the 25th.
Sarah Thurgood (an Infant) was bury'd December the 2^d.
Elizabeth Whitehead was bury'd February the first.

Godfrey Jones, Rector.

Burials 1732.

John Bonham was bury'd May the 24th.
Sarah Fog was bury'd June the 7th.
Richard Cary was bury'd October the 5th.
Thomas Powell was bury'd December the 13th.
Martha Sheed & William Sadler were bury'd Jan^ry the 25th.
John Bridges was bury'd Feby the 14th.
Sarah Thurgood was bury'd March the 13th.

Godfrey Jones, Rector.

1733.

William Thurgood (an Infant) was buryd March the 29th.
Anne Clarke (an Infant) & Thomas Barnard were bury'd April the 3^d.
Sarah Stane (an Infant) was bury'd April the 20th.
James Whitehead was bury'd April the 29th.
Mary Parish was bury'd April the 30th.
Isaac Stracey was bury'd July the 19th.
Master William Bull was bury'd July the 28th.
Doctor Godfrey Jones, Rector of this Parish, buried Augt 15th, 1733.
    The Affidavit was brought according to the Form prescribed.
Elizabeth Besouth was buried Septr 23^d, 1733. Affidavit made accord-
    ing to the Form prescribed.
Mrs Mary Velley was buried Decr 20th, 1733. Affidavit was made of
    her being buried in woollen, according to ye Act of Parliament.
    Died Decr 15th.

Thomas Velley, Rector.

William Shed, Infant, buried Feb: 5th, 173¾. Affidavit was made of
    being Buried in Woollen.
Ann Bernard, alias Mole, was buried Feb: 17th, 173¾. Affidavit was
    made of her being buried in Woollen.

1734.

Miss Elisabeth Bull was buried April 30th, 1734. Affidavit was made of her being buried in Woollen, according to ye Act of Parliament.

John Stapler, of this Parish, was buried May 30th, 1734. Affidavit was made of his being buried in Woollen, according to Act of Parliament.

Matthew Stapler, an Infant, was buried June 10th, 1734. Affidavit was made of his being buried in Woollen, according to the Act of Parliament.

Robert Walker, of this Parish, Sojourner, was buried June 20, 1734. Affidavit was made of his being buried in Woollen, according to ye Act of Parliament.

Anne Shead, of this Parish, was buried July [*blank*], 1734. Affidavit was made of her being buried in Woollen, according to ye Act of Parliament.

John Wennell, of this Parish, was buried Aug: 8, 1734. Affidavit was made of his being buried in Woollen, according to ye Act of Parliament.

Sarah Browne, of this Parish, Infant, was buried Aug. 23, 1734. Affidavit was made of her being buried in Wollen, according to ye Act of Parliament.

Elizabeth Nettleton, of this Parish, was buried Septr 6th, 1734. Affidavit was made of her being buried in Woollen, according to Act of Parliament.

William Hains, Infant, of this Parish, was buried Novr 8th, 1734. Affidavit was made of his being buried in Wollen, according to Act of Parliament.

Ann Searle, Infant, of this Parish, was buried Nov^r [*blank*] 1734. Affidavit was made of her being buried in Wollen, according to ye Act of Parliament.

Henry Graves, of the Parish of Brentwood, Infant, was buried Nov^r [*blank*], 1734, in this Parish. Affidavit was made of his being buried in Woollen, according to Act of Parl.

Mary Munday, of this Parish, was buried Jan: 19th, 1734. Affidavit was made of her being buried in Woollen, according to ye Act of Parliament.

Elisabeth Clift, of this Parish, was buried Feb: 25th, 1734. Affidavit was made according to Act of Parliament.

Mrs Anne Ayloffe, of this Parish, was buried Feb^r: 28th, 1734. Affidavit was made of her being buried in Woollen, according to Act of Parliament.

Burials 1735.

Thomas Pegg was buried Mar. 30th, 1735. Affidavit was made of his being buried in Woollen, according to Act of Parliament.

George Stane, the son of Richard Stane & [*blank*] his wife, was buried May [*blank*], 1735. Affidavit was made of his being buried in Woollen, according to Act of Parliament.

John Salmon, of this Parish, was buried June 15th, 1735. Affidavit was made of his being buried in Woollen, according to ye Act of Parliament.

Elizabeth Royston, of this Parish, was buried June 25th, 1735. Affidavit of her being buried in woollen, according to Act of Parliament.

Robert Young was buried July 2d, 1735. Affidavit was made of his being [buried] in Woollen, according to ye Act of Parliament.

Mary Throughgood was buried Augst 28th. Affidavit was made of her being buried in woollen, accord : to Act of Parl :

William Cramphorne, of this parish, was buried Septr 1mt. Affidavit was made of his being buried in woollen, according to the Act of Parliament.

Jeoffrey Throughgood was buried Septr. 19, 1635. Affidavit was made of his being buried in Woollen, according to the Act of Par.

Abigail Cooper, of the Parish of High Ongar, was buried in this Parish Octobr [blank] 1735. Affidavit was made of her being buried in woollen, according to Act of Par :

William Stane, of this Parish, was buried Octr 24, 1735. Affidavit was made of her being buried in Woollen, according to Act of Par:

Stephen and Anne Finch, Infants, were buried Octobr . . . th, 1735. Affidavit was made of their being buried in Woollen, according to Act of Parliament.

Mary Madle, Infant, was buried Novr 13th, 1735. Affidavit was made of her being buried in woollen, according to the Act of Parl :

Robert Clift was buried Dec. [blank], 1735. Affidavit was made of his being buried in Woollen, according to Act of Parliament.

Mr James Shepherd was buried Decr 31, 1735. Affidavit was made of his being buried in Woollen, according to Act of Parliament.

Ann Brown, Infant, was buried Feb : [blank] 1735. Affidavit.

Thomas Velley, Rector.

Burials 1736.

Mary Stane, Infant, was buried Apr : 21, 1736. Affidavit was made of her being buried in Woollen, according to Act of Parliament.

Timothy Todd was buried May 3d, 1736. Affidavit was made of his being buried in Woollen, according to Act of Parliament.

John Nettleton, Infant, was buried Aug : 7th, 1736. Affidavit was made of his being buried in Woollen, accor : to Act of Par.

Lodwell Macglothwell was buried Aug : [blank], 1736. Affidavit was made of his being buried in woollen, according to Act of Parliament.

Susannah Gouldsbourgh, from Chelmsford, was buried Aug : 31mt, 1736. Affidavit was made of her being buried in Woollen, according to ye Act of Parliament.

Mary Wiseman, of the Parish of Shenfield, in ye County of Essex, was buried Aug : 29, 1736. Affidavit was made of her being buried in woollen, according to Act of Parliam'.

Cornell & Elizabeth Shed (Infants) were buried Octhr [blank], 1736. Affidavit was made of their being buried in woollen, according to Act of Par.

Mary Allen, of this Parish, was buried Octbr 31st, 1736. Affidavit was made of her being buried in Wool :, acco : to Act of Parliament.

Mary Thurgood, of this Parish, was buried Novr 3d, 1736. Affidavit was made of her being buried in Woollen, ac : to Act of Parliament.

Elizabeth Eylet was buried Novr 9th, 1736. Affidavit was made of her being buried in Woollen, according to Act of Parl.

Elizabeth Shed, of this Parish, was buried Novr 25th, 1736. Affidavit was made of her being buried in Woollen, ac: to Act of Parliament.

Mary Helmes, of ye Parish, was buried Novr 27th, 1736. Affidavit was brought of her being buried in woollen, ac: to Act of Parl.

Thomas Whitehead, of this Parish, was buried January 16th, 1736. Affidavit was brought of his being buried in Woollen, ac: to Act of Parl.

Widow Jane South was buried March 1st, 1736/7. Affidavit was made ac: to Act of Parliament.

Ephraim Knight, Infant, was buried Mar. 11th, 1736. Affidavit was made of his being buried in Woollen, according to Act of Parl.

Abigail Stane, of this Parish, was buried Mar: 13, 1736. Affidavit was made of her being buried in Woollen, acc: to Act of Parl.

Thos Valley, Rector, 1736.

Burials 1737.

Mr John Bull, Son of Sr John Bull, was buried April 22^d, 1737. Affidavit was made of his being buried in Woollen, according to Act of Parliament.

Richard White, alias Crabb, was buried April 24th, 1737. Affidavit was made, etc.

James Burrell was buried April 29th, 1737. Affidavit was made of his being buried in Woollen, according to Act of Parliament.

Ann Francis, Infant, was buried May 11th, 1737. Affidavit was made of her being buried in Wooll: ac: to Act of Parl.

Elizabeth Carey was buried June 9th, 1737. Affidavit was made of her being buried in Woollen, according to Act of Parliament.

Dorothy Borne, of this Parish (Infant), was buried June 26th,'1737. Affidavit was made of her being buried in Woollen, according to Act of Parl.

William Bettys, Infant, was buried Aug. 4, 1737. Affid: made of his being buried in Woollen, acc: to Act of Parl.

Mrs Anne Bincks was buried July 31, 1737. Affidavit was made of her being buried in Woollen, according to Act of Parliament.

Mrs Elizabeth Turner was buried Aug. 5, 1737. Affidavit was made of her being buried in Woollen, according to Act of Parliament.

Mrs Binckes & Mrs Turner, two sisters, died both July 29th.

Sarah Hills, Infant, was buried Oct: 20, 1737. Affidavit was made of being buried ac: to Act of Parl.

Thomas Velley, Rector, 1737.
Robt Wren, Church Ward.

Burials 1738.

Grace Bournes, of this Parish, was buried April 13th, 1738. Affidavit was made of her being buried in Woollen, acc: to Act of Parl.

Mrs Ann Harper, of ye parish, was buried June 17th, 1738. Affidavit was made of her being buried in Woollen, acc: to Act of Parl.

Mr Abraham Havers, of ye Parish of High Ongar, was buried July 9th, 1738. Affidavit was made of his being buried in Woollen, according to Act of Parl.

Mary Shed, Infant, was buried Sep^{lr} 11th, 1738. Affidavit was made of her being buried in Sheep's Wooll, according to Act of Parliament.

Sarah Thurgood, of this Parish, was buried Septr 17th, 1738. Affidavit was made of her being buried in sheep's Wooll, according to Act of Parliament.

William Searle, of this Parish, was buried Oct^{br} 13th, 1738. Affidavit was made of his being buried in Woollen, according to Act of Parliament.

Anne White was buried Novr 21st, 1738. Affidavit was made of her being buried in Woollen, ac : to Act of Parl.

Dame Elizabeth Bull, wife of Sir John Bull, Kn^t, was buried Thursday, Decr 21st, 1738. She died Decr 7th. Affidavit was made of her being buried in Woollen, accord : to Act of Parlia.

Thomas Madle, of y^e Parish, was buried Jan : 5th, 1738-9. Affidavit was made of his being buried in Woollen, according to Act of Parliament.

James Carey, of y^e Parish, was buried Feb : 15th, 173$\frac{8}{9}$. Affidavit was made of his being bur^d in Wool^n, ac : to Act of Parl.

Thos Velley, Rector.

Burials 1739.

Anne Hanchet, Infant, was buried April 12th, 1739. Affidavit was made of her being buried in Woollen, according to Act of Parliament.

John Hoskins, of Lewis in Sussex, was buried May 15th, 1739. Affidavit was made of his being buried in Woollen, according to Act of Parliament.

John Shaels, of ye Kingdom of Ireland, was buried May 28th, 1739. Affidavit was made Acco : [sic].

M^{rs} [blank] Havers was buried June ye 5th, 1739. Affidavit was made of her being buried in Wool : ac : to Act of Parliament.

Sarah Stanes, of this Parish, was buried Nov^r [blank], 1739. Affida : was m : ac : to A : Parl.

William Worsegate, of ye Par : of H : Ongar, was buried Dec^r [blank], 1739. Affid : was m : ac : to A : Parl :

Thos Velley, Rect^r.

Burials 1740.

Martha Guye was buried Mar : 27, 1740. Affid : was made of her being buried in Wool : ac : to Act Par.

John Leverit was buried Apr : 1, 1740. Affidavit was made, &c.

Sarah Tod was buried Apr. 9th, 1740. Affidavit was brought, &c.

Mrs Margaret Alexander was buried April 30th, 1740. She died Apr. 24th at Smith's Hall. Affidavit was made of her being buried in Woollen, acc : to Act of Parliament.

Robert Stane, of this Parish, was buried May 2nd, 1740. Affidavit was made of his being bur^d in Wool : ac : to Act of Parl :

James Hogg, Infant, was buried May 14th, 1740. Affidavit was made of his being buried in Wool : ac : to Act of Parl :

Sarah Tod buried Apr. 9, 1740. Received ye Affidavit.

Sarah Wiseman buried May 21, 1740.   Received ye Affidavit.
Anna Maria Fytch buried May 25, 1740.   Received ye Affidavit.
Susan Stane buried June 1^{nt}, 1740.   Received ye Affidavit.
Olive Fog buried 7 (?) July, 1740.   Received the Affidavit.
Sarah Stoke buried Oct : 26, 1740.
[*blank*] Bones (?), Infant, 19th Oct., 1740.   Affidavit Received.
Ann Cramphon bur : Nov : 7, 1740.   Received Affidavit.
M^n Camp buried Decr 12th, 1740.   Affidavit received.
Mary Maidwell buried Jan. 4th.   received Affidavit.
Ann Bret, Infant, buried Jan. 6.   Affidavit received.
Widow Guye buried Jan : 18, 1740.   Affidavit received.
Sarah Maidwell buried Feb : 15, 1740.   Affidavit.
William Lee buried Feb : 21, 1740.   Affidavit.
John Ephraim Knight, Infant, buried Mar : 19.   Affidavit.
Thomas Velley, Rector.

Burials 1741.

James Woolmer, buried Apr. 5.   Affidavit received.
Eliza Speller buried Apr. 17.   Affidavit received.
Jane Burrell buried Apr. 23^d.   Affidavit received.
James Chopping bur : Apr. 24, 1741.   Affidavit received.
Eliza : Nichols buried May 25, 1741.   Affidavit received.
Eliz : Finch buried May 25, 1741.   Affidavit received.
Ann Clark buried May 27, 1741.   Affidavit received.
Sarah Wheeler buried May 29, 1741.   Affidavit.
Sarah Standish buried June 21, 1741.   Affidavit received.
Eliz : Clark, Infant, bur : June 24, 1741.   Affidavit was received.
Hannah Guye buried June 24, 1741.   Affid.
Sarah Allen buried June 25, 1741.   Affidavit received.
Richard Stane buried July 6th.   Affidavit received.
Richard Guye buried July 18, 1741.   Affidavit received.
Mary Lawrence, Inf., bur. July 27.   Affidavit received.
Thomas Knight, Stage Coachman, buried Aug. 15, 1741.   Affidavit
     received.
John Knight, Stage Waggoner, bur. Aug. 14, 1741.   Affidavit received.
Clem : Munday buried Aug. 16.   Affidavit received.
Eliz : Wennell bur. Aug. 16, 1741.   Affidavit received.
George Buchanan buried Aug. 20.   Affidavit received.
John Stane buried Aug. 30, 1741, aged 97.   Affidavit received.
Richard Snatt buried Aug. 31, 1741.   Affidavit received.
Mary Fogg, wid :, buried Oct. 17, 1741.   Affidavit received.
William Thurgood buried Oct. 20, 1741.   Affidavit received.
Ann Nettleton buried Oct. 22. 1741.   Affidavit received.
Sarah Porter, Wid :, buried Novr 19, 1741.   Affidavit received.
Mary, the wife of Edward Fogg, was buried Decr 25, 1741.   Affid :
     received.
Philippa Warren, Infant, was buried Jan. 3^d, 1741.   Affidavit received.
John Anger was buried Jan : 15, 1741.   Af : rec^d.
Sarah Trahern buried Jan : 26, 1741.   Af : rec.
Elizabeth Ainger buried Mar. 3^d, 1741.   Aff : rec.
Thos Velley, Rect^r, 1741.

Burials 1742.

Sir John Bull, Kn^t, was buried April 7th, 1742. He died Apr. 4th. Affidavit receiv'd.
Thos Royston buried Ap : 29, 1742. Affid : received.
Sarah, Daughter of George Smith, buried May 3^d, 1742. Af : rec.
Susan Miller, of Hornchurch, was buried May 11th, 1742. Aff : received.
Mary Ting, Widow, of ye Parish, was buried May 23^d, 1742. Aff : rec.
John Bridges, of this Parish, was buried May 20, 1742. Affi : rec.
Sarah, the wife of James Turner, buried May 26, 1742. Affid : received.
William Stane buried July 4th, 1742. Affid : received.
James Chaplain buried July 21, 1742. Affidavit received.
Ann Thorogood buried Sept^r [*blank*] 1742. Affid : received.
Elizabeth Smyth, wife of George Smyth & Elizabeth Smyth, Daughter of the said George Smith, were buried Jan^{ry} 14th, 1742. Affid : received.

Thos Velley, Rector, 1742.

Burials 1743.

Sarah Howgate, Infant, buried April 6, 1743. Af : rec.
Sarah Howgate, ye Mother, bur : Apr. 8, 1743. Af : rec.
Robert, son of J^n Thurgood & Mary his wife, buried Apr : 25, 1743. Af : rec.
Sheffield, son of George Warren & Mary his wife, buried July 26. Af : rec :
Stock Hamseed buried Aug : 26, 1743. Af : rec :
Mary Smith, Infant, buried Sep. 14. Af : rec :
Lydia, wife of Nat : Allen, buried Sep. 15. Af :
George, son of John Bettyes, bur. Oct. 7, 1743. Af : rec :
Amy Gillet bur. Oct. 11th. Aff : rec :
Will :, son of Jos : Allen, bur. Oct. 14. Aff : rec :
Ann, Daught. of Jos : Allen, Oct. 16. Af : rec :
Mary Brown, Widow, bur. Oct. 17, 1743. Af : rec :
Nathaniel Allen buried Oct. 17th, 1743. Aff : rec :
William Angier bur. Oct. 25th, 1743. Aff : rec :
Elizabeth Stephens, Infant, bur. Oct. 30. Aff : rec :
Cordelia, Wife of Hen. Corney, Nov. 23. Af. rec :
Samuel Mathams bur. Jan. 30th, 1743. Aff : rec :
Thomas, the Son of Thos Velley, Min : of y^s Par :, died Feb : 5th, buried Feb : 7th, 1743. Affid : rec :
Eleanor Bridgeman bur. Feb : 10th. Aff : rec :
Timothy Todd bur^d Mar. 19. Aff : rec :

Burials March 25, 1744.

Walter Buchanan buried Apr : 2^d, 1744. Affid : received.
Olive, Daughter of Pet^r Speller & Mary his wife, bur. Ap : 11. Aff : rec :

Tho', son of Tho' Warren & Mary his Wife, buried June 14, 1744.
Aff: received.
Tho' Ross bur^d Jul: 8, 1744. Aff: rec:
Mary Ross bur^d Jul: 15, 1744. Aff: rec:
John, son of James Buckland & Eliz: his wife, buried Novr 18th.
Elizabeth West, of Chelmsford, was buried May 20th, 1744. Affid: rec:
Ann Velley, Daughter of Tho' Velley, Min: of ye Parish, died Jan: 15,
buried Jan^ry 17th, 1744. Affid: rec:
James Elmes buried Jan^ry 29th. Af: rec:
Thomas Onion, the son of Tho' Onion, buried Feb: 5th, 1744. Affid:
rec:
Elizabeth Jasper bur: Mar. 11th, 1744.
Henry Thurgood buried Mar. 12th, 1744. Aff: rec:
Elizabeth Wood buried Mar. 22.

Burials March 25, 1745.

Susannah Belchier buried March 31. Af: rec:
Elizabeth Cowel, wife of Sam: Cowel, bur. Ap: 2^d.
Eliza: Stane, wid:, bur. Apr. 3^d, 1745.
Ann Emerson, wife of Rich: Emer:, bur: Apr: 10.
Thomas Gillet buried Apr. 13th, 1745.
Mary Wennell buried Apr: 14, 1745.
John Knight, son of wid: Knight, bur. Apr. 17. Af: rec:
Samuel Nichols buried Apr: 28. Af: rec: 1745.
Richard Chopping buried June 13.
Ann, Daughter of Edw: Harper, bur. June 21.
Abraham, son of Peter Speller & Mary his wife, Bur. Aug. 30. Af: rec:
Sarah, Daughter of Tho' Bridges & Sarah his wife, Bur. Sept. 3^d.
Dutch Soldier buried Oct. 1st.
Tho', son of Tho' Onion & Eliz: his wife, buried Oct. 6, 1745. Af: rec:
Jeoffry Austin bur. Oct. 16. Af: rec:
Thomas Sandford bur. Oct. 17th, 1745. Aff: rec:
Richard Houchin bur: Oct. 27, 1745.
Jane Bridges bur. Oct. 30. Aff: rec:
John Bridges bur. Nov. 29, 1745.
Mary Bonham bur. Novr 30. Aff: rec.
John Stane bur^d Decr 19. Aff: rec:
Zachary Brown bur^d Jany 8. Af: rec:
Ann Searle bur. Feb. 2^d. Af: rec:
John, Bastard Child of Mary Clift, Feb: . . . . ?

Burials Mar: 25, 1746.

Ann Finch, Daughter of Ste: & Jane, bur. Apr. 2, 1746.
Alexander Velley, the Son of Thomas Velley, Rect^r of this Parish, &
Jane his wife, died Tuesday Apr. 15, aged 3 years 11 months & 5
days, & was buried Apr: 18 at High Laver.
Esther, wife of John Say, buried July 24, 1746. Affid: received.
Mary Guy, from Stanford Rivers, buried Aug: 10, 1746.
John, Son of John Mitchel & [blank] his wife, buried Aug^st 15, 1746.
136

Mary Bannister, Infant, buried Sepr 28, 1746. Af: rec:
Will: Peacock buried Octr 16, 1746. Af: rec:
John Sadler buried Novr 21, 1746. Af: rec:
Francis Ross bur^d Decr 1, 1746. Af: rec.
Ann, Daughter of Thos Alsup, bur. Jan. 7. Af: rec:
John Phillips buried Jan: 16. Af: re: 1746.
Richard Unwin, Infant, bur^d Jan. 21. Af: re:
John Phipps buried Nov^r [blank], 1746.
Richard Houchen bury'd Feb. 19, 1746. Aff: Rec^d.
Margaret Conn, an infant, bury'd Feb. 19, 1746. Aff: Rec^d.
John Brown Bury'd March 12, 1746. Aff: Rec^d.
Mary Pyke, an infant, bury'd March 20, 1746. Aff. Rec^d.
Mary Phillips bury'd March 14, 1746. 1746. Aff: Rec^d.

Thomas Velley, Rector, Mar. 24th, 1746.

Burials March 25th, 1747.

Richard Daniel, an infant, buryd April 17. Aff. Rec^d.
Robert Wren bur^d June 3, 1747. Aff. Rec^d.
Mary Knight buryd Augt 31, 1747. Aff. Rec^d.
Eliz: King, an infant, buryd July 12, 1747. Aff.
Catherine Orson bury'd July 20, 1747.
Robert Searle buryd Augt 24, 1747.
Eliz: Havers buryd Sepr 6, 1747. Aff. R^d.
Justinian Hanchet, Gent., buried Septr 24th, 1747. Aff. rec^d.
Isaac Salwood bur^d Octr 7th, 1747. Aff. rec^d.
Ann Christy, Infant, bur^d Novr 1, 1747. Aff. Rec.
James Meredith, Inf^t, bur^d Dec^r [blank], 1747. Af. Rec^d.
Henry Thorogood Bur^e Feb. 3^d, 1747. Af: Rec^d.
Henry Munday, Infant, bur^d Dec^r [blank], 1747. Af. Rec^d.
Dorothy Unwin, Infant, bur. Mar: 23, 1747. Aff. Rec^d.

Thos Velley, Rector, Mar. 24th 1747

Burials Mar. 25, 1748.

Ann, Infant Daughter of Rich^d & An: Carey, buried Apr. 3^d, 1748.
    Af. rec:
Ann Pyke, Infant, buried Apr. 29, 1748. Af: Re:
Damaris Wrenn buried May 18, 1748. Af: Re:
John Goody buryed June 3^d, 1748. Af: Rec:
Elizabeth King, Infant, buried June [blank], 1748. Af: Rec:
Stephen Finch buried Aug. 9. Af: Rec:
Mary Boodle, Infant, bur^d Oct: 9, 1748. Af: Rec:
Susan Wasket, wid., bur. Novr 8, 1748. Af: rec:
[blank] Long, Infant, bur^d Jan. 6, 1748. Af. Rec:
Willm Baron, Infant son of Bar :, bur. Jan. 30. Af: Rec:
Willm Spicer bur. Feb : 7th, 1748. Af: rec:
Lydia Bedford bur. Feb. 5th, 1748. Af: rec:

Thos Velley, Rect^r, Mar. 24, 1748.

Burials Mar. 25, 1749.

Stephen Bridgman buried Mar. 29, 1749. Af: Rec:
William Shead, Senior, bur⁴ May 19ᵗʰ, 1749. Af: Rec:
James Meredith bur⁴ June 16. Af: Rec:
John Woolmer, Infant, bur⁴ Sepᵇʳ 17, 1749. Af: Rec:
Ann Baron, Infant, bur⁴ Octʳ 20. Af: Rec⁴.
William Cramphorn bur⁴ Novʳ 26. Af. Rec:
Eliz. Baily, Widow, bur⁴ Jan. 4ᵗʰ, 1749. Af: Rec⁴.
Sarah Finch bur⁴ Jan. 5, 1749. Af: Rec⁴.
Emma Bridgman buried Jan. 11, 1749. Af: Rec:
Mary Francis buried Jan. 15, 1749. Af: Rec:

Burials Mar. 25, 1750.

Benjamin Uthwayt buried Apr. 23, 1750. Aff: Rec:
John Lenham, Infant, buried April 24ᵗʰ, 1750. Aff: Rec:
John Bourn buried May 3⁴, 1750. Aff: Rec:
Sarah Monday buried June 7ᵗʰ, 1750. Affid: Received.
John Buckland, Infant, buried Aug. 20, 1750. Af: Rec:
Susannah Stane, of the Lion, bur. Sep. 24, 1750. Af: Rec:
William Littel buried Octʳ 10, 1750. Af: Rec:
Thomas Clark bur. Octʳ [*blank*]. Af: re:
2ⁿᵈ Decʳ. Rev⁴ Tho: Velley, Dʳ, Rector of this pish.
Thomas Emerson Bridges, an infant, bury'd Decʳ 18, 1750. Affᵗ Rec⁴.
Stephen Daniel (an infant) buryd Janʳʸ 9, 1750.
Kitty Lenham bur⁴ Jan. 19.
Robert Conn, an infant, buryd ffebʳʸ 5.
Elisabeth Evans Willis (an infant) buryd ffebʸ 24.
Catherine Angier, ffebʸ 28.

Index.

INDEX.

Abbatt.
  Joan, 93.
Abbot.
  Anne, 98.
Abbott.
  Hugh, 5, 7, 96.
  John, 5.
  Margett, 7.
  Thomas, 94.
Abell.
  Grace, 83.
  John, 83.
  Martha, 78.
Acres.
  Mary, 106.
  William, 106.
Adams.
  Ales, 94.
  Edmund, 94.
  James, 5.
  Joan, 6, 93, 94.
  Lionel, 119.
  Mother, 95.
  Thomas, 5, 6, 95.
Addams.
  Elisabeth, 83.
  Henry, 83.
Ailet.
  Thomas, 99.
  Vmfry, 99.
Ailett.
  Elizabeth, 6.
  Giles, 6.
  Thomas, 6.
Ainger.
  Elizabeth, 134.
Aker.
  Joane, 28.
  Jone, 36.
  Mary, 27, 28, 85.
  Rebecka, 27.
  Robert, 36.
  (Widdow), 115.
  William, 27, 28, 107.
Alexander.
  Ann, 125.
  Edward, 83, 107.
  Henry, 128.

Alexander—*continued.*
  Johanna, 128.
  Margaret, 133.
  Nicholas, 115.
  William, 109.
  Vidua, 83.
Allen.
  Abigail, 60, 61, 87, 124.
  Ann, 86, 135.
  Elizabeth, 58.
  George, 37.
  James, 58.
  Jane, 58.
  John, 59.
  Joseph, 53, 68, 135.
  Lydia, 51, 53, 58, 59, 135.
  Mary, 35, 37, 60, 131.
  Nathanaell, 37, 51, 53, 55, 58, 123, 135.
  Sarah, 68, 134.
  Thomas, 55, 60, 61, 87, 124.
  Walter Neil, 59.
  William, 135.
Allexander.
  Elizabeth, 109.
  Margarete, 84.
  Margrett, 114.
  Nicolas, 123.
  Thomas, 84.
  William, 109.
Allin.
  Esther, 64.
  Joseph, 64, 65.
  Sarah, 64, 65.
Allinn.
  Henry, 42, 114.
  Mary, 42, 44.
  Nathanniell, 42, 44, 114, 126.
  Thomas, 44.
Almond.
  Sarah, 86.
Allsop.
  Daniell, 37, 40.
  Elizabeth, 37.
  Sarah, 40.
Allsup.
  Danniell, 113.
  Elizabeth, 113.
  Judie, 114.

141

Allsup—*continued.*
   Widow, 114.
Alsop.
   Ann, 71.
   Annys, 95.
   Daniell, 36, 38, 39.
   Dorothey, 18.
   Elizabeth, 18, 22, 36, 77, 78, 99.
   Fr., 9, 97.
   Fra., 9.
   Ffrances, 22, 24, 26.
   Ffrancis, 7, 18, 19, 20, 21, 77, 81,
      97, 98, 99, 100.
   Frauncis, 7, 9.
   Grace, 77.
   Jeffrey, 7, 77, 94, 95, 97.
   Joan, 94.
   John, 93, 94, 97.
   Judeth, 21.
   Judith, 38.
   Katherine, 7.
   Margaret, 24.
   Mary, 18-22, 24, 26, 39.
   Mother, 97.
   Richard, 9.
   Sarah, 26.
   Thomas, 18, 71.
   William, 20, 36.
Alsopp.
   Alice, 5.
   Elizabeth, 8.
   Fr—, 7, 8, 10.
   Grace, 7.
   John, 5, 10.
   Jeffrey, 5.
   Nathaniel, 5.
   Nicholas, 5.
   Thomas, 8.
   William, 8.
Alsup.
   An, 72.
   Ann, 72.
   Daniel, 35.
   Elizabeth, 35.
   Thomas, 72.
Alsupp.
   Ann, 137.
   Thomas, 137.
Andrew.
   James, 53.
   John, 53.
   Mary, 53.
Andrewes.
   John, 101, 102.
   Mary, 102.
Angeir.
   Elisebeth, 123.
   William, 123.
Anger.
   Abigail, 69.
   Ann, 69.
   Anne, 29, 30, 33, 108.
   Elizabeth, 26, 35, 37.
   Ellin, 105.
   Francis, 96.
   George, 41.

Anger—*continued.*
   Jaine, 35.
   Jane, 37, 41.
   John, 35, 37-39, 41, 105, 134.
   Mary, 26, 110.
   Sarah, 31-35, 108.
   Susanna, 34.
   Thomas, 26, 29-35, 39, 108, 111, 113.
   Widow, 109.
   William, 109.
Angier.
   Abraham, 25.
   Ann, 121.
   Catherine, 77, 138.
   Elizebeth, 57, 62, 86.
   Ellin, 26, 106.
   Jane, 23, 36, 127.
   John, 26, 36, 106, 117.
   Katerine, 36.
   Mary, 23, 25, 78.
   Sarah, 26.
   Thomas, 23, 25, 104.
   Widdow, 119.
   William, 57, 62, 86, 135.
Anjer.
   Anne, 21.
   Ellen, 21.
   Elizabeth, 80.
   John, 18-23, 98.
   Margaret, 98.
   Mary, 19-22, 82.
   Sara, 19-21.
   Sarah, 18, 19, 23.
   Thomas, 19-23, 80, 82, 100.
Ansell.
   Mother, 95.
   William, 94, 96.
Anzer.
   Marie, 10.
   Mary, 96.
   Thomas, 10, 11, 96.
Anzor.
   John, 11.
   Mary, 10.
   Thomas, 10, 11.
Apletun.
   Sir William, 86.
Archer.
   Benjamin, 26.
   Elizabeth, 20, 103.
   Ffrances, 104.
   Ffrancis, 19, 20, 22, 103.
   Henrie, 102.
   Jacob, 19-23, 26, 27, 82, 102, 106,
      110, 113.
   John, 22, 100, 101.
   Joseph, 23.
   Mary, 19, 20, 22, 101, 104.
   Margaret, 20, 22, 23, 26, 27, 82,
      102.
   Margrett, 113.
   Thomas, 20.
   Widdow, 105.
Arnold.
   Ann, 73.
   Thomas, 73.

Ash.
  Anne, 62, 126.
  Benjamin, 60, 62, 128, 129.
  Benjamine, 57, 58, 122.
  Cordelia, 57, 58, 60, 62, 122.
  Elizabeth, 60, 124.
  John, 57, 122.
  Mary, 60.
Attaridge.
  Edward, 59.
  John, 59.
  Susanna, 59.
Attaway.
  Elizabeth, 128.
  John, 126.
Attawey.
  Benjamin, 60.
  Elizabeth, 60.
  John, 60.
Attredg.
  Edward, 58.
  Mary, 58.
  Susan, 58.
Attridg.
  Edmund, 59.
  Edward, 59.
  Susan, 59.
Atwood.
  Essex, 117.
Austin.
  Jeoffry, 136.
Ayloffe.
  Anne, 130.
Aynger.
  Sarah, 84.
  Thomas, 84.

Babb.
  Anne, 18.
  Nicolas, 18.
Babbs.
  Elizabeth, 24, 83.
  George, 24, 78, 83, 105, 106.
  John, 35.
  Mary, 35, 110.
  Nicholaus, 105.
  Phillis, 78.
  Thomas, 35, 110.
  ——— 124.
Babs.
  Anne, 33.
  Mary, 28, 30, 33, 34, 82, 107-109.
  Phyllis, 82.
  Sarah, 30.
  Thomas, 28, 30, 31, 33, 34, 106-109.
  Virginie, 31.
  Widow, 109.
  William, 33, 34, 108, 109.
  ——— 85, 106.
Babtharston.
  Rose, 78.
Bacon.
  Amy, 82.
  Philip, 82.
  Thomas, 116.

Baily.
  Elizabeth, 138.
Baker.
  Annis, 80.
  Annys, 77.
  John, 77.
Ballard.
  Mary, 127.
  Sarah, 87.
Bancks.
  Jone, 98.
Banister.
  Edward, 78.
  Rose, 78.
Bannister.
  Margery, 86.
  Mary, 72, 89, 137.
  Susan, 72.
  Thomas, 86.
  William, 72.
  Yates, 89.
Barbar.
  James, 102.
  Prudence, 102.
  Sarah, 89.
Barefoot.
  Ellen, 80.
  John, 80, 95.
Bareford.
  Anne, 100.
  John, 100.
Barefote.
  Easter, 80.
  Edward, 13, 80.
  Mary, 13.
Barker.
  Jane, 19.
  Jone, 16, 18, 20.
  Margerett, 84.
  Mary, 19, 20, 102.
  Robert, 16, 18-20, 102.
  William, 18.
Barnard.
  Damaris, 10.
  Elizabeth, 9, 78.
  George, 11.
  Henry, 6, 77.
  John, 11.
  Katharine, 10.
  Martha, 79.
  Mary, 6, 10, 78.
  Richard, 6.
  Thomasin, 77.
  William, 9-11, 79, 95.
Barnes.
  Richard, 74, 93.
  Sarah, 74.
Baron.
  Ann, 73, 138.
  John, 73.
  (Widow), 86.
  William, 73, 137.
Barrel.
  John, 125.

Barrell.
  Rebecca, 115.
Barrett.
  Ellin, 78.
  Ellyn, 79.
  John, 11, 78, 96, 101.
  Richard, 95.
  Sara, 11.
Barrison.
  Temperance, 19.
  Theophilus, 19.
  Thomas, 19.
Barter.
  Sarah, 89.
  Thomas, 89.
Barwicke.
  Anthonie, 77.
  Margery, 77.
  William, 6.
Bash.
  George, 82.
  Mary, 82.
Bass.
  Sarah, 87.
  Thomas, 87.
Basse.
  Jane, 16.
  Jone, 16.
  Katherine, 16.
  Robert, 16.
Bastick.
  Elizabeth, 86.
Bateman.
  Grace, 11.
  Marie, 10, 96.
  Margaret, 10, 96.
  Mary, 10.
  Zacharie, 96.
  Zachary, 10, 11, 96.
Bathrip.
  Sarah, 89.
Batsford.
  Ann, 45-47, 50, 51, 54, 56, 120, 122.
  Anne, 12, 44, 86, 105.
  Annis, 78.
  Catherine, 10.
  Christopher, 27.
  Elizabeth, 14, 25-29, 31, 44, 99.
  Giles, 12, 82.
  Jacobi, 104.
  James, 11, 19, 21, 25, 29, 44-47, 50,
    51, 54, 56, 82, 110, 120, 122, 123.
  Jeames, 31, 86.
  Joane, 11.
  Jone, 19, 21, 82.
  Joseph, 45.
  Judith, 51, 120.
  Lyonell, 54.
  Margaret, 10.
  Mary, 10, 26, 98.
  Philip, 26-28, 50, 109.
  Phillip, 13.
  Phyllis, 82.
  Robert, 10, 13, 99.
  Sara, 21.
  Sarah, 31.

Batsford—*continued*.
  Thomas, 11, 98.
  William, 10-14, 28, 47, 78, 82, 98, 99.
  [*Blank*], 25.
Battle.
  Ann, 74.
  Elizabeth, 73.
  Jane, 74.
  Isaac, 73, 74.
  [*Blank*], 73.
Baxter.
  Amy, 46.
  Calebb, 46, 48.
  Elizabeth, 48.
  Sarah, 46, 48.
Bayford.
  Millecent, 61.
  Sarah, 61.
  William, 61.
Baynham.
  John, 108.
Bazen.
  Thomas, 109.
Beans.
  Elizabeth, 84.
  Henry, 84.
Beard.
  Agnes, 16, 18, 19, 21.
  Ann, 30, 32, 107, 119.
  Christopher, 16, 18, 19, 21, 104.
  Elizabeth, 23, 30, 97.
  John, 18, 20, 21, 23, 31, 103, 107.
  Joshea, 21.
  Joshuah, 112.
  Josiah, 19, 30, 119, 120.
  Josias, 31, 32, 107.
  Katherin, 20, 21, 23.
  Katherine, 32.
  Mary, 21, 104.
  Sarah, 80.
  Thomas, 16, 20, 80, 86, 97, 99, 102,
    103.
  Widdow, 118.
Beasing.
  Elizabeth, 74
  James, 74.
Bedford.
  Lydia, 137.
Bedle.
  Elizabeth, 39.
  James, 39.
  Joseph, 39.
Beety.
  Ann, 66.
  George, 66.
  John, 66.
Belcher.
  Mary, 87.
Belchier.
  Susannah, 136.
Bell.
  Mary, 49.
  Thomas, 49.
Bennet.
  Ann, 15.
  Jane, 79.

144

Bennet—*continued.*
Jone, 81.
Moses, 93.
Sarah, 15.
Thomas, 79.
William, 15, 79, 81.
Bennett.
Annis, 79.
Benson.
Henry, 42, 115.
Mary, 42.
Benten.
Sarah, 48.
Susan, 48.
Benton.
Emme, 84.
Jane, 126.
Susan, 86.
Bernard.
Ann, 129.
Anne, 66.
Besouth.
Elizabeth, 129.
Thomas, 128.
Best.
Joane, 79.
Jone, 103.
William, 13, 79, 97, 103.
Thomas, 13, 97.
Bett.
Susan, 78.
William, 78, 97.
Bettis.
Anne, 63-65, 88, 128.
James, 64, 127.
John, 63-65 88.
Betts.
Elizabeth, 94.
Jeffrey, 94.
Betty.
Susan, 21.
Susannah, 82.
William, 21, 82.
Bettye.
William, 105.
Bettyes.
Ann, 70, 73.
George, 135.
Elizabeth, 73.
John, 70, 73, 135.
[*Blank*], 70.
Bettys.
Elizabeth, 72.
John, 72.
William. 132.
Bibbe.
Anne, 86.
Rebecca, 86.
Bidges.
Rebecca, 115.
Big.
Anne, 81.
Biggs.
Ann, 89.
Bilt.
Elizabeth, 10.

Bilt—*continued.*
Isaac, 12, 28.
Katherine, 25.
Mary, 25, 27, 82, 83.
Nathaniel, 11, 28, 83.
Nathaniell, 25, 27.
Richard, 10, 28, 100.
William, 10-12, 28, 82, 100, 105.
Bincks.
Anne, 132.
Binckes.
———, 132.
Binder.
Alice, 94.
Binion.
Sarah, 121.
———, 121.
Binks.
Georg, 57.
Hannah, 55.
Jacob, 58.
Mary, 54, 56, 57, 121.
Sarah, 55-58.
Thomas, 54-58, 121.
Blaxe.
Richard, 101.
Blewett.
Thomas, 114.
Blomer.
Anne, 81.
Charles, 81.
Bloomer.
Anne, 16.
Charles, 16.
Ellen, 16.
Blyten.
Joan, 93.
Bolt.
Anne, 61.
Richard, 61.
Bones.
Ffrances, 87.
Mary, 85.
Samiell, 120.
Samuel, 85.
[*Blank*], 134.
Bonham.
John, 129.
Mary, 125, 136.
Boodle.
John, 72-74.
Mary, 73, 137.
Richard Bernard, 72.
Sarah, 72-74.
Thomas, 74.
Booth.
Barton, 87.
Hester, 87.
Booyd.
John, 118.
Bora.
Elizabeth, 25, 27.
Richard, 25, 27.
Robert, 27.
Thomas, 25.

Boram.
  Abigail, 33, 34, 108.
  Clemence, 83.
  Elizabeth, 33, 108.
  Emme, 84.
  Henry, 83.
  John, 33, 34, 108.
  Robert, 84.
  —n, 34.
Borar.
  Elizabeth, 23.
  Richard, 23.
Borne.
  Dorothy, 132.
Bornes.
  Frances, 69.
  Grace, 69.
  John, 68, 69.
  Wi——, 68.
  [Blank], 68.
Borst.
  John, 59.
  Thomas, 59.
  [Blank], 59.
Boste.
  Anne, 99.
  John, 99.
Bouchee.
  Elizabeth, 111.
Bound.
  Abigaill, 28.
  George, 28.
Bounds.
  Thomas, 109.
Bourn.
  John, 138.
Bourne.
  Elizabeth, 7.
  Grace, 65, 66.
  John, 65, 66.
  Katherine, 77.
  Marie, 77.
  Mary, 95.
  Morice, 7.
  Robart, 77.
  Thomas, 65.
  William, 7, 65, 77, 95.
Bournes.
  Grace, 132.
Bowns.
  Susan, 109.
Bowtel.
  Samuel, 123.
Bowtell.
  Elizabeth, 52.
  Robert, 57.
  Samuel, 54.
  Samuell, 52, 57, 118, 121, 122.
  Susan, 52, 57.
  Susanna, 54.
  Thomas, 57, 122, 123.
Bowyer.
  Anne, 80.
Bradbent.
  Mary, 79.
  Richard, 79.

Brainwood.
  Alice, 80.
  Anne, 88, 125.
  Elizabeth, 78, 102, 128.
  Grace, 5.
  James, 14, 80, 97, 126.
  Jane, 6.
  Jeffray, 81, 102.
  Jone, 93.
  Mary, 97.
  Thomas, 5, 97.
Brainwoode.
  Joane, 5.
  Thomas, 5.
Brand.
  Isabel, 77.
Brandwood.
  James, 40.
  Mary, 40.
Brandwoods.
  Anne, 44.
  James, 44.
  Katerine, 44.
Branwood.
  Ann, 39, 41, 114.
  Elizabeth, 29, 32, 106, 108.
  James, 32, 39, 106, 108.
  Jeame, 114.
  Jeames, 41, 114.
  Jeane, 29.
  Joan, 94.
  John, 39.
  Katherine, 32, 108.
  Lidiah, 41, 114.
  Marey, 106.
  Mother, 97.
Brasier.
  John, 110.
  Sammuel, 41.
  Sarah, 41.
  Thomas, 41.
Braynard.
  James, 111.
Brazier.
  Sammuell, 40, 118.
  Sarah, 40, 118.
Breach.
  Charles, 20.
  Elizabeth, 20.
  John, 20.
Bredges.
  Joseph, 118.
Breme.
  Joan, 77.
  Robart, 77.
Bret.
  Ann, 70, 134.
  [Blank], 70.
Brewer.
  Anne, 61, 94.
  Charles, 61, 125.
  Elizabeth, 60-62, 65.
  James, 58.
  Mary, 58, 62.
  Nathanael, 60, 61.
  Nathaneel, 124.

Brewer—*continued.*
    Nathaniel, 61, 62, 65, 129.
    Nathaniell, 58.
    Susannah, 65.
    William, 108.
Brickly.
    Mary, 122.
Bridge.
    Henery, 85.
    Henry, 40.
    Johana, 85.
    Johannah, 40.
    William, 40.
Bridgeman.
    Eleanor, 135.   ·
Bridges.
    Benjamin, 64.
    Edward, 62.
    Elizabeth, 39, 41, 43, 44, 60-65, 72,
      127.
    Elizebeth, 45, 47.
    Francess, 107.
    Francesse, 31.
    James, 62, 126.
    Jane, 60-63, 87, 136.
    John, 30-32, 41, 60-65, 87, 107, 109,
      129, 135, 136.
    Joseph, 49.
    Mary, 43, 61.
    Olive, 88.
    Rebecka, 49.
    Rebeckah, 32.
    Samuel, 60, 125.
    Sarah, 30, 32, 44, 71-73, 86, 128,
      136.
    Susannah, 65.
    Thomas, 61, 71-73, 136.
    Thomas Emerson, 73, 138.
    William, 29, 39, 41, 43-45, 47, 49,
      117, 119.
Bridgman.
    Damaris, 123.
    Eleanor, 62.
    Elizabeth, 60.
    Emma, 60, 138.
    Mary, 60-63.
    Nem, 122.
    Richard, 123.
    Stephen, 60-63, 138.
    Thomas, 63, 122, 123.
Bringhurst.
    ——, 108.
Brown.
    Alexander, 64, 127.
    Ann, 57, 59, 60, 68, 73, 123, 131.
    Anne, 61-64.
    Elizabeth, 60, 63, 125, 126.
    John, 20, 57, 82, 87, 99, 137.
    Joseph, 47-50, 52, 54-57, 59 64, 73,
      117, 119-123, 125, 127.
    Margaret, 20, 36, 82.
    Mary, 62, 66, 73, 87, 126, 128, 135.
    Mathew, 36.
    Olive, 47, 48, 52, 54-56, 119, 120,
      121.
    Ollive, 49, 50, 52.

Brown—*continued.*
    Philip, 52, 56, 120.
    Sarah, 47, 55, 117, 121.
    Trahearn, 62.
    Trahern, 66.
    Trehern, 49.
    Zachary, 136.
Browne.
    Ann, 39.
    Anne, 8, 64, 96.
    Annis, 79.
    Daniell, 39, 112.
    Dennis, 97.
    Edward, 107.   ·
    Elizabeth, 9, 96.
    Frances, 79.
    Frauncis, 8.
    Joan, 77.
    John, 8-10, 79, 95-97.
    Joseph, 52, 64, 128.
    Margaret, 110.
    Marie, 96.
    Mary, 8, 64, 79.
    Mathew, 110.
    Matthew, 10, 96.
    Ollive, 52.
    Rebecca, 10.
    Sara, 9.
    Sarah, 83, 130.
    Thomas, 83.
Bryan.
    Josiah, 58.
    Mary, 58.
Bryon.
    Josiah, 59, 60, 124.
    Mary, 59, 60.
    Rebecca, 59.
Buchanan.
    Alexander, 56.
    David, 53.
    George, 134.
    Isaac, 53.
    James, 49.
    John, 53.
    Joseph, 57.
    Mary, 49, 51, 53, 56-58.
    Rose, 58.
    Walter, 49, 51, 53, 135.
    Walther, 56-58.
    Wather, 53, 120.
    Williams, 53, 120.
Buchannan.
    Elizabeth, 64.
    George, 52, 64.
    Mary, 52, 62, 64.
    Sarah, 64, 90.
    Walter, 52, 62.
Buchannon.
    Benjamin, 62.
Buckland.
    Elizabeth, 136.
    James, 136.
    John, 136, 138.
Built.
    Mary, 23.
    Nathaniel, 23.

Bull.
  Elizabeth, 64, 66, 130, 133.
  James, 64, 129.
  John, 66, 132.
  Sir John, 64, 132, 133, 135.
  Kitty, 66.
  Richard, 125.
  Thomas, 127.
  Turner, 127.
  William, 129.
Bunn.
  Mary, 87.
Bunnell.
  Mary, 66.
Bunnington.
  Joane, 93.
Burling.
  John, 113.
Durre.
  Jone, 78.
  Mary, 79.
Burrel.
  Anne, 64.
  Jane, 18, 61, 65.
  Jone, 18.
  Joseph, 65.
  Mary, 60, 61, 64, 87.
  Philip, 60, 61, 64, 87.
  Simon, 18.
Burrell.
  Anne, 127.
  Elizabeth, 66.
  James, 132.
  Jane, 15, 17, 19, 20, 22, 25, 66, 68,
    70, 88, 134.
  John, 20, 70, 104.
  Joseph, 66-68, 70, 88.
  Lettice, 62, 129.
  Mary, 62, 67, 68.
  Newland, 15.
  Philip, 62.
  Simon, 15, 17, 19, 20, 22, 25, 102,
    104, 105.
  William, 22, 104.
  [. . . . .], 25.
  ———, 105.
Burrill.
  John, 33, 84.
  Mary, 84.
Burton.
  Benjamin, 121.
  Benjamine, 119.
  David, 89.
  Dorathy, 78.
  Elizabeth, 78, 121.
  Gamaliell, 27, 105.
  John, 27.
  Mary, 89.
  Rebekah, 105.
  ———, 25, 27, 105.
Bury.
  Elizabeth, 7.
  Joseph, 7.
Bush.
  Anne, 83.

Bush—continued.
  Elizabeth, 87.
  Thomas, 98.
Butcher.
  John, 9, 93.
  Samuel, 9.
Butler.
  Anne, 78.
  George, 78.
  Jeffrey, 6, 93.

Cackbread.
  Widdow, 112.
  William, 112.
Cakebread.
  Martha, 78.
  Mary, 83.
  Thomas, 78.
  William, 83.
Calis.
  Anne, 77.
Calys.
  Anne, 5.
  William, 5.
Camp.
  James, 46.
  John, 45, 46, 48, 125.
  Susanna, 45, 48.
  Susannah, 46.
  Thomas, 48.
  ———, 134.
Campe.
  Thomas, 125.
Campion.
  Elizabeth, 79.
  John, 98.
Capell.
  Charles, 113.
  Gammaliell, 113.
Carey.
  Ann, 72, 137.
  Anne, 74.
  Elizabeth, 132.
  James, 133.
  Richard, 72, 74, 137.
Carie.
  Elizabeth, 42.
  Katherine, 86.
  Mary, 41, 42.
  Richard, 41, 42.
Carter.
  Alice, 32, 128.
  John, 32, 107.
Cary.
  Ann, 72, 89.
  Anne, 43.
  Elizabeth, 37, 39, 43, 44, 47, 57-59,
    112, 120.
  Elizebeth, 54, 55.
  James, 54, 55, 57-59, 120, 127.
  John, 122.
  Jolly, 56, 122.
  Katherine, 39.
  Martha, 47, 118.
  Mary, 38, 58, 112.

148

Cary—*continued.*
    Richard, 37-39, 43, 44, 47, 59, 72,
        89, 112, 118, 129.
    Sarah, 56, 122.
    Susanna, 44, 115.
    Thomas, 57.
    William, 56.
Castle.
    Margaret, 101.
Chadweeke.
    Edmond, 77.
    Isabel, 77.
Chadwick.
    Edmund, 93.
Chaillet.
    David, 125.
Chake.
    Ffortune, 82.
    Rebecka, 85.
Chamberlin.
    Sarah, 90.
    Thomas, 90.
Chambers.
    John, 87.
    Mary, 87.
    Thomas, 98.
Champnes.
    Debora, 9.
    Ellin, 13.
    Isaac, 9.
    Joane, 83.
    John, 13.
    Robert, 9.
    Thomas, 13, 105.
Champnis.
    Ellyn, 79.
    Thomas, 79, 100, 101.
Chaplain.
    James, 135.
Chaplin.
    Benjamin, 69.
    Elizabeth, 31, 62-65, 69.
    James, 62-65, 69, 87, 125.
    John, 65.
    Mary, 62, 87, 125.
    Robert, 31.
    Sarah, 64.
Chaplinn.
    ——, 114.
Chaplyn.
    James, 61.
    Mary, 61.
    Thomae, 104.
Chapman.
    Ann, 52.
    Bartholomew, 11, 12, 80, 97, 100.
    Bartlemew, 100.
    Benjamin, 42.
    Daniel, 33, 34, 43, 115.
    Daniell, 37, 38, 40, 51, 86, 110, 111.
    Danniell, 42, 114.
    Elizabeth, 67.
    Hannah, 40.
    James, 12, 67.
    Jane, 33, 34, 37, 114.
    Jean, 40.

Chapman—*continued.*
    John, 11, 51, 52.
    Jone, 100.
    Margery, 80.
    Marjory, 103.
    Mary, 37, 42, 43, 67, 97.
    Samuell, 111.
    Susan, 51, 52.
    William, 43.
    Widdow, 117.
    ——, 115
Charuill.
    Margery, 80.
Chaucke.
    Ann, 35.
    Susan, 35.
    Thomas, 35.
Chaunsey.
    Philip, 77.
    Robert, 77.
Chervill.
    Joane, 79.
Cheston.
    Joan, 8.
    John, 8, 9.
    Mary, 9.
    Richard, 8, 94.
    Thomas, 8.
Chidwick.
    Brigit, 93.
Chifens.
    Elizabeth, 64.
    Mary, 64, 128.
    William, 64.
Childs.
    Anne, 22, 23.
    Ffrances, 22.
    Frances, 104.
    Grace, 23.
    Robert, 22, 23, 104.
Chivers.
    Mary, 126.
Choping.
    Catherine, 37.
    Elizabeth, 35, 37.
    Jane, 32.
    John, 35, 37.
    Mary, 35.
    Richard, 32.
Choppen.
    Elizabeth, 35.
    John, 35.
    Sarah, 35.
Choppin.
    Elizabeth, 21, 34.
    John, 34.
    Richard, 21, 34.
Choppine.
    Mary, 127.
Chopping.
    Elizabeth, 22, 23, 31-34, 84, 112,
        126.
    James, 33, 134.
    Jane, 22, 33.
    John, 23, 31-34, 38, 84, 108, 112,
        123.

Chopping—*continued.*
   Katherine, 85.
   Richard, 22, 23, 33, 38, 109, 136.
   William, 34.
Choppinge.
   Elizabeth, 25.
   Jane, 30.
   Katherine, 25, 30.
   Richard, 25, 30.
Christy.
   Ann, 71, 137.
   Daniel, 71, 73, 74, 89.
   Jane, 71, 73, 74, 89.
   Sarah, 74.
Chrocherood.
   Charles, 117.
Clark.
   Ann, 67, 134.
   Elizabeth, 53, 67, 134.
   Garnet, 53.
   Jeffray, 103.
   John, 23, 82, 103.
   Mary, 23.
   Samuel, 53.
   Susannah, 82.
   Thomas, 67, 138.
Clarke.
   Anne, 65, 66, 88, 129.
   Bennet, 7.
   Clemence, 84.
   Dorothy, 61.
   Elizabeth, 87.
   Ffrances, 27.
   John, 27, 104, 105.
   Joseph, 88.
   Margaret, 95.
   Mary, 88.
   Richard, 7.
   Thomas, 65, 66, 88.
   William, 61, 84, 123.
   [*Blank*] 27.
   ——, 104, 115.
Clay.
   Susan, 89.
Cleaveland.
   Rebecca, 82.
Cleveland.
   Anne, 83.
Clemence.
   John, 60.
   Mary, 60.
Clements.
   Mary, 125.
Clerk.
   Ales, 96.
   Alice, 8, 11.
   Dorithy, 56, 57, 59, 121.
   Elizabeth, 11, 56, 121.
   Garnett, 120.
   Henry, 10.
   Katherine, 7.
   Laurence, 96.
   Mary, 59.
   Nicolas, 10.
   Richard, 7, 97.
   Samuell, 120.

Clerk—*continued.*
   Thomas, 7, 8.
   William, 56, 57, 59, 121.
Clerke.
   Alice, 11.
   Anne, 8.
   Henry, 10.
   Lawrence, 11.
   Lettice, 10.
   Margaret, 7.
   Mother, 95.
   Richard, 6-8, 94.
   Thomas, 61, 94.
Cliff.
   Elizabeth, 59.
   Rebecca, 59.
   Robert, 59.
Cliffe.
   James, 30, 33, 34, 108.
   John, 13, 33.
   Rebecca, 33, 34, 108.
   Rebecka, 30.
   Robert, 34.
Clift.
   Abigale, 86.
   Abigayle, 32.
   Ann, 46, 117.
   Anne, 64.
   Elizabeth, 53, 56, 130.
   Elizebeth, 46, 52.
   James, 29, 32, 63-65, 67, 84, 88.
   John, 53, 65, 136.
   Lettice, 63-65, 67, 88.
   Marah, 29.
   Mary, 50, 56, 63, 72, 86, 119, 127,
     136.
   Phillis, 65.
   Rebeca, 32.
   Rebeccah, 84.
   Rebecka, 29.
   Robert, 46, 50, 52, 53, 56, 72, 86,
     117, 119, 131.
Clifft.
   Elizebeth, 116.
   James, 49.
   Mary, 47, 49.
   Robert, 47, 49, 116.
Cllift.
   Phillis, 90.
Cock.
   Danniell, 41, 43, 44.
   James, 44.
   Jane, 41.
   Jone, 41, 43, 44.
Cocke.
   Daniel, 45.
   Gabriel, 45.
   Joan, 45.
Coe.
   Edward, 48.
   Elizabeth, 45.
   John, 46, 87.
   Mary, 43-46, 48, 87.
   Sammuell, 43.
   Samuel, 44.

Coe—*continued.*
Samuell, 45, 46, 48.
Thomas, 44.
Coke.
Henry, 97.
William, 97.
Cole.
Grace, 6.
John, 6, 94, 95.
Jone, 83.
Mary, 87.
Richard, 87.
Robart, 6.
Sarah, 85.
William, 83.
Colford.
Annis, 79.
Colins.
Mary, 63.
Collins.
Dennis, 127.
Jeffery, 17.
Mary Bales, 17.
——, 106.
Collis.
Mary, 80.
William, 80.
Collyn.
Jane, 79.
Colmer.
Mary, 73.
Richard, 73.
Samuel, 73.
Con.
Ann, 71.
Margaret, 71.
Robert, 71.
Conn.
Margaret, 137.
Robert, 138.
Cooper.
Abigail, 44, 131.
Abigaill, 43.
Abigale, 86.
Abigall, 45, 46.
Elizabeth, 43.
John, 46.
Jesse, 128.
Thomas, 43-46, 86, 121.
Widdow, 119.
Corbet.
Jone, 98.
Walter, 98.
Corby.
Daniel, 14.
Water, 14.
Cordall.
Grace, 83.
Cornell.
Ann, 115.
Cordeliah, 42.
Elizabeth, 38, 40, 42, 128.
James, 38, 40, 120.
Jeames, 42, 114, 115.
William, 38, 126.

Corney.
Cordelia, 64, 135.
Elizabeth, 62.
Henry, 62-64, 135.
Mary, 62-64.
Sprainger, 62.
Cottyn.
Elisabeth, 83.
Courtney.
Ellin, 5.
Courtnole.
Mary, 83.
Coward.
Ann, 47.
Georg, 47.
James, 47.
Cowel.
Elizabeth, 136.
Cowland.
James, 88.
Martha, 88.
Cowper.
Abigail, 63.
Joan, 80.
Mary, 62, 63.
Thomas, 62, 63.
Crab.
Alice, 96, 107.
Aune, 79, 99.
Edward, 96.
Elizabeth, 11.
Henry, 8, 14, 104.
John, 8, 11, 13, 15, 77, 79, 94, 96, 98.
Margaret, 14, 15, 17.
Margeret, 79.
Mary, 15, 81, 87.
Nicholas, 107.
Robart, 79, 94.
Robert, 12-15, 17, 97, 99, 101.
Solomon, 12, 97.
Walter, 17, 101.
William, 15, 87, 99.
[*Blank*], 77, 96.
Crabb.
Edward, 7.
Elizebeth, 56.
John, 7, 8, 57, 79.
Mary, 79.
Richard, 68, 132.
Robart, 7.
Robert, 8.
William, 56, 57.
[*Blank*], 57.
Crafts.
Margarett, 32.
Thomas, 32.
Crampen.
Ann, 50, 51.
William, 50, 51.
Cramphon.
Ann, 134.
Cramphorn.
William, 138.

Cramphorne.
  John, 127.
  William, 131.
Crampin.
  Ann, 56.
  John, 56.
  William, 56.
Crampion.
  Ann, 54.
  Elizebeth, 54.
  William, 54.
Crampon.
  Elizabeth, 122.
  William, 122.
Cravin.
  Francis, 97.
  Mary, 97.
  William, 97.
Crofts.
  Anne, 32, 34, 108, 109.
  Margaret, 32-34, 109.
  Marget, 107, 108.
  Michael, 33.
  Thomas, 32-34, 107-109.
Crooke.
  James, 33, 84, 108.
  Sarah, 83.
Crookes.
  Sarah, 105.
Crouchman.
  Charles, 73.
  Daniel, 73.
  Susannah, 73.
Crow.
  Elizebeth, 86.
  Joan, 95.
  Mother, 96.
  Susan, 88.
Curds.
  Martha, 127.
  Sarah, 63.
Cutler.
  Ffrancis, 85.
  Katherine, 85, 114.
Cuts.
  Margaret, 80.

Dan.
  Luce, 110.
Dane.
  Ann, 86.
  Georg, 86.
Daniel.
  Ann, 73.
  Edward, 71.
  Elizabeth, 71.
  Mary, 71, 74.
  Richard, 72-74, 137.
  Stephen, 74, 138.
  [Blank], 72.
Darvile.
  Daniell, 23.
  David, 24.
  Elizabeth, 23-27.
  James, 22-27, 104.
  Jane, 22, 26, 104.

Darvile—continued.
  Joane, 25.
  Sarah, 27.
Davies.
  Anne, 88.
  Catherine, 88.
  Elizabeth, 124.
  John, 88.
Davis.
  John, 99.
Dawes.
  Priscilla, 106.
  ——, 106.
Day.
  Susanna, 88.
Dellon.
  Katheren, 87.
Dellower.
  Samuel, 69.
  [Blank], 69.
Dennis.
  Joan, 78.
Denys.
  John, 94.
Derington.
  Abdiel, 18.
  Anne, 7.
  Annis, 79.
  Bartholomew, 8-10, 78, 95, 98.
  Elizabeth, 13, 14, 95, 78, 79, 103.
  Ffrancis, 18, 102.
  Frauncis, 10.
  George, 9.
  Gilbert, 10.
  Grace, 77.
  James, 11-14, 79, 99, 103.
  Jane, 80.
  Joane, 79.
  Jone, 78.
  John, 11, 13, 103.
  Katherin, 18.
  Katherine, 102.
  Mary, 10, 12, 79, 98, 103.
  Martha, 80, 101.
  Peter, 9, 10, 78.
  Priscilla, 9.
  Richard, 7, 9, 80, 99, 101.
  Ruth, 13.
  Sarah, 80.
  Theophilus, 9, 80.
  Thomas, 9, 14, 18, 79, 95.
Derrington.
  Anne, 83.
  Barthlemew, 95.
  Bartholomew, 96.
  Elizabeth, 95.
  Ffrancis, 17.
  James, 7, 83.
  Katherin, 17.
  Martha, 9.
  Mary, 8.
  Obadiah, 106.
  Richard, 7-9, 102.
Deryngton.
  Jane, 8.
  Richard, 8.

Dew.
    Mary, 86.
Dickinson.
    John, 98.
Ditton.
    Katherine, 78.
    Richard, 78.
Dongar.
    Antonius, 71.
    Johannes Antonius, 71.
    Maria, 71.
Dore.
    Ann, 67.
    George, 67.
    Luke, 67.
    Olive, 73, 74.
    Richard, 73.
    William, 73, 74.
Dountin.
    Mary, 86.
Dowsett.
    Mary, 79.
Dowly.
    Mary, 79.
    William, 79.
Dowthy.
    Mary, 87.
Draper.
    Anne, 63.
    James, 63.
    Martha, 63.
Ducket.
    Jane, 6, 94.
    Joan, 93.
    Robart, 94.
Duckett.
    Elizabeth, 5.
    Robert, 5.
Duckfield.
    Grace, 80.
    John, 80.
Duddesborow.
    Mary, 12.
    Sara, 11.
    William, 11, 12, 97.
Duke.
    John, 83.
    ———, 83.
Dunmowe.
    Susan, 96.
    Thomas, 96.
Durentone.
    John, 28.
Durringtone.
    John, 28.
Dyer.
    John, 84.
    Susan, 84.

Eates.
    Anne, 62.
    Barnaby, 62.
    John, 126.
    Mary, 62, 126, 127.

Edmunds.
    Elizabeth, 6.
    William, 5, 93.
Edward.
    Philip, 98.
    Sara, 98.
Elderton.
    Annis, 79.
    Edward, 97.
Elkin.
    Henry, 104.
    Mary, 82.
Ellett.
    Mary, 120.
Elmes.
    James, 136.
Emberson.
    Anne, 126.
    Thomas, 124.
Embeson.
    Ann, 86.
Emerson.
    Anne, 136.
    Richard, 136.
Emsonn.
    Ann, 41.
    Thomas, 41, 114.
Enever.
    Ann, 121.
    John, 112, 119.
    William, 117.
Eniver.
    John, 44.
    Mary, 44.
    Robert, 44.
Ennyveer.
    John, 29.
    Sarah, 29.
    William, 30.
Ennyver.
    John, 51.
    Sarah, 51.
    Susanna, 28.
Erwin.
    Simon, 108.
Esterley.
    Francis, 96.
Estick.
    Henry, 79.
    Mary, 79.
Eue.
    Elizabeth, 114.
    Samuel, 114.
Euerard.
    Hugh, 12.
    James, 14.
    John, 13.
    Martha, 14.
    Mary, 13.
    Philip, 12-14.
    Sara, 14.
Euerist.
    Steven, 97.
    William, 97.

x

Evans.
 Olive, 88.
 Sarah, 128.
 Thomas, 88.
Eve.
 Elizabeth, 37.
 Esther, 88.
 Richard, 88.
 Samuell, 37, 110.
Everard.
 Daniel, 14.
 Joan, 15.
 Jonathan, 16.
 Martha, 14-16.
 Philip, 14-16.
Evered.
 Mother, 97.
Ewer.
 Anne, 107.
Ewin.
 Anne, 105.
 ——, 105.
Exeter.
 Mary, 82.
Eylet.
 Elizabeth, 132.

Fane.
 Charlotte, 90.
 Henry, 90.
Farrington.
 George, 9.
 William, 9.
Farrinton.
 Collonell, 117.
Faulker.
 Frances, 87.
Feild.
 William, 106.
 [*Blank*], 106.
Felpes.
 Catherine, 79.
 Richard, 79.
Fensam.
 Alice, 80.
Ffibs.
 Edward, 30.
 Marey, 30.
Ffinch.
 Dennis, 6.
 Dorathy, 43, 44.
 Elizabeth, 44.
 Grace, 5.
 James, 87.
 John, 125.
 Mary, 87.
 Robart, 6.
 Robert, 5.
 Thomas, 43, 44, 115.
Ffipps.
 Edward, 111.
Ffoard.
 Jane, 109.
 Thomas, 109.
Ffog.
 James, 43.

Ffog—*continued*.
 Mary, 43.
 William, 43.
Ffogg.
 Elizabeth, 45.
 Jeames, 41, 45.
 Jeams, 42.
 Mary, 41, 42, 45.
 Sarah, 41.
Ffoot.
 Jone, 98.
 Thomas, 98.
Ffootman.
 John, 105.
 Thomas, 105.
Fford.
 Elizabeth, 33, 123.
 Jane, 33, 34.
 John, 34.
 Mary, 33.
 Thomas, 33, 34, 123.
Ffosbury.
 Edward, 81.
Ffosten.
 John, 5.
 Thomas, 5.
Ffoster.
 Jacob, 84.
 Richard, 44.
 Rose, 84.
 Sarah, 44.
Ffrancis.
 Elizabeth, 34.
 George, 34, 109.
 Jane, 34.
 Margrett, 41.
 Susan, 33.
 Susanna, 33, 34, 41, 84.
 William, 33, 34, 41, 84, 125.
Ffynch.
 Emma, 100.
 Mary, 101.
 Prudence, 99.
 Robert, 99.
 William, 99, 100, 101.
Field.
 John, 93.
Finch.
 Ann, 136.
 Anne, 67, 72, 131.
 Elizabeth, 70, 134.
 Elizebeth, 50.
 Esther, 69.
 George, 54, 66, 88.
 Henery, 49, 52, 118.
 James, 47.
 Jane, 65-67, 69, 70, 72, 136.
 John, 45.
 Margaret, 54, 128.
 Marget, 47, 50, 52, 55.
 Margett, 45, 47.
 Mary, 65.
 Richard, 10.
 Samuell, 121, 122.
 Sarah, 66, 138.

Finch—*continued.*
 Stephen, 55, 65-67, 69, 70, 72, 131, 136, 137.
 Susanna, 66, 88.
 Thomas, 45, 47, 49, 50, 52, 54, 55, 118, 121.
 William, 10, 47, 104.
Fipps.
 Edward, 32.
 George, 32.
 Mary, 32.
Fips.
 Edward, 36.
 Mary, 36.
Fog.
 Anne, 66.
 Edward, 51, 63, 66 67.
 Elizabeth, 63.
 James, 51.
 Mary, 51, 63, 66, 67.
 Olive, 118, 134.
 Sarah, 66, 67, 129.
Fogg.
 Edward, 64, 68, 70, 134.
 Elizabeth, 126.
 Elizebeth, 122.
 James, 47, 49, 64.
 John, 49.
 Joseph, 54, 120.
 Mary, 49, 64, 68, 70, 134.
 Olive, 47, 68.
 Sarah, 47, 54.
 Widdow, 120.
Foord.
 Jane, 84.
 Thomas, 84.
Foot.
 Thomas, 12.
Foote.
 John, 97.
 Jone, 79.
 Thomas, 79, 97.
Forbett.
 Margarett, 126.
Forde.
 Elizebeth, 47.
 Mary, 47.
 Thomas, 47.
Forman.
 Phenenna, 96.
Forrington.
 William, 10.
Forster.
 Jone, 78.
Fosten.
 George, 93.
Foster.
 Catherine, 123.
 Henry, 5.
 Joane, 5.
 Martin, 94.
 Richard, 115.
 Sarah, 115.
Foston.
 George, 5.
 Joan, 6.

Foston—*continued.*
 John, 5, 6.
Fote.
 John, 12.
 Thomas, 12.
Fowler.
 Anne, 126.
 Charles, 126.
 Elizabeth, 88.
Fox.
 Frances, 70.
 Joan, 93.
 Joane, 5.
 John, 5.
 Margaret, 69.
 Sarah, 70.
 Thomas, 69, 70.
 [*Blank*], 69.
Frances.
 Ann, 69.
 Anne, 68.
 Elizabeth, 36.
 Frances, 116.
 Mary, 53.
 Richard, 38, 53, 68, 69.
 Sarah, 53.
 Susan, 36.
 Thomas, 69, 119.
 William, 36, 38, 53, 116.
Francis.
 Abigail, 64, 88.
 Ann, 132.
 George, 35.
 Mary, 55, 58, 64, 138.
 Richard, 54, 120, 121.
 Sarah, 54.
 Susan, 35, 125.
 Susanna, 37.
 Thomas, 37, 55, 58, 128.
 William, 35, 37, 55, 58, 64, 128.
Freshwater.
 John, 37.
 Susanna, 37.
 William, 37.
Fryer.
 Ann, 114.
Fuellin.
 Peter, 109.
Fyfield.
 Alice, 5.
 John, 5.
Fynch.
 Andrew, 11, 96.
 Annys, 77.
 Emma, 9.
 George, 11, 96.
 Grace, 9, 77, 94, 95.
 James, 6.
 Joan, 77.
 Margett, 78.
 Prudence, 10, 97.
 Robart, 6, 9.
 Robert, 5, 94.
 Stephen, 5, 95.
 William, 9-11, 96, 97.

Fytch.
  Anna Maria, 134.

Gabel.
  ——, 128.
Galloway.
  Mary, 80.
Gardiner.
  Elizabeth, 89.
  William, 89.
Garrett.
  Alice, 80.
  Henry, 80.
  ——, 83.
Garriott.
  Elizabeth, 84.
  Phillipp, 84.
Gary.
  Joane, 79.
Geff.
  Mary, 86.
Georg.
  Edward, 59.
  Martha, 59.
  Anne, 88.
Gibson.
  Frances, 82.
Gillet.
  Amy, 62, 135.
  Ann, 67.
  Anne, 61, 62, 63, 64.
  Samuel, 61, 62, 63, 64, 67.
  Samuell, 119.
  Sarah, 64, 128.
  Susanna, 62.
  Thomas, 61, 136.
Gillett.
  Prudence, 49.
  Samuell, 49.
  Susan, 49.
Gladden.
  Robiat, 117.
Gladwin.
  Henry, 9.
  William, 9.
Glascock.
  Alice, 6, 17.
  Ann, 49, 52, 53, 120.
  Anne, 6, 79.
  Bartholomew, 59, 124.
  Christopher, 24, 25, 26, 27, 106.
  Clemence, 27.
  Dorathy, 59, 60.
  Elizabeth, 25, 106, 125.
  Ffrancis, 15.
  George, 17.
  Hannah, 51.
  James, 6.
  Joan, 77.
  John, 6, 15, 48, 59, 60.
  Joseph, 122.
  Judeth, 24, 25, 26, 27.
  Margarett, 26, 106.
  Mary, 15, 55.

Glascock—*continued*.
  Matthew, 77.
  Prudence, 47, 48, 49, 50, 51, 55, 86, 122.
  Robert, 52, 119.
  Samuel, 55, 59, 62, 86.
  Samuell, 47, 48, 49, 50, 51, 118, 122.
  Sarah, 62, 128.
  Thomas, 17, 49, 52, 53, 60, 119, 120.
  [*Blank*], 59.
Glascocke.
  Elizabeth, 7.
  John, 7.
  Rose, 84.
Glascok.
  Dorithy, 59.
  Elizebeth, 54.
  John, 59.
  Joseph, 58.
  Prudence, 52, 54, 55, 58.
  Samuell, 52, 54, 55, 58.
  Sarah, 52.
Godfrey.
  John, 116, 119.
  Philip, 119.
  William, 111.
Godfrie.
  Samuell, 35.
  Sarah, 35.
  William, 35.
Godfry.
  John, 51, 119.
  Susan, 51, 86.
  William, 31, 106.
Godson.
  Susan, 84.
Goldesberg.
  Elizebeth, 48.
  John, 48.
  Richard, 51.
  Susan, 48, 51.
  Susanna, 48.
  Thomas, 48, 51, 119.
Goldesburgh.
  John, 63.
Goldsberg.
  Thomas, 119.
Golsberg.
  Charles, 49.
  Susan, 49.
  Thomas, 49.
Goodding.
  Mary, 79.
Goodell.
  Mary, 85.
  Robert, 85.
Goodwin.
  Elizabeth, 78.
  Georg, 78.
  George, 9.
  John, 122.
  Katherine, 9.
Goody.
  John, 137.

156

Gosling.
Anne, 83.
Gouldesburgh..
Charles, 126, 128.
Elizabeth, 28, 45, 63.
Mary, 63.
Richard, 63.
Thomas, 28, 45.
———, 124.
Gouldsbourgh.
Susannah, 131.
Gouldsburgh.
Anne, 30.
Elizabeth, 32.
Thomas, 30, 32, 41.
———, 114.
Gowers.
Ruth, 87.
Graehawe.
George, 5.
Richard, 5.
Grainge.
Andrew, 105.
Katharine, 83.
Grainger.
Jacob, 23.
Joane, 23.
Richard, 23.
Grange.
Andrew, 8, 15, 16, 17.
Anne, 15, 16, 17.
John, 7.
Katharine, 16.
Raffe, 8.
Richard, 8.
[Blank], 17.
Granger.
Joane, 25.
Richard, 25, 105.
[Blank], 25.
———, 105.
Granjer.
Elizabeth, 22.
Jone, 22.
Richard, 22.
Grapes.
Samuel, 8.
William, 8.
Graue.
John, 8.
Mary, 11.
Sara, 79.
Thomas, 10.
William, 8, 10, 96.
Grave.
Mary, 81.
Sara, 10.
Thomas, 96.
William, 10, 96.
Graves.
Abigail, 17.
Agnes, 16, 17, 19.
Anne, 80.
Henry, 130.
James, 16.
Theophilus, 19.

Graves—continued.
Thomas, 16, 17, 19, 21, 80, 81, 82,
98, 100, 102, 104.
———, 109.
Gray.
Anne, 65.
Edward, 62, 63, 64, 65, 66.
Elizabeth, 62-66.
John, 62.
Martha, 66.
Mary, 63.
Green.
Mary, 86, 89.
Olive, 89.
Vic, 89.
Greene.
Anne, 88.
Dorethy, 78.
George, 80.
Jane, 88.
Joan, 80.
Thomas, 96.
Grene.
Richard, 95.
Griffin.
Alice, 94.
John, 14.
Robert, 14.
Samuel, 14.
Griffinhoffe.
Abraham, 39, 112.
Martha, 39, 112.
Griffinhoof.
Abraham, 41.
Abram, 116.
Elizabeth, 41.
Martha, 41.
Griffinhoofe.
Abraham, 40, 42, 43.
Martha, 40-43.
William, 43.
———, 115.
Griffinnhoofe.
Abraham, 41.
Mary, 41.
Groves.
Dennis, 89.
Grubb.
Anne, 33.
John, 29, 33.
Rebecka, 29.
Sarah, 33, 107.
Sarrah, 29.
Gryffyn.
Anne, 100, 101.
John, 98, 101.
Love, 98.
Robert, 98.
William, 100.
Guailen.
Goodman, 48.
Rebecka, 48.
Gualter.
Ales, 78.
Richard, 78.

Gunson.
 Richard, 123.
Guy.
 Abigall, 86.
 Elizabeth, 42, 64, 128.
 George, 39, 42, 43, 44, 115, 116.
 Hannah, 63, 64, 65, 69, 87.
 John, 69.
 Joseph, 65.
 Martha, 39, 42, 43, 44.
 Mary, 65, 136.
 Richard, 44, 63, 64, 65, 69, 87.
Guye.
 Hannah, 70, 134.
 Martha, 133.
 Rebeccah, 70.
 Richard, 70, 134.
 Widow, 134.
Gwin.
 John, 108.
Gyn.
 Henry, 124.

Haggar.
 Ann, 58.
 Elizabeth, 14.
 Joshua, 14, 98.
 Mary, 98.
 Richard, 58, 123.
 Rose, 14, 58.
Hagger.
 Richard, 57, 59.
 Rose, 57.
 ———, 59.
Haince.
 Ann, 50, 51, 119.
 Elizebeth, 52, 55.
 Jonas, 52, 55.
 William, 50, 51, 55, 119.
 [Blank], 50.
Haines.
 George, 27, 37, 38, 85, 118.
 Goodwiffe, 116.
 Joane, 27.
 Martha, 37.
 Mary, 38, 119.
 Sarah, 37, 38, 85.
 Susan, 38.
Hains.
 Goodman, 117.
 William, 130.
Halceter.
 ———, 44.
Hale.
 Martha, 96.
Hales.
 ———, 114.
Hallingworth.
 Elizabeth, 94.
Hammerstone.
 Mary, 81.
Hampshire.
 Edward, 88.
 Margaret, 88.
Hamseed.
 Stock, 135.

Hance.
 Elizabeth, 127.
 Jonas, 124.
Hanchet.
 Anne, 133.
 Justinian, 137.
Hancock.
 ———, 109.
Hancocke.
 John, 108, 110.
Hansaker.
 John, 5.
 Joseph, 5.
Hardie.
 Margerett, 84.
 William, 84.
Hardman.
 Martha, 13, 80.
 William, 13, 80.
 Sara, 13.
Hardred.
 David, 104.
 ———, 104.
Harper.
 Ann, 132, 136.
 Edward, 136.
Harris.
 Edward, 13, 15, 81.
 Elizabeth, 13, 110.
 Ellen, 80.
 James, 66.
 John, 13, 110, 120.
 Jone, 101.
 Joseph, 15.
 Mary, 77.
 Sarah, 66.
 Thomas, 120.
 William, 66, 77.
 Zephora, 13.
 Zipporah, 15.
Harrison.
 Anne, 65, 127.
 Elizabeth, 94.
 Sarah, 64, 65, 89.
 William, 64, 65, 94.
Harrys.
 Edward, 80.
 John, 95.
 Zephora, 80.
Hart.
 William, 105.
Harwood.
 Anne, 23, 24, 104, 105.
 Anthonie, 101.
 Anthony, 19, 20, 21, 26, 27, 104.
 Anthonye, 22, 23, 24.
 Dulcibella, 27.
 Elizabeth, 20, 21, 22, 23, 24, 26, 27,
 104.
 Giles, 103.
 Jane, 22.
 Jone, 21, 103.
 Margarett, 26.
 Mary, 19, 101.
 Marye, 20.

Haryson.
 George, 97.
Haselwood.
 Elizabeth, 79.
 George, 11, 12, 79.
 Martha, 11.
 Robert, 12.
 Thomas, 11.
Hasley.
 Elizabeth, 14, 101.
 George, 14, 98, 101
 Martha, 98.
 William, 14.
Hasplam.
 Mary, 123.
Hastler.
 Humphrey, 112.
Hathwaie.
 Elizabeth, 78.
Hauers.
 Charles, 40, 41, 42.
 Ffrancis, 42.
 John, 41.
 Mary, 41, 42.
 Thomas, 40.
Havers.
 Abraham, 55, 133.
 Charles, 43, 44, 45, 46, 48, 49, 53,
  116, 121, 125.
 Elizabeth, 137.
 Henery, 49.
 Jacob, 45, 116.
 James, 46.
 John, 53, 55, 58, 59, 60, 121.
 Joseph, 44.
 Mary, 43, 44, 45, 46, 48, 49, 53, 55,
  58, 59, 60, 87, 116, 124, 126.
 Sarah, 46.
 Susanna, 58.
 William, 43.
 ———, 133.
Havos.
 Ann, 56.
 John, 56.
 Mary, 56.
Haynes.
 Elizabeth, 42, 115.
 George, 29, 39, 41, 42, 114, 115.
 Jane, 29.
 Joseph, 29.
 Mary, 113.
 Sarah, 39, 41, 42, 115.
 Sussanna, 39.
Hays.
 Ann, 59.
 Richard, 59.
 Stafford, 59.
Hawers.
 Charles, 39.
 Mary, 39.
Hawes.
 Andrew, 24.
 Jane, 24.
 Margarett, 24.

Hawkins.
 Elizabeth, 61.
 John, 61.
Hazel.
 George, 106.
Hazelwood.
 Elizabeth, 12.
 George, 12.
Heard.
 Elizabeth, 11.
 Thomas, 11.
Heardman.
 Abigail, 16.
 Martha, 16.
 William, 16.
Hellan.
 Allice, 95.
Helms.
 James, 54, 56.
 Jeames, 53.
 John, 53.
 Mary, 53, 54, 56, 132.
Herne.
 Elizabeth, 69.
 Rawlins, 69.
Herrington.
 John, 101.
Hewes.
 Anne, 98.
 Dennis, 82.
 Grace, 102.
 Thomas, 82.
Hewet.
 Alice, 15.
 Elizabeth, 15.
 Nathaniel, 15.
Higgs.
 Ann, 51.
 James, 50.
 John, 49.
 Mary, 45, 46, 49, 50, 51, 117.
 Richard, 118.
 Robert, 45, 117.
 Thomas, 45, 46, 49-51, 117, 118.
Hill.
 Anne, 83.
 Elizabeth, 88.
 John, 127.
 ———, 83.
Hills.
 Edward, 112.
 Elizabeth, 86, 112.
 Elizebeth, 56.
 James, 56.
 Margaret, 79.
 Mary, 97.
 Richard, 97, 126.
 Sarah, 132.
 Widdow, 118.
 ———, 108.
Hinton.
 Mary, 85.
 Robert, 85.
Hobbs.
 Joseph, 71.

Hobbs—*continued*.
  Mary, 71.
  William, 71.
Hockley.
  Joane, 95.
  Jonathan, 118.
  Jone, 79.
  Lydia, 85.
Hockly.
  Johnathan, 51.
  Mary, 51, 86.
Hodskin.
  Dorethy, 78.
  Thomas, 78.
Hogg.
  James, 133.
Hogge.
  Elisabeth, 83.
  Rebekah, 104.
  William, 83, 104.
Hokly.
  Jonathan, 120.
Holbrooke.
  William, 112.
Holibred.
  Jane, 79.
Holmes.
  Elizabeth, 41.
  Thomas, 41.
Holt.
  Joseph, 83.
  Martha, 83.
  Sarah, 36.
  Thomas, 36, 110.
Holte.
  Sarah, 112.
Hore.
  Anne, 15.
  Ffrancis, 15.
  John, 15.
Horne.
  Joan, 77.
  William, 77.
Horrard.
  Anne, 82.
  Annis, 81.
  George, 99.
  Giles, 81, 82, 99, 100.
  Thomas, 81, 100.
Horsenayle.
  Nicholas, 31.
Horsnail.
  Elizabeth, 34.
  Nicholas, 34.
  William, 34.
Horsnaile.
  Elizabeth, 32, 33.
  John, 32.
  Marget, 86, 121.
  Mary, 33.
  Nicholas, 32, 33, 121.
  Thomas, 86, 121.
Horsnaill.
  Elisebeth, 35, 120.
  Nicolas, 35, 120.
  Thomas, 35.

Horsnaylle.
  Elizabeth, 30.
  Nickholas, 30.
Horwood.
  Giles, 13.
  Joane, 13.
Hoskins.
  John, 133.
Houchen.
  Anne, 68.
  Richard, 68, 137.
  Stane, 68.
Houtchin.
  Anne, 63, 64, 65, 66.
  Edward, 64.
  John, 64.
  Richard, 63, 64, 65, 66, 136.
  Susanna, 65.
  Thomas, 66.
Houte.
  Sara, 36.
  Sarah, 36.
  Thomas, 36.
How.
  Johanna, 88.
Howard.
  Elizebeth, 86.
  Martha, 88.
  Mary, 122.
  Robert, 86.
Howbroke.
  Isaac, 13.
  John, 12, 97.
  William, 12, 13, 97.
Howgate.
  Sarah, 71, 135.
Hubbard.
  Francis, 94.
Hubbock.
  William, 81.
Hughes.
  Margery, 77, 94.
Hull.
  Danell, 29.
  Francis, 29.
  Mary, 29.
Humphrey.
  Mary, 87.
Humstone.
  Edward, 12.
Hungate.
  Mary, 36.
  Robert, 36.
Hunt.
  Elizabeth, 57.
  Mathias, 57.
  Sarah, 57.
Huntington.
  Jone, 77.
  William, 93.
Hurle.
  Edward, 94.
Hurrell.
  James, 20, 82.
  Mary, 20, 82.

Hurt.
  Margaret, 77.
  William, 77.
Hutchinson.
  Charles, 71.
  Elizabeth, 71.
  Henry John, 71.
Hutley.
  Elizabeth, 9, 78.
  John, 9.
  Richard, 9, 78.
Hutton.
  Elizabeth, 26.
  Richard, 26.
  [Blank], 26.
Hynes.
  Annis, 81.

Ince.
  Anne, 96.
  Henry, 98.
  Hugh, 7, 8, 9, 10, 95, 96.
  James, 9.
  John, 8.
  Martha, 9.
  Rebecca, 8.
  William, 7.
Ingoal.
  John, 98.
Ingold.
  Mary, 82, 85.
Ingram.
  Elizabeth, 62.
  Georg, 93.
  John, 62.
  Martha, 62.
Inhivor.
  Sarah, 85.
Innivere.
  Elizabeth, 33.
  John, 33.
  Susan, 33.
Innyver.
  John, 31.
  Robert, 31.
Irons.
  Mary, 87.
Isbroke.
  Marie, 78.

Jacob.
  Anna, 14.
  Edward, 14.
Jackson.
  Thomas, 81.
Jasper.
  Abigail, 63, 126, 128.
  Abigal, 62.
  Elizabeth, 62, 66, 83, 136.
  Martha, 66, 88.
  William, 62, 63, 66, 88.
Jenkin.
  James, 84.
  Mary, 84.
Jiggins.
  John, 100.

John.
  Poore, 123.
Johnson.
  Daniell, 25.
  Francis, 96.
  Goodman, 105.
  Richard, 24, 25.
  William, 24.
  [Blank], 24, 25.
Jones.
  Anne, 78.
  Avery, 95.
  Godfrey, 60, 61, 62, 63, 65, 66, 127, 129.
  Jane, 60.
  John, 120.
  Mother, 95.
  Robert, 10.
  William, 10.
  ——, 124.
Jonson.
  Mary, 87.
Joyner.
  Anne, 25.
  Cordelia, 23, 24, 25.
  Dan, 24, 25.
  Daniell, 23.
  Isaac, 24.

Keale.
  John, 106.
Keel.
  Elizabeth, 16, 99.
  John, 16, 82, 99, 100.
  Mary, 82.
  Thomasyn, 100.
  Thomasyne, 16.
Kempton.
  Mary, 112.
  Samuel, 112.
  Samuell, 38, 112.
  Sarah, 112.
Kendale.
  Edmund, 31.
Kendall.
  Edmund, 107.
  Edmunde, 30.
  Joan, 107.
  Joane, 30.
  John, 30.
Kent.
  Andrew, 95.
  Ann, 67.
  Elizabeth, 68, 70.
  Ellin, 95.
  Samuel, 67, 68, 70.
  Sarah, 68.
  William, 70.
Kenton.
  Samuel, 111.
Kettle.
  Aron, 52.
  John, 52.
  Martha, 52.

Kettlewell.
Aron, 86.
Martha, 86.

Key.
Elias, 115.

Kildar.
Earle of, 80.

King.
Abigail, 17.
Ann, 34, 35, 40, 41, 42, 43, 45, 86, 106, 113, 119, 122.
Anna, 28.
Anne, 11, 15, 16, 18, 19, 20, 21, 43, 88, 113.
Dorothie, 14.
Dorothy, 97.
Edward, 13.
Ealizabeth, 34.
Elizabeth, 12, 14, 15, 17, 19, 28, 34, 35, 36, 85, 123, 126, 137.
Elizebeth, 57.
Ffrancis, 15.
Frances, 84.
James, 21, 33, 34, 36, 43, 85, 108, 110, 115.
Jeames, 34, 113.
Joane, 95.
John, 11, 12, 13, 14, 15, 17, 28, 41, 45, 65, 67, 82, 97, 98, 115.
Jone, 7, 82.
Joseph, 14, 40, 41, 42, 43, 45, 61, 111, 113, 115, 119, 122, 127.
Joyce, 15.
Lionel, 66.
Margaret, 12, 82.
Margett, 78.
Mary, 16, 33, 43, 59, 60, 61, 63, 65, 66, 67, 108, 109.
Richard, 19, 20, 21, 36.
Robert, 13, 15, 16, 18, 19, 21, 103, 108.
Sammuell, 43.
Samuel, 43, 63, 86, 115.
Samuell, 28, 35, 110.
Sarah, 61.
Susan, 57, 86, 122.
Susana, 45.
Susanah, 116.
Susanna, 116.
Thomas, 14, 78, 98, 106.
Widow, 116.
William, 45, 57, 59, 60, 61, 63, 65, 66, 67, 86, 116, 122.

Kinge.
Anne, 23, 24, 26, 83, 104.
James, 30, 85.
John, 30, 83.
Jonas, 26.
Mary, 30, 83.
Rebecka, 85.
Richard, 23, 24, 26, 104, 105.
Sary, 104.
William, 23.

Knight.
Cave, 61, 125.
Denis, 43.

Knight—*continued.*
Denness, 52.
Dennis, 42, 44, 46, 48, 114, 117.
Denniss, 54.
Elizabeth, 44.
Ephraim, 70, 132.
James, 46, 117.
John, 42, 43, 44, 46, 48, 52, 54, 65, 70, 114, 117, 121, 123, 134, 136.
John Ephraim, 134.
Katherine, 86.
Mary, 48, 68, 137.
Margarett, 54.
Marget, 121.
Sarah, 43, 86.
Thomas, 52, 134.
Widow, 136.

Lacey.
Elizabeth, 29.
Hannah, 30, 109.
Joan, 29.
Joane, 29.
Jonah, 29.
Jonas, 29.
William, 30, 109.

Lacie.
Auery, 85, 114.
Doritie, 85.

Lacy.
Auery, 17, 80, 100.
Averie, 19.
Avery, 13, 16, 17, 31, 82, 101.
Elizabeth, 13, 81.
Hannah, 33.
Henery, 29.
James, 29.
Jane, 16, 17, 19, 33, 80, 83, 101.
Jeane, 85.
John, 16.
Jonas, 33, 115.
Jone, 100.
Margere, 118.
Mary, 50, 119, 120.
Mathew, 101.
Nathan, 17.
Rebeka, 49.
Ruth, 29.
Susanna, 49.
Thomas, 49.
William, 19, 31, 33, 50, 100, 111, 119, 120, 121.

Lagden.
Anne, 77.

Lambe.
Thomasin, 77.

Lambert.
Robert, 7.
William, 7.

Lamborne.
Margaret, 8.

Lanckfeild.
Joseph, 106.

Lane.
Alice, 83.
Auery, 42.

Lane—*continued*.
   Dorritie, 42.
   Ffrancis, 83.
Langfield.
   Katherin, 14.
   Richard, 14.
   Thomasyn, 14.
Langfyeld.
   John, 17, 100.
   Katherin, 15, 17.
   Margaret, 15.
   Richard, 15, 17, 100, 103.
Langley.
   Ales, 78.
Lankfield.
   Anne, 25, 26.
   Edward, 97.
   Giles, 12.
   Joseph, 11, 25, 26.
   Margarett, 26.
   Philip, 25.
   Richard, 11, 12, 13, 105.
   Thomas, 13, 97.
Lankford.
   Edward, 12.
   Elizabeth, 11.
   Giles, 97.
   Richard, 11, 12, 97.
Larking.
   Benjamin, 89.
   Sarah, 89.
Larkin.
   Thomas, 111.
Lasy.
   Avery, 13.
   Matthew, 13.
Lathom.
   Elizabeth, 78.
Lauender.
   Mother, 98.
   William, 97.
Lauerett.
   Mary, 39.
   Thomas, 39.
Laurence.
   Francis, 65.
   Thomas, 98.
Lavender.
   John, 24.
   Margaret, 24.
   Rebekah, 24.
   William, 96.
Lawrence.
   Francis, 66, 70, 71.
   Jane, 65, 66, 70, 71.
   Joseph, 72.
   Mary, 70, 134.
   William, 66.
   [*Blank*], 71, 72.
Laybank.
   Anne, 88.
   John, 88.
Lee.
   Ellin, 93.
   Esther, 88.
   William, 134.

Lees.
   Johñ, 98.
Leger.
   Anne, 79.
Legget.
   Ann, 86.
Leigh.
   Ann, 121.
   John, 121.
   Mary, 127.
   ——, 124.
Lenham.
   Dorothy, 73, 74.
   John, 73, 74.
   Kitty, 74, 138.
   ——, 138.
Leonard.
   How, 87, 88.
Leueret.
   Elizabeth, 114.
   Thomas, 114.
Leuerett.
   Elizabeth, 113.
   Mary, 113.
   Thomas, 113.
Leueritt.
   Elizabeth, 42.
   Mary, 42.
   Thomas, 42.
Leuitt.
   Mary, 43.
   Thomas, 43.
   William, 43.
Leverett.
   Mary, 44.
   Thomas, 44.
Leverick.
   Richard, 40.
   Thomas, 40.
Leverit.
   Elizabeth, 119.
   John, 133.
   Thomas, 119.
Leveritt.
   Ann, 41.
   Elizebeth, 49.
   Mary, 41, 45, 49.
   Sarah, 45.
   Thomas, 41, 45, 49, 116.
   William, 116.
Levett.
   Mary, 44.
   Thomas, 44.
Levirit.
   John, 47.
   Mary, 47.
   Thomas, 47.
Lewis.
   Abygaile, 32.
   James, 30, 32.
   Jeames, 31.
   Joane, 30, 32.
   John, 59.
   Sarah, 30.
   [. . . .], 59.

Lewsly.
    Ann, 86.
    Henery, 86.
Lilbrim.
    Henrie, 82.
    Mary, 82.
Lillbourne.
    Rebeckah, 85.
Littel.
    Anne, 69.
    Margarett, 71.
    William, 69, 71, 138.
Little.
    Mary, 66, 68, 69, 71, 88.
    Sarah, 68.
    William, 66, 68.
Lloyd.
    Mary, 128.
Louett.
    Jane, 7.
    John, 7.
Long.
    ———, 137.
Lorkyn.
    Elizabeth, 83.
    John, 104.
Lorrance.
    Henry, 80.
    Lidia, 80.
Lucas.
    Anne, 63, 65.
    Charles, 108.
    Daniell, 107.
    Elizabeth, 60, 87.
    Israel, 108.
    John, 33, 46, 48, 52, 60, 87, 110, 115, 120, 124, 125, 126, 128.
    Mary, 45, 46, 48, 52.
    Samuel, 63, 65.
    Samuell, 48.
    Sarah, 33, 45, 63, 110, 120.
    Widow, 108.
Luck.
    Benjamin, 88.
    Mary, 88.
Lucke.
    John, 35, 85.
Lukas.
    Ann, 28, 29, 30.
    Charles, 29.
    Christian, 28.
    Daniell, 28, 29, 30.
    Elizabeth, 29.
    Israell, 30.
Luther.
    Charlotte, 90.
    Elizabeth, 83.
Lynd.
    Margaret, 77.

Mace.
    Edmund, 18.
    Mary, 18.
Macglothwell.
    Lodwell, 131.

Madewell.
    John, 46.
    Martha, 51, 125.
    Mary, 64, 65, 67, 69.
    Mathew, 47, 117.
    Sarah, 45, 46, 47, 48, 49, 51, 52.
    Thomas, 45, 46, 47, 48, 49, 51, 52, 64, 117.
    William, 49, 64, 65, 67, 69.
Madle.
    Ann, 71.
    John, 86.
    Katherine, 86.
    Mary, 71, 73, 131.
    Thomas, 133.
    William, 70, 71, 73.
    [Blank], 70.
Madwell.
    Elizebeth, 54, 120.
    John, 116.
    Sarah, 54.
    Thomas, 54, 117, 121.
Maidwell.
    Mary, 134.
    Sarah, 134.
Maior.
    Edward, 12, 79.
    Martha, 12.
    Mary, 12, 79.
Major.
    Hannah, 28.
    Timothy, 28.
Malcott.
    Elizabeth, 32, 33, 34, 111.
    Elizabeth Anna, 34.
    Elizebeth, 119.
    James, 34.
    John, 33.
    Thomas, 32, 34.
Malery.
    Henry, 109.
Mallery.
    Agnes, 7.
    Annis, 78.
    Ffrances, 15, 16, 17, 18, 20, 21, 22, 99.
    Francess, 106.
    George, 22.
    Henrie, 15, 17, 18, 20, 99.
    Henry, 8, 16, 21, 22, 80, 106.
    Jone, 101.
    Margaret, 21.
    Mary, 15.
    Phil, 8.
    Philip, 98.
    Phill, 7.
    Phillip, 7, 20.
    Richard, 8.
    Sarah, 18, 44.
    William, 44.
Marcold.
    Rose, 88.
Mare.
    Edward, 14, 15, 16, 98.
    Martha, 16, 98.
    Mary, 14, 15, 16.

Mare—*continued.*
 Sara, 14.
 Timothy, 15.
Martin.
 Elizabeth, 29, 36.
 Elizebeth, 35.
 Joan, 94.
 John, 29, 35, 36.
 Katherine, 29.
 Margarett, 36.
 Mother, 95.
 Sarah, 88.
 Thomas, 29.
Martyn.
 Joan, 94.
Mason.
 Josias, 79.
 Mary, 79.
Mathams.
 Samuel, 135.
Matthew.
 ——, 20.
Mathewes.
 Benedict, 18, 101.
 Benet, 19, 101.
 Peter, 101.
 Robert, 19.
 Sarah, 18, 19.
 William, 18, 101.
Matthews.
 Edward, 73.
 Edward Parnell, 73.
 Elizabeth, 73.
May.
 Jane, 87.
Mayer.
 Edward, 31, 102, 103, 106.
 Mary, 102, 103.
 Sara, 102.
 Timothy, 31, 106.
Mayor.
 Ann, 32.
 Anne, 32.
 Edward, 18.
 Mary, 18.
 Nymphas, 32.
 Rebecka, 32.
 Timothy, 32, 108.
 Widdow, 112.
 William, 18.
Mead.
 James, 44, 115.
 John, 38, 40, 44, 115, 116.
 Mary, 40.
 Sarah, 38, 44.
 Sary, 40.
Meade.
 Elizabeth, 95.
 Jane, 42.
 John, 39, 41, 42, 115.
 Sarah, 39, 41, 42.
Medley.
 Katherine, 77.
 Margaret, 78.
Meggs.
 . . . ., 107.

Meller.
 Sarah, 84.
Meredith. .
 James, 73, 74, 137, 138.
 John, 74.
 Olive, 73.
Meridith.
 James, 72.
 [*Blank*], 72.
Merrills.
 John, 114.
 Martha, 114.
 Mary, 86.
Michal.
 John, 61.
 Mary, 61.
Midleton.
 Margaret, 94.
Milford.
 Ales, 77.
Miller.
 Ann, 56.
 Elizebeth, 56.
 Giles, 11, 12, 82.
 John, 56.
 Katherine, 12.
 Margaret, 11, 82.
 Mary, 11, 86.
 Mathew, 114.
 Sarah, 82.
 Susan, 135.
 Thomas, 86.
 (Widow), 97.
Milles.
 Ann, 84.
 Robert, 84.
Mitchel.
 Anne, 66, 68.
 James, 66.
 John, 66, 68, 136.
 Mary, 68.
 ——, 136.
Mitchell.
 Anne, 63-65.
 Elizabeth, 65.
 John, 61-65.
 Martha, 62.
 Mary, 61, 62.
 Septame, 63.
 William, 61, 126.
Mole.
 Anne, 66, 129.
Monday.
 James, 71.
 John, 59, 71, 87.
 Mary, 71.
 Sarah, 59, 87, 138.
 Widow, 123.
Monk.
 Edward, 86.
 Sarah, 86.
Monson.
 Alice, 70.
 Samuel, 70.
 Susannah, 68.
 [*Blank*], 68.

165

Moore.
Christopher, 65.
Mary, 65.
Robert, 65.
More.
John, 5.
Thomas, 5.
Morice.
Anne, 6, 7, 77.
Catherine, 78.
Edward, 6.
Elizabeth, 6, 9, 78.
Henry, 6, 7, 94.
James, 6, 7, 10, 95.
Jane, 7.
John, 9, 10, 78, 94.
Margaret, 77.
Marie, 77.
Thomas, 6, 7, 77.
Morrell.
Ann, 89.
Joan, 77.
Thomas, 89.
Morse.
Danniel, 114.
Morton.
Elizabeth, 27.
Katharine, 83.
Katherine, 27, 83.
Laurence, 27, 83.
Morrice.
Elizabeth, 96.
James, 96.
John, 6.
Mott.
Joyce, 11.
Marget, 12.
Robert, 11, 12.
Munday.
Ann, 38.
Anna, 112.
Anne, 36, 37.
Clemence, 134.
Clement, 62.
Elizabeth, 38, 44, 111, 112.
Elizebeth, 116.
Henry, 72, 137.
James, 48, 120.
John, 42, 59, 69, 70, 72, 73, 89.
Mary, 37, 58, 59, 60, 69, 70, 72,
    73, 86, 89, 113, 124, 130.
Philip, 45, 116.
Rebecca, 86.
Rebecka, 48.
Sarah, 40, 42, 44, 45, 110, 116,
    117.
Susannah, 67.
Thomas, 62, 72.
William, 36, 37, 38, 40, 42, 44, 45,
    48, 58, 59, 60, 62, 70, 86, 110,
    112, 116, 117, 118, 126.
Mundey.
An, 36.
Ann, 36.
William, 36.

Munke.
John, 83.
Martha, 83.
Munsel.
Mary, 80.
Thomas, 80.
Nailor.
Sarah, 89.
Nash.
James, 87.
Mary, 87.
Nayler.
Jane, 83.
John, 83.
Naylor.
Jane, 107.
John, 107, 109.
Neale.
Edward, 83.
Elisabeth, 83.
Margarete, 84.
Mary, 84.
Nelson.
Anne, 79.
Nettleton.
Ann, 134.
Anne, 70.
Elizabeth, 130.
John, 70, 131.
Sarah, 70.
Neue.
Robert, 114.
Newton.
John, 24, 25.
Mary, 24.
[Blank], 24, 25.
Niccolls.
John, 104.
Niccolson.
Anne, 99.
Elizabeth, 19, 20, 21, 99.
Ffortune, 82.
John, 19, 20, 21, 82, 99, 102, 103.
Nicholls.
Anna Maria, 64.
Mary, 64, 89.
William, 64.
Nichols.
Ann, 70.
Elizabeth, 70, 134.
Ffortune, 107.
John, 108.
Samuel, 69, 70, 136.
Sarah, 69.
William, 69.
Nicholson.
Elizabeth, 81.
Geffrey, 79.
John, 81.
Nicolds.
Hugh, 86.
Mary, 86.
Nicolls.
Elizabeth, 104.
Ffortune, 22.

Nicolls—*continued*.
John, 22, 104.
Nicols.
Phillip, 77.
William, 97.
Nicolson.
Anne, 16.
Elizabeth, 16, 18, 103.
Frances, 79.
John, 16, 18, 103.
Mercia, 18.
Millesant, 16.
Norden.
Elizabeth, 39, 41, 43, 44, 112, 116, 117.
Elizebeth, 45, 46.
John, 39, 116.
Margeret, 46.
Preston, 112.
Rebecca, 45, 114.
Rebecka, 43.
Rebekah, 44.
Westenn, 39.
Weston, 39, 41, 43, 44, 45, 46, 112, 114, 116, 117.
. . . ., 116.
Norington.
Elizabeth, 32.
Penellipe, 32.
Thomas, 32.
Norrington.
Sarah, 85.
Thomas, 85.
Norris.
Elizabeth, 88.
Richard, 88.
Northen.
Elizabeth, 40.
Westin, 40.
Northey.
Elizabeth, 21.
Mary, 21.
Nicolas, 21.
Not.
William, 107.
Nowell.
Phillis, 78.
Nunney.
Elizebeth, 50.
Francis, 50, 51.
Martha, 50, 51.
Nunny.
Maria, 51.

Odwell.
Elizabeth, 84, 85.
Thomas, 85.
Offyn.
Abraham, 100.
Olin.
Andrew, 8.
Joan, 7.
John, 8; 95.
Onion.
Elizabeth, 72, 136.
Thomas, 72, 136.

Oram.
Bartholomew, 71.
Joseph, 71.
Mary, 71.
Orson.
Catherine, 137.
Osborn.
Jane, 26.
Mary, 26.
Samuel, 102.
Thomas, 26.
Osborne.
Jane, 22.
Margaret, 88.
Mary, 22, 25.
Mercie, 102.
Thomas, 22, 25.
Ottaway.
Abigail, 54.
Elizabeth, 54, 59.
Elizebeth, 55, 56, 58.
John, 54, 55, 56, 58, 59, 121.
Susan, 124.
Susanna, 56.
Overill.
Elizabeth, 83.
Mary, 85.
Thomas, 83.
Owen.
David, 82.
Elizabeth, 83.
John, 83, 106.
Rebecca, 82.
Widow, 108.
Oye.
Elizabeth, 114.
George, 114.
. . . ., 114.

Pagett.
John, 47, 48.
Mary, 47, 48.
Sarah, 48.
Paine.
Georg, 77.
Jone, 77.
Painter.
Jone, 94.
Palinge.
John, 101.
Marian, 101.
Pallavicine.
Horacio, 106.
Jane, 104.
Palm.
John, 7.
Thomas, 7.
Palmer.
Anne, 77, 95.
Joan, 77.
John, 77, 78, 103.
Marian, 78.
Pane.
Georg, 94.

Paperill.
John, 61.
Sarah, 61.
Parkes.
Joana, 32.
Joane, 32.
Jone, 29, 31.
Mary, 31.
William, 29, 31, 32.
Parker.
Alice, 18, 23, 104.
Anna, 12.
Edward, 23.
Elizabeth, 18.
John, 12, 17, 18, 100, 102.
Nicholas, 11, 12.
Nicolas, 79.
Robert, 23, 104.
Sara, 79.
Sarah, 100.
Thomas, 11.
Parkes.
(Widow), 86.
Johana, 85.
Parks.
Joanna, 32, 34.
Joannah, 112.
Johannah, 112.
John, 32, 112.
Mary, 34, 107.
William, 32, 34, 107, 112.
Parmeter.
Elizabeth, 78.
Georg, 9, 78, 95.
Margaret, 9.
Parnbe.
John, 19, 20, 102.
Richard, 19, 20, 102.
Sarah, 19, 20.
Parish.
Dorothee, 28.
Joyce, 28.
Mary, 87, 129.
Thomas, 126.
Parrish.
Ann, 52, 120.
Mary, 50, 52, 86, 118.
Thomas, 50, 52, 86, 116, 118, 120.
Parsons.
Elizabeth, 14.
Hannah, 18.
Jacob, 17, 102.
John, 16.
Jone, 20.
Margaret, 15.
Mary, 14, 15, 16, 17, 18, 20, 24.
Rafe, 16, 17, 18, 20, 102.
Ralph, 24.
Rodolph, 14, 15.
Thomas, 24.
Widow, 107.
Paveley.
Elizabeth, 89.
James, 89.
Maria, 65.
Mary, 64, 65.

Paveley—*continued*.
Thomas, 64, 65.
Victory, 64, 128.
Pavit.
Damaris, 124.
Pawlson.
Elizabeth, 50.
Nathaniel, 50.
Peachy.
Mary, 80.
Peacock.
Barnabas, 16, 19, 21, 101.
Barnabe, 17, 18, 100.
Barnaby, 81.
Benjamin, 19.
Edward, 14, 15, 16, 28, 31, 100, 101, 110, 113, 115.
Elizabeth, 14, 15, 16, 100, 110.
Ffrances, 105.
Henry, 16.
Jane, 28.
Jeane, 113.
John, 18, 97, 100, 101.
Margaret, 16, 18, 19, 21, 81.
Mary, 45, 117, 127.
Sarah, 31.
Steven, 15.
Thomas, 16, 118.
William, 14, 17, 45, 100, 117, 137.
Peate.
Joseph, 63.
Margaret, 63.
Richard, 63.
Pechie.
Elizabeth, 9, 78.
Georg, 9, 10.
George, 10, 78, 95.
Marie, 10, 95.
Mary, 10, 78.
Pecock.
Edward, 80.
Elizabeth, 80.
Peg.
Ffrances, 87, 125.
Georg, 38.
George, 38, 87, 110.
Rebekah, 38.
Sarah, 38, 110.
Thomas, 38.
Pegg.
Georg, 55.
George, 41, 123, 128.
Martha, 55, 56, 58, 60.
Mary, 60, 125.
Rebekah, 41, 123.
Susana, 41.
Thomas, 55, 56, 58, 60, 130.
Pegge.
George, 85.
Rebecca, 85.
Pegram.
John, 117.
Joseph, 40, 115, 117.
Sarah, 40.
Pegrome.
Joseph, 39.

Pegrome—*continued.*
  Sarah, 39.
Pegrum.
  John, 47.
  Joseph, 41, 42, 46, 47, 114, 116,
    117.
  Mary, 41, 42, 46, 114, 115, 117.
  Sarah, 41, 42, 46, 114, 116.
Peniman.
  George, 11.
  James, 11.
Penington.
  James, 119.
Pennington.
  James, 50, 51, 119.
  Mary, 50, 51, 58, 119.
Penny.
  Katherine, 77.
Pennyman.
  George, 23, 26, 105.
  James, 10, 23.
  John, 10.
  Joane, 26.
  Mary, 23, 26, 105.
  ——, 104.
Penyman.
  Annis, 78.
  Elizabeth, 12, 102.
  George, 19, 20, 21, 22, 24.
  James, 12, 78, 100, 102.
  John, 24.
  Laurence, 12.
  Mary, 19, 20, 21, 22, 24.
  Richard, 21.
  Sarah, 20.
Pepper.
  George, 30, 31, 107.
  John, 19, 30.
  Martha, 19.
  Roase, 30.
  Rose, 107.
  Sarah, 31.
Perrey.
  William, 124.
Perry.
  Abraham, 89.
  Elizabeth, 88, 89.
  Francis, 55.
  John, 88.
  Mary, 55, 60, 126.
  Susan, 89.
  William, 60.
Perryer.
  [*Blank*], 108.
Persons.
  Ralph, 107.
Peters.
  Lettice, 88.
  Mary, 87.
Petitt.
  Ann, 89.
Pettit.
  John, 97.
Philips.
  Anne, 127.
  Mary, 88.

Phillips.
  Ann, 53.
  John, 53, 137.
  Joseph, 124.
  Mary, 53, 137.
  Sara, 53.
Phipps.
  Edward, 34, 35, 115, 117, 120.
  John, 137.
  Mary, 34, 35, 117.
  Rebecca, 34.
  Sarah, 120.
Phips.
  Edward, 33, 36, 38, 108, 109.
  George, 86.
  John, 33, 36, 108.
  Mary, 33, 36, 108, 109.
  William, 38.
  [*Blank*], 109.
Phypps.
  Edward, 124.
Pickerine.
  Elizabeth, 33, 108.
  George, 108.
  Lawrence, 33, 84.
  Winifred, 33, 84.
  [*Blank*], 107.
Piper.
  George, 107.
  John, 107.
Plat.
  Alice, 15, 103, 104.
  Anne, 18.
  Elizabeth, 15, 17, 18, 19.
  Margaret, 80.
  Robert, 29.
  Thomas, 15, 17, 18, 19, 29, 103,
    106.
  William, 19.
  Winifred, 29.
Platt.
  Anne, 29, 107.
  Annis, 80.
  Elizabeth, 16.
  Jone, 83.
  Margarett, 28.
  Robert, 16, 28, 114.
  Sara, 13, 97.
  Thomas, 13, 16, 28, 29, 80, 97.
  William, 80.
  Winifred, 84.
  Winnefred, 117.
  Winnifred, 29.
Pledger.
  Elias, 28.
  Elizabeth, 28.
Pole.
  Bennet, 94.
Polley.
  Elizabeth, 12.
  Robert, 12.
  Thomas, 93.
Polly.
  Elizabeth, 99.
  Margaret, 93.
  Mary, 99.

Pomfret.
 Elizabeth, 98.
Pomfrett.
 Jane, 7.
 Thomas, 7, 94.
Poole.
 Daniel, 105.
 Daniell, 24.
 Edward, 80.
 Elizabeth, 83.
 James, 25.
 Joan, 80.
 John, 104.
 Philip, 24, 25, 104, 105.
 [Blank], 24, 25.
Pooll.
 Mary, 122.
Pope.
 Elizabeth, 18.
 Jonathan, 17, 18, 19, 20, 81.
 Mary, 17, 18, 20, 81.
 William, 20.
Poreter.
 Janne, 45.
 Thomas, 45.
 William, 45.
Porter.
 Ann, 50.
 Charles, 71, 72, 74.
 Elizabeth, 61, 62, 125.
 George, 72.
 Hannah, 41, 114.
 Jane, 41, 42, 43, 49, 50, 114, 116,
  122.
 Jeane, 85.
 John, 116.
 Mary, 71, 72, 74.
 Robert, 61, 62, 87, 128.
 Sarah, 134.
 Steward, 42, 115.
 William, 41, 42, 43, 49, 50, 85, 114,
  116, 119.
Portor.
 Jane, 45.
 John, 45.
 Steward, 49.
 William, 45.
Potter.
 Charles, 74.
 Elizabeth, 46, 51, 52, 54, 74.
 Isabell, 54.
 Jane, 125.
 Mary, 51.
 Sarah, 52, 129.
 William, 46, 51, 52, 54, 74, 121.
Potts.
 John, 88.
 Sarah, 88.
Poulter.
 Jane, 17..
 Samuel, 17.
 Thomasyn, 17.
Pouter.
 Widdow, 120.
Powel.
 Barbary, 78.

Powel—continued.
 Robart, 78.
Powell.
 Thomas, 129.
Poynes.
 Catherine, 78.
Prentice.
 Marget, 86.
 Mary, 16, 17, 81, 82.
 Thomas, 16, 17, 81.
Prentis.
 Mary, 98.
 Thomas, 98.
Prentise.
 Elizabeth, 97.
 Henry, 96.
 Marie, 97.
 Mary, 11.
 Thomas, 11, 96, 97, 103.
Preston.
 Christopher, 24, 83, 105.
 Lydia, 24, 83, 105.
Price.
 John, 89.
 Mary, 89.
Priket.
 William, 86, 112.
Pyke.
 Ann, 72, 137.
 John, 72.
 Mary, 72, 137.

Questel.
 John, 94.
Questell.
 Anne, 7.
 Elenor, 7.
 Elizabeth, 6.
 James, 6.
 Jane, 6, 94.
 Joane, 6.
 John, 6, 7, 8, 94, 95.
 Katherine, 7.
 Margett, 6.
 Mary, 6.
 Rebecca, 7.

Racheld.
 Nathanill, 116.
Rachell.
 James, 44.
 Margrett, 40, 44.
 Nathaniell, 40, 44.
Ram.
 Daniell, 54, 55.
 John, 54.
 Katherin, 54.
 Katerine, 55, 123.
 William, 123.
Ramm.
 Daniell, 56, 57, 86, 122.
 Elizebeth, 56.
 Katherine, 56, 57, 86.
 William, 57.
Ramsay.
 John, 65.

Ramsay—*continued.*
Olive, 65.
Ramsey.
Elizabeth, 78.
Joan, 110.
John, 78, 88.
Josua, 9.
Olive, 88.
Thomas, 9.
Rand.
Richard, 5.
Thomas, 5.
Raynbeard.
Ann, 105.
Raynold.
Mary, 80.
Raynoldes.
Margaret, 80.
Samuel, 80.
Read.
Abigail, 21.
Ann, 46.
Anne, 128.
Elizabeth, 21, 22, 3 26, 103, 104, 106.
Jeffray, 98, 99.
John, 22, 99, 104.
Jone, 98.
Josiah, 23.
Robert, 26, 106.
Susan, 79.
Thomas, 46.
William, 21, 22, 23, 26, 103, 104, 106.
Reading.
Anne, 79.
John, 79.
Redman.
Mary, 35.
Thomas, 35.
Readmel.
Mary, 35.
Thomas, 35.
Rednell.
Thomas, 110.
Reese.
Ffeby, 35.
William, 35.
Reeves.
Frances, 82.
William, 82.
Renalds.
Ffrancis, 99.
Mary, 19.
Susan, 19, 20, 21.
Thomas, 19, 20, 21, 99, 103.
Renolds.
Ann, 87.
Reynolds.
Abigail, 88.
Elizabeth, 85.
Francis, 106.
George, 88, 89.
Sarah, 89.
Susan, 89.
Thomas, 104.

Reynolds—*continued.*
William, 106.
Rice.
John, 116.
Richardson.
Alice, 80.
Thomas, 121.
Richoll.
Elisabeth, 83.
Right.
Anne, 34.
George, 34.
Hannah, 34.
Rivers.
Elizabeth, 13.
John, 13,
Roaffe.
John, 41, 42.
Mary, 42.
Sarah, 42.
Roberds.
Goody, 118.
Willi, 118.
Robjon.
Elizabeth, 86.
Roberts.
Anne, 16.
David, 19.
John, 15, 16, 18, 19, 99, 103.
Joyce, 16, 18, 19.
Margaret, 15, 99.
Mary, 18.
[*Blank*], 15.
Rock.
George, 128.
Rofe.
John, 43, 111.
Mary, 43.
William, 43.
Roffe.
John, 38.
Robart, 6.
Roffey.
Ann, 89.
Henry, 89.
Rogers.
Elisabeth, 83.
Grace, 77.
Joan, 6.
John, 83.
Marie, 78.
Mary, 87.
Richard, 6, 77.
Robert, 87.
Thomas, 78.
Rose.
Susan, 84.
Ross.
Francis, 137.
Katherine, 55, 121.
Mary, 136.
Thomas, 55, 120, 136.
. . . ., 55.
Rosse.
Frances, 54.
Mary, 54.

Rosse—*continued*.
  Prudence, 56.
  Thomas, 54, 56.
  . . . ., 56.
Rous.
  Elizabeth, 42.
  Mary, 42.
  Simon, 42.
Rouse.
  Simon, 115.
Rowden.
  Ann, 42, 112.
  Anna, 42.
  John, 112.
Rowland.
  Catherine, 79.
Rowley.
  Ann, 73.
Rowse.
  Elizabeth, 113.
  Simond, 41, 113.
  William, 41, 113.
Royston.
  Elizabeth, 131.
  Thomas, 135.
Ruck.
  Adam, 16.
  Elizabeth, 15, 16.
  John, 15.
  Robert, 15, 16.
Russell.
  Mary, 55, 117.
  Susan, 53, 55, 86.
  Susana, 53.
  William, 53, 55, 86, 123.
Rust.
  Susan, 88.
  William, 88.

Sadler.
  Ann, 42, 46, 47, 48, 51, 53, 117.
  Anna, 64.
  Anne, 43, 44, 45, 61, 62, 63, 64.
  Frances, 47, 48, 114, 117.
  Francies, 51.
  Ffrancis, 42, 43, 44, 45, 46, 47, 53,
    64, 115, 121, 123.
  Jesse, 53, 121.
  John, 61, 115, 137.
  Olive, 42, 88.
  Ollive, 46, 114.
  Philip, 44, 122.
  Rowland, 121.
  Rowlun, 45.
  William, 48, 61, 62, 63, 64, 126,
    129.
Saling.
  Elizabeth, 5.
  John, 94.
  Thomas, 5, 6.
Salmon.
  Ann, 87.
  Christopher, 87.
  John, 130.
  Widow, 108.

Salwood.
  Isaac, 137.
Samford.
  Anne, 22, 27.
  Edward, 22, 27.
  Thomas, 27.
Sammon.
  Anne, 17, 18, 28, 82.
  Francis, 28.
  John, 17, 18, 28, 82.
  Jone, 17.
Sampson.
  Elizabeth, 88.
  Thomas, 88.
Samuel.
  Dorothey, 15.
  Elizabeth, 14.
  Mary, 14, 15, 16, 17, 82, 101.
  Matthew, 16.
  Richard, 14, 15, 16, 17, 100, 101.
Sanders.
  John, 43, 50, 115, 120.
  Prudence, 50.
  Richard, 43, 115.
  Sarah, 43, 50, 120.
  William, 94.
Sandford.
  Edward, 87.
  Elizabeth, 60.
  Mary, 60, 87.
  Thomas, 59, 60, 136.
  ——, 125.
Sanford.
  Anne, 21.
  Edward, 21.
  Elizebeth, 56, 59.
  John, 21.
  Thomas, 56.
Santlow.
  Hester, 87.
Santon.
  Joane, 80.
Sarrett.
  Mary, 37.
  Richard, 37.
  [*Blank*], 37.
Sarrutt.
  Richard, 110.
Saunders.
  Abigail, 87.
  Abigall, 57, 86.
  John, 46, 48, 57, 86, 116, 119.
  Prudence, 86, 119.
  Sarah, 46, 48.
  Thomas, 57.
Saward.
  Anne, 62, 65, 127, 128.
  Dorothy, 63, 128.
  Elizabeth, 60, 61, 62, 63, 64, 65,
    66, 128.
  Isaac, 60-66.
  Jacob, 60.
  Martha, 61.
  Sarah, 64, 66, 127.
  Susannah, 65.

Sawkin.
  Elizabeth, 78.
  Thomas, 78.
Sawkins.
  James, 87.
  Ruth, 87.
Saxie.
  Alice, 103.
  John, 81, 99.
  Mary, 81.
  Thomas, 101.
Say.
  Benjamine, 57.
  Easter, 120, 136.
  Hester, 53, 55, 57.
  John, 53, 55, 57, 120, 136.
  Mary, 123.
Sayer.
  William, 127.
Saywell.
  Roger, 97.
Scambler.
  James, 36, 37, 39, 85.
  John, 39.
  Mary, 36, 37, 39, 85.
Scampion.
  Anne, 79.
  Elizabeth, 13, 100.
  Henrie, 100.
  Henry, 14.
  Jeremy, 13, 97.
  John, 12, 13, 96, 97.
  Martha, 12, 14, 96.
  Mary, 80.
  Samuel, 12, 80, 97.
  . . . ., 113.
Scholley.
  Mary, 81.
  Thomas, 81.
Searl.
  Ann, 72.
  Elizebeth, 48.
  Henery, 118.
  Henry, 72.
  Mary, 72.
  Sarah, 46, 117.
  William, 46, 48, 117, 118.
Searle.
  Ann, 69, 71, 130, 136.
  Anne, 67, 68, 69, 89.
  Harry, 67, 68, 69, 71, 89.
  Robert, 68, 137.
  Sarah, 71.
  William, 133.
Searll.
  Ann, 58.
  Easter, 55.
  Elizabeth, 47, 55, 118.
  Elizebeth, 49, 52, 54, 56, 58.
  Harrie, 54.
  Henery, 47.
  John, 56.
  Mary, 52.
  William, 47, 49, 52, 54, 55, 56, 58,
    118.

Sedgewick.
  Anne, 103.
  Elizabeth, 11.
  John, 103.
  Mary, 13.
  Philip, 12.
  Thomas, 11.
Sedgewicke.
  James, 11.
  John, 10.
  Thomas, 10, 11.
Sedgwick.
  Anne, 21.
  Daniell, 22, 104.
  Edward, 25-28.
  Elizabeth, 22, 25, 27, 105.
  Horatio, 28.
  James, 22, 25, 104, 105.
  John, 21.
  Robart, 12.
  Robert, 93.
  Susanna, 25-28.
  Thomas, 12, 13, 25, 100.
Sell.
  Abraham, 59.
  Anne, 32.
  Elizabeth, 36, 116.
  Elizebeth, 50.
  Hellen, 32, 34.
  Margaret, 77.
  Mary, 50, 54, 57, 59, 86, 128.
  Sarah, 87.
  Thomas, 32, 34, 36, 50, 54, 57, 59,
    86, 113, 122.
  Widdow, 123.
Sells.
  Elizabeth, 35.
  Thomas, 35.
Setch.
  John, 88.
  Rose, 88.
Sewell.
  Anne, 79.
  Roger, 79.
Shaels.
  John, 133.
Sharpe.
  Tabitha, 79.
  Thomas, 79.
Shead.
  Ann, 67.
  Anne, 130.
  Elizabeth, 67.
  Georg, 57.
  John, 69.
  Martha, 73.
  Mary, 57, 58, 69, 73.
  William, 57, 58, 67, 69, 73, 138.
Sheadd.
  Edward, 86.
  Mary, 86.
Shed.
  Cornel, 72.
  Cornell, 131.
  Elizabeth, 71, 131, 132.
  Georg, 124.

Shed—*continued.*
John, 60.
Mary, 60, 69, 71, 72, 124, 133.
William, 60, 69, 71, 72, 129.
Sheed.
John, 129.
Martha, 66, 129.
William, 66.
Sheffield.
Samson, 104.
Shefford.
Frances, 112.
Peter, 112.
Shepherd.
James, 131.
Shingleton.
William, 12.
Shipton.
Ellyn, 12.
Ffrancis, 17.
John, 12, 13, 14, 15, 17, 99, 102.
Katherin, 14, 15, 17.
Mary, 14.
Stephen, 15.
Steven, 99.
Thomas, 13, 102.
William, 13.
Siday.
Sarah, 87.
Sigersgill.
James, 32.
Katherine, 32.
Robert, 32.
Siluester.
Robart, 6.
Skiner.
Ffrances, 39.
John, 39.
William, 39.
Skinner.
Ann, 52, 119.
Elizabeth, 36, 124.
Elizebeth, 48, 49, 52, 53, 122.
Ffrances, 36, 38.
John, 48, 49, 52, 53, 122, 124, 125.
Mary, 53.
William, 36, 38, 116.
Slight.
Henery, 108.
Smal.
Giles, 80.
Grace, 80.
Jone, 17.
Margaret, 19.
Samuel, 16.
Sarah, 14, 16, 17, 19.
William, 14, 16, 17, 19, 98.
Smale.
Lidia, 14, 80.
Sarah, 15, 106.
William, 14, 15, 104, 106.
Small.
Alice, 8, 95.
Cornelius, 8, 96.
Elizabeth, 7, 13, 79.
Giles, 7, 8, 9, 96.

Small—*continued.*
Grace, 8.
Gyles, 98.
Gy—, 8.
Henry, 13.
John, 12, 13, 79, 103.
Lidia, 9.
Lydia, 83, 104.
Margaret, 21, 102, 103.
Mary, 79.
Prudence, 9.
Samuel, 99.
Sarah, 21.
Susan, 7.
Thomas, 8, 95.
William, 7, 8, 21, 97, 99, 102, 103, 104.
Smeth.
Martha, 88.
Smiggersgill.
James, 84.
Smith.
Easter, 30.
Elizabeth, 34.
Frances, 104.
George, 135.
Henry, 79.
Jasper, 108.
Jane, 39.
Jeames, 42.
Jenny, 118.
Joan, 37.
Joana, 108.
Joane, 79.
Joanna, 32-34.
Johanna, 129.
John, 33, 108.
Jone, 30, 42.
Lydia, 32.
Martha, 37.
Mary, 85, 135.
Sarah, 37, 39, 135.
Thomas, 66, 116.
William, 30, 32, 33, 34, 37, 39, 42, 107, 108, 120.
Smithson.
Elizabeth, 47.
Elizebeth, 47.
John, 47.
Smyth.
Elizabeth, 17, 80, 135.
George, 135.
James, 98, 124.
Jasper, 17, 80, 103.
John, 100.
Snatt.
Richard, 134.
Sorrell.
Alice, 83.
Soule.
Anne, 77.
John, 77.
South.
Edward, 48.
Jane, 132.
Thomas, 48, 118.

South—*continued.*
   [*Blank*], 48.
Spalding.
   Annis, 79.
   John, 79.
Spark.
   Dorothey, 13.
   Esther, 100.
   John, 12, 102.
   Joseph, 13, 102.
   Mary, 12.
   Nicholas, 13.
   Nicolas, 12, 14, 99, 100, 102.
   Thomasyn, 14, 102.
   William, 14.
Sparke.
   Easter, 14.
   Nicolas, 13, 14, 101.
   Thomas, 13.
Sparkes.
   Nicholas, 98.
Sparks.
   Dorothy, 101.
   Nicolas, 101.
   Thomas, 104.
   William, 113.
Speller.
   Abraham, 72, 136.
   Anna Maria, 66.
   Elizabeth, 69, 70, 134.
   John, 72.
   Mary, 66, 68, 69, 72, 135, 136.
   Olive, 135.
   Peter, 66, 68, 69, 70, 72, 135, 136.
   [*Blank*], 70.
Spicer.
   Elizabeth, 40.
   John, 42.
   Sarah, 37, 40, 41, 42, 44, 45, 123.
   Susanna, 44.
   Thomas, 37, 40, 41, 42, 44, 45, 125.
   William, 41, 137.
Spiller.
   Mary, 64, 65.
   Olive, 64.
   Peter, 64, 65.
Spilman.
   John, 9.
Spiser.
   Katherine, 39.
   Thomas, 39.
Spooner.
   Elizebeth, 52.
   Henery, 52.
   Mary, 52.
Spranger.
   Andrew, 8.
   Marian, 8.
   Martha, 83.
   Mary, 32, 87, 114.
   Sarah, 109.
   William, 31, 32, 33, 107, 117.
Sprangier.
   ——, 117.

Spunner.
   Henry, 50.
   Mary, 50.
Squire.
   Mary, 82.
Staine.
   Rebekah, 23.
   Robert, 23.
Staines.
   Anne, 62, 63.
   Elizabeth, 39, 63, 65.
   George, 39.
   John, 105.
   Katherine, 39.
   Mary, 62, 126.
   Robert, 65, 105.
   Sussan, 112.
   William, 62, 112.
Stains.
   Anne, 64.
   George, 34, 109.
   John, 64, 113.
   Katherine, 34, 108, 109.
   Robert, 34, 108.
   Susan, 113.
   William, 34, 64, 85, 108, 113.
Stane.
   Abigail, 132.
   Abigaill, 44.
   Alice, 68.
   Anne, 65.
   Austin, 68.
   Brigitt, 95.
   Elizabeth, 26, 67, 68, 69, 78, 113, 136.
   Frances, 84.
   George, 67, 113, 130.
   James, 26.
   John, 10, 25, 65, 66, 67, 68, 69, 97, 102, 128, 134, 136.
   Katherine, 69, 113.
   Margaret, 11.
   Mary, 44, 66, 68, 131.
   Rebecca, 21, 22.
   Rebecka, 107.
   Rebekah, 25, 26.
   Richard, 44, 65, 66, 67, 68, 129, 130, 134.
   Robert, 21, 22, 25, 26, 44, 67, 68, 69, 84, 103, 133.
   Sarah, 65, 66, 67, 68, 69, 129.
   Seppy, 66.
   Susan, 30, 84, 134.
   Susannah, 138.
   William, 10, 30, 44, 65, 67, 84, 107, 119, 131, 135.
   [*Blank*], 67, 130.
   (Boy), 95.
Stammer.
   Mary, 77.
Standish.
   Sarah, 134.
Stanes.
   Ann, 49, 60.
   Anne, 61, 63.
   Abigall, 45, 46, 47, 51.

175

Stanes—*continued.*
 Abygall, 49.
 Elizabeth, 37, 120, 127.
 Elizebeth, 51.
 Georg, 35, 36, 124.
 George, 33, 35, 37, 85.
 John, 33, 36, 38, 47, 51, 52, 54, 63,
  64, 119, 122, 127.
 Katerine, 35, 36, 48, 49, 53, 84,
  120.
 Katharine, 37, 124.
 Katherin, 33.
 Margaret, 81.
 Marian, 38.
 Mary, 35, 45, 46, 48, 51, 53, 56,
  60, 119, 120, 125.
 Maryon, 36.
 Rebecca, 84.
 Rebekah, 24.
 Richard, 33, 45, 46, 47, 49, 51, 52,
  54, 56, 63, 115, 117, 118, 119,
  122, 127.
 Robert, 24, 35, 36, 47, 49, 51, 55,
  61, 86, 105, 117, 118, 119.
 Sarah, 47, 49, 51, 52, 54, 55, 63,
  64, 86, 125, 133.
 Susan, 33, 86.
 Susana, 33.
 Susanna, 36, 46, 63, 115.
 Susannah, 31.
 Thomas, 36, 51, 53, 119, 120.
 William, 21, 31, 33, 45, 46, 48, 51,
  53, 56, 60, 61, 63, 115, 118, 125.
Stanley.
 Elizabeth, 85.
Stapeler.
 John, 60.
 Mary, 60, 89.
Stapler.
 John, 130.
 Matthew, 130.
Stapleton.
 [*Blank*], 94.
Starecroft.
 Eleanor, 89.
Starky.
 Mary, 81.
Stayns.
 William, 98.
Steabing.
 Abigell, 35.
 Benjamin, 35.
 Susen, 35.
Stebbin.
 Abigail, 36, 110.
 Anne, 110.
 Benjamin, 36, 110.
Stebing.
 Abigall, 36.
 Agatha, 36.
 Ann, 36.
 Benjamin, 36.
Stebbing.
 Abbegeirle, 40.
 Abigail, 38.
 Abigal, 113.

Stebbing—*continued.*
 Abigale, 113.
 Abigeiall, 39.
 Ann, 122.
 Benjamin, 38, 39, 113, 122.
 Benjamine, 40.
 Elizabeth, 39.
 Sarah, 40, 113.
 Theophilus, 38.
Stephen.
 Mary, 60.
Stephens.
 Ann, 67, 71, 128.
 Anne, 65.
 Charlotta, 72.
 Dennis, 72.
 Elizabeth, 71, 135.
 Georg, 48, 65, 67, 71, 72.
 Katherine, 48.
 Mary, 86.
 Susanna, 48.
Stepping.
 Abigail, 34.
 Abigall, 35.
 Benjamin, 34, 35.
 Daniel, 82.
 Daniell, 18.
 Nathaniel, 35.
 Sarah, 18, 82.
Stevens.
 Anne, 66.
 Dennis, 89.
 Georg, 47, 50.
 George, 66, 89.
 Katherine, 47, 50.
 Stanes, 50.
St. John.
 Rowland, 117.
Stoakes.
 Abigail, 88.
 Ann, 42.
 Elizabeth, 41.
 Georg, 40.
 George, 40, 41, 42, 44, 114, 115.
 Johannah, 40.
 Jone, 40, 41, 42, 44.
 Martha, 87.
 Mary, 32, 40.
 Thomas, 44, 115.
 Widow, 108.
Stoaks.
 Ann, 109.
 George, 109.
 Mary, 109.
Stoddard.
 Devora, 80.
 John, 13, 80.
 Richard, 13.
Stoddart.
 Andrew, 105.
Stoke.
 Sarah, 134.
Stokes.
 Amy, 82.
 Elizabeth, 32.
 George, 32.

176

Stokes—*continued*.
    Jane, 89.
Stone.
    Ann, 59.
    Elizabeth, 22, 23, 24, 82.
    James, 22, 23, 24, 82.
    Margaret, 31.
    Mary, 23.
    Rebeccah, 31.
    Sarah, 24.
    William, 31, 59.
Story.
    Anne, 98.
Stracey.
    Isaac, 129.
    Sarah, 89.
Stracy.
    Luce, 97.
    Thomas, 13, 97.
Stringer.
    John, 87.
    Martha, 87.
Strutt.
    Edward, 50, 54, 56, 119.
    Mary, 50, 54, 56, 119.
    Richard, 54.
    Samuell, 54.
    William, 50.
Sugdin.
    John, 95.
    Mother, 97.
Sutton.
    Rebecca, 82.
Sweateapple.
    John, 35.
    Mary, 35.
Sweetapple.
    Elizabeth, 34.
    John, 34, 85, 119.
    Mary, 34, 85.
    Widdow, 120.
Sweeten.
    Elizabeth, 60, 87.
    Henry, 60, 87.
    John, 60.
Sweeting.
    Anne, 61.
    Elizabeth, 61, 62, 64, 65.
    Henry, 61, 62, 64, 65, 129.
    Mary, 64, 79, 103.
    William, 65.
Sweting.
    Easter, 80.
Swinow.
    Susan, 78.
Symson.
    John, 6.

Taber.
    Amy, 61.
    Elizabeth, 35, 61.
    John, 31, 35, 61.
    Roberd, 35.
    Thomas, 61.
Tabor.
    Amy, 125.

Tabor—*continued*.
    Catherine, 110.
    Clemence, 27, 84.
    Elizabeth, 21, 22, 24, 25, 27, 32, 34, 53, 78, 84.
    Elizebeth, 122.
    George, 34, 53.
    John, 21, 32, 33, 34, 108, 109, 114, 123, 124, 125.
    Katherine, 33, 34, 108.
    Mary, 34.
    Mary Anne, 25.
    Susanna, 84.
    Thomas, 34, 53, 104, 120, 122, 123, 125.
    William, 21, 22, 24, 25, 27, 32, 33, 34, 78, 84, 103, 105, 107, 108, 110, 113.
    . . . ., 123.
Tabour.
    Elizabeth, 36, 50.
    Elizebeth, 59.
    Georg, 122.
    John, 59.
    Kathrine, 36.
    Mary, 117.
    Susan, 121.
    Thomas, 50, 59, 118, 121.
    William, 36, 50.
Tagell.
    Richard, 93.
Tailor.
    Henry, 77.
Talcot.
    Mary, 34.
    Richard, 34.
Talcut.
    John, 35.
    Mary, 35, 36.
    Richard, 35, 36.
    Thomas, 36.
Tanner.
    Thomas, 83.
    Joane, 83.
Tariar.
    Debora, 80.
Tarling.
    Mary, 89.
Tasker.
    Elizabeth, 94.
Tayler.
    John, 83.
    Sarah, 83.
Taylor.
    Elizabeth, 83.
Tedder.
    Henery, 126.
Thayer.
    Mary, 84.
    William, 84.
Thomas.
    Elizabeth, 6.
    Josua, 6.
    Mary, 6, 93.
    William, 6.
    ——, 94.

Thomlinson.
  Nathan, 116.
Thomson.
  Elizabeth, 105.
Thom.
  Mary, 87.
Thornton.
  Jone, 81.
  Katherine, 78.
  Richard, 81.
Thorogood.
  Elizabeth, 128.
  Henry, 137.
  John, 67, 68.
  Martha, 127.
  Mary, 67, 68, 89.
  Philip, 69.
  Robert, 68.
  Sarah, 69, 88.
  William, 69.
Thorowgood.
  Henery, 88.
  Rebecca, 88.
Throughgood.
  Jeffery, 31.
  Jeoffrey, 131.
  John, 31.
  Mary, 131.
Throwgood.
  Richard, 83.
  Elisabeth, 83.
Thrayen.
  Philip, 36.
  William, 36.
Thrgood.
  Ann, 32.
  Jeffery, 32.
Thurgood.
  Agnes, 33, 109.
  Ann, 70, 135.
  Anne, 32, 33.
  Dorothy, 34.
  Eliner, 35.
  Elizabeth, 30, 32, 33, 34, 35, 109.
  Ffrancis, 29, 32, 114.
  Henry, 42, 70, 136.
  Jeffery, 114.
  Jeffry, 33.
  John, 51, 54, 67, 70, 114, 135.
  Joyce, 29.
  Margerett, 32.
  Mary, 29, 32, 42, 67, 70, 131, 135.
  Phillip, 42.
  Rachell, 51.
  Robert, 135.
  Sarah, 54, 65, 66, 67, 68, 70, 88,
    129, 133.
  William, 30, 32, 33, 34, 35, 65, 66, 67
    68, 70, 85, 88, 108, 109, 129, 134.
  [Blank], 108.
Thurogood.
  Ann, 52.
  Dorethy, 120.
  Elizebeth, 121.
  Em, 118.
  John, 52, 55, 56, 116, 119.

Thurogood—continued.
  Mary, 55, 119.
  Rachell, 52.
  Sarah, 55, 56, 129.
  William, 119.
Thuroogood.
  John, 120.
Thurowgood.
  Ffrancis, 30.
  John, 30.
  Mary, 30.
Tiday.
  Thomas, 83.
  Elizabeth, 83.
Tidie.
  Thomas, 103.
Tidy.
  Robert, 14.
  Thomas, 14.
Tiler.
  Anne, 13, 79.
  Elizabeth, 12.
  Mary, 48.
  Richard, 13.
  Thomas, 48.
  William, 12, 13, 79.
Till.
  Edmund, 60, 124.
  Elizabeth, 60.
  Jeffery, 39, 116, 117, 123.
  Jeffrey, 41.
  Jeffry, 43.
  John, 39, 57, 58, 59, 60.
  Pearson, 60.
  Sarah, 39, 41, 43, 57, 58, 59, 60,
    127.
  Sammuell, 41.
  Samuell, 117.
  Stracey, 59.
Ting.
  Anne, 7.
  Elizabeth, 78, 95.
  Ellin, 77.
  George, 7.
  Henry, 5, 6, 7, 8, 9, 77, 94, 95.
  Joan, 77, 94.
  Mary, 8, 135.
  Thomas, 6, 9, 78, 95.
  William, 5.
Tod.
  Sarah, 133.
Todd.
  Timothy, 131, 135.
Tode.
  Sarah, 59.
  Timothy, 59.
  Thiomothy, 59.
Tomlinson.
  Lydia, 85.
  Nathan, 85.
  Widdow, 117.
Tomson.
  Bennett, 24.
  Elizabeth, 12.

Tomson—*continued*.
    Ffather, 104.
    Jane, 11.
    John, 10.
    Marie, 11.
    Mary, 24.
    Nicholas, 10, 11, 12.
    Nicolas, 11.
    Robert, 24.
Tovey.
    Frances, 87.
    John, 87.
Trahern.
    Sarah, 134.
Traherne.
    Joan, 110.
    Olive, 38.
    Philip, 38, 110, 120.
    Sarah, 38.
Trappes.
    Thomas, 6.
Trapps.
    Ann, 46, 86.
    Edward, 46.
    James, 46, 86.
    Mary, 82.
Traps.
    Henry, 84.
    Jane, 84.
Travel.
    Abigail, 72, 73, 74.
    Elizabeth, 73.
    James, 62, 73.
    John, 61, 62, 72, 73, 74.
    Mary, 72.
    Sarah, 61, 62.
    William, 61.
    [*Blank*], 74.
Traveler.
    Elizabeth, 60, 124.
    John, 60.
    Sarah, 60.
Traveller.
    John, 60.
    Sarah, 60.
Trayhern.
    Elizabeth, 50.
    Elizebeth, 46, 47.
    Philip, 46, 47, 50.
    Phillipp, 46, 117, 118.
    Sarah, 47, 117.
    William, 50.
Trayherne.
    Philip, 36, 37, 110.
    Rowland, 37, 110.
    Sarah, 110.
    William, 36.
Treyhern.
    Elizabeth, 48.
    Elizebeth, 48.
    Philip, 48, 118.
    Philipp, 48.
    Rowland, 48, 118.
    William, 48, 118.
Tricket.
    William, 119.

Tucker.
    Elizebeth, 58.
    Job, 58.
    John, 58.
    Thomas, 122.
Tuke.
    Brian, 9.
    Morice, 9.
Tumner.
    Margery, 41.
    Mary, 41.
    Micall, 41.
Tunbridg.
    Zephora, 80.
Tunbridge.
    Edward, 96.
Turke.
    Thomas, 105.
Turner.
    Ann, 89.
    Anne, 64, 93, 115.
    Boyde, 114.
    Elizabeth, 38, 114, 132.
    James, 64, 66, 135.
    John, 89.
    Margery, 86.
    Martha, 37, 38, 86, 110, 112.
    Marthe, 36.
    Mary, 40, 85, 113.
    Michael, 37, 38, 110, 112.
    Michall, 40, 113.
    Michell, 118.
    Mihill, 36.
    Richard, 115, 116, 126.
    Robart, 93, 94.
    Sarah, 64, 66, 135.
    Susannah, 66.
    [*Blank*], 110.
Turnes.
    Elizabeth, 81.
    Thomas, 98.
Turnish.
    Elizabeth, 9, 93.
    John, 5, 7, 8, 94, 95.
    Mary, 7, 94.
    Robert, 5.
    Thomas, 9.
    William, 93.
Turnor.
    Anne, 77.
    Arthur, 8.
    Edward, 8, 77.
    Morice, 8.
Turuish.
    Ales, 77, 78.
    Ellin, 77.
    Grace, 78.
    Joan, 78.
    John, 77.
    Thomas, 78.
Twene.
    Jane, 89.
Twinn.
    Rebecka, 87.
    Robert, 87.

Ty.
Ales, 78.
Christopher, 78.
Tyday.
Robert, 104.
Tydie.
Anna, 14.
Elizabeth, 100.
Katherine, 14, 15.
Robert, 14, 15.
Samuell, 15.
Thomas, 100.
Tydy.
Elizabeth, 78.
Robart, 12.
Robert, 13, 97.
Thomas, 12, 78, 97.
Tyler.
Abigail, 33.
Agnes, 12, 15.
David, 106.
Elizabeth, 32.
Martha, 15.
Mary, 31.
Priscilla, 32, 33, 110.
Richard, 31, 32, 33.
William, 12, 15.

Umphrye.
John, 82.
Umwell.
Elizabeth, 89.
Unwin.
Dorathy, 72, 137.
Elizabeth, 72.
Richard, 72, 137.
Thomas, 72.

Vaid.
William, 115.
Vauks.
Elizebeth, 122.
——, 122.
Vayl.
Frances, 80.
Velley.
Alexander, 70, 136.
Ann, 71, 136.
Elizabeth, 36.
Jane, 70, 71, 136.
Mary, 71, 129.
Sarah, 36.
Thomas, 36, 67, 68, 69, 70, 71, 72, 73, 74, 89, 129, 133, 134, 135, 136, 137, 138.
Vinton.
Abigail, 88.
John, 88.
Vmphrye.
Mary, 82.

Wadley.
George, 63.
Thomas, 63.
Waggstaff.
Sarah, 87.

Waggstaff—continued.
Thomas, 87.
Wailet.
An, 36.
Ann, 36.
Henry, 94.
John, 36.
Wailett.
Ann, 37.
Bennett, 7.
Daniell, 37.
Edward, 8.
Henry, 8.
Joan, 7, 37.
Waillet.
Elizabeth, 38.
John, 38.
Wakelin.
Johanna, 88.
Walker.
Robert, 130.
Wall.
Sarah, 89.
Samuel, 89.
Waller.
Margaret, 79.
Wallice.
(Widow), 115.
Wallis.
Anne, 26.
Gregorie, 20.
Gregory, 21, 24, 26, 82.
John, 20.
Martha, 24.
Mary, 20, 21, 24, 26, 82, 83.
Walys.
Katherine, 77.
Richard, 77.
Wamsley.
Andrew, 12, 13, 78, 97.
Benjamin, 12, 13, 97.
Dorathy, 78.
Wanner.
Francis, 32.
Mary, 32.
Sarah, 32.
Ward.
Dennis, 58.
Edward, 29, 31, 32, 33, 34, 107, 109.
Elizabeth, 32.
Ellen, 29.
James, 34, 109.
Joseph, 87.
Marget, 33.
Mary, 29, 32, 33, 34, 109.
Rebecca, 6.
Richard, 56, 58, 86, 123.
Sarah, 56, 58, 86, 123.
Susan, 87.
Thomas, 93.
William, 31, 107.
Warmesley.
Rebecca, 88.
Warmsley.
Hannah, 87.

Warner.
    Andrew, 33.
    Francis, 30, 31, 32, 33, 34, 84.
    John, 32, 83.
    Margaret, 80.
    Mary, 34, 83, 108.
    Ruth, 34.
    Sarah, 31, 32, 33, 34.
    Seraj, 30, 84.
Warren.
    Elizabeth, 71.
    George, 135.
    Mary, 70, 71, 135, 136.
    Philippa, 70, 134.
    Sheffeld, 70.
    Sheffield, 135.
    Thomas, 70, 71, 136.
Wasket.
    Elizabeth, 120.
    Elizebeth, 54.
    Mary, 67.
    Susan, 137.
    William, 54, 67, 120.
Waskett.
    Susan, 54, 86.
    William, 54, 86.
Waters.
    Robert, 26.
    [Blank], 26.
Watson.
    Mary, 13.
    Robert, 13.
    Tabitha, 79.
Waylet.
    Anne, 34, 37, 112.
    Daniel, 37.
    John, 34, 37, 112.
    Mary, 108.
    Sarah, 108.
Waylett.
    Ann, 86.
    Anne, 35, 83.
    Avery, 83.
    Griffee, 114.
    Griffidd, 42.
    John, 26, 35, 113, 114.
    M . . . ., 113.
    Sarah, 26, 35, 113.
    (Widow), 42, 114.
    William, 109, 113.
Waynsworth.
    Abel, 98.
    Anne, 98.
Weal.
    Ann, 71.
    Mary, 71.
    William, 71.
Weald.
    John, 72.
    Sarah, 72.
    William, 72, 73.
Wease.
    Elliner, 113.
Weaver.
    Elizabeth, 77.

Webster.
    John, 95.
Weldon.
    Abigall, 96.
    Alice, 94.
    Anne, 8.
    Anger, 8.
    Catherine, 77.
    Elizabeth, 79, 80, 95.
    John, 7, 8, 9, 10, 11, 77, 94, 96, 97, 100, 103.
    Katherin, 103.
    Katherine, 97.
    Mary, 7, 8, 79, 94.
    Robert, 11, 97.
    Samuel, 9.
    Samuell, 100.
    Thomas, 10, 96.
    Timothy, 10.
Wells.
    Elizabeth, 36, 40, 111.
    Grace, 36.
    Isaac, 40, 83.
    John, 36, 38, 40, 111, 112.
    Richard, 112.
Wels.
    John, 93, 99.
Wennel.
    James, 70.
    John, 70.
    Mary, 66, 82.
    Rachel, 69.
    Richard, 70.
    Sarah, 65, 66, 69, 70.
    Susannah, 70.
    Thomas, 65, 66, 69, 70, 82.
Wennell.
    Elizabeth, 53, 86, 134.
    Elizebeth, 50, 52, 56.
    Ellin, 23, 116.
    George, 27, 113.
    James, 52, 56, 89, 119.
    John, 21, 50, 52, 53, 56, 86, 119, 130.
    Magnus, 68.
    Margaret, 18.
    Mary, 18, 20, 21, 23, 25, 27, 68, 136.
    Susan, 89.
    Thomas, 18, 20, 21, 23, 25, 27, 68, 104.
    Widdow, 120.
West.
    Daniell, 85.
    Elizabeth, 61, 62, 63, 136.
    James, 61, 62, 63.
    Mary, 63.
    Sarah, 85.
    Susan, 79.
    Susanna, 61.
    Thomas, 79.
Westwood.
    Clemence, 83.
    Grace, 78.
    Nicolas, 78.
    Sarah, 89.

Westwood—*continued.*
Thomas, 120.
William, 89.
Whasket.
William, 127.
Wheeler.
Ann, 69.
Mary, 69, 89.
Sarah, 69, 134.
Thomas, 69, 89.
Whetsone.
Christofer, 17.
Whetston.
Sarah, 83.
Whetstone.
Christopher, 107.
Elizabeth, 17.
[*Blank*], 17.
White.
Agnes, 99.
Alice, 38.
Andrew, 17, 100.
Ann, 49, 51, 54, 55, 57, 58, 59, 123.
Anna, 37.
Anne, 133.
Dennis, 82.
Elezabeth, 27, 28.
Elisabeth, 25.
Elizabeth, 22, 26, 34, 43, 45, 58, 61, 65, 86, 128.
Elizebeth, 121.
George, 12, 82, 114.
Grace, 38, 40.
Henery, 27, 33, 34, 35, 38, 49, 51, 54, 58, 120.
Henry, 36, 37, 40, 55, 57, 108, 124, 125.
Isaac, 105.
James, 28, 36, 55, 61, 65.
Jane, 26, 84.
Jeames, 43.
Joan, 37.
Joana, 34.
Joane, 34, 36.
Joanna, 33, 34.
John, 13, 51, 93, 99, 120.
Jone, 35.
Loue, 40.
Margaret, 13, 17, 18, 20, 34, 79, 101.
Marian, 78.
Martha, 13, 83.
Mary, 20, 33, 49, 82.
Michael, 12, 13, 14, 17, 18, 20, 78, 99, 100, 101.
Michaell, 12.
Richard, 68, 132.
Robert, 12, 22, 25, 26, 27, 28, 43, 45, 86, 118, 127.
Sarah, 34, 58, 123.
Thomas, 12, 111.
Widdow, 114.
William, 17, 33, 108.
Whitehead.
Ann, 124.
Doritie, 85.

Whitehead—*continued.*
Dorothy, 33, 34, 111.
Elisebeth, 36, 52, 55.
Elizabeth, 37, 39, 40, 41, 42, 110, 113, 123, 129.
Hannah, 113.
James, 52, 129.
John, 42, 115.
Katerine, 36.
Robert, 37, 52, 55, 121, 124.
Samuel, 33, 34, 85, 107, 111, 113, 124.
Susan, 86.
Susanna, 39.
Thomas, 33, 38, 111, 132.
William, 36, 37, 38, 39, 40, 41, 42, 111, 113, 118.
Whitheade.
Dorathy, 32.
Samuell, 32.
Whithorn.
Edward, 81.
Whitte.
Grace, 116.
Hennery, 116.
Love, 116.
Whitteridge.
Henry, 127.
Whyte.
Elezabeth, 28.
Robert, 28, 105.
Whetstone.
John, 105.
Wial.
Henry, 8.
Thomas, 8.
Wiatt.
Jane, 7.
Thomas, 7, 8.
Wibert.
Rebeckah, 85.
Wignall.
Elizabeth, 78.
William, 78.
Wilcock.
Annis, 78.
Wilkin.
John, 109.
Katherine, 85.
Wilkinn.
Katherine, 114.
Wilkinson.
John, 119.
Willand.
Avelin, 93.
Clemence, 12.
Edmond, 5, 11, 12, 78.
Edmund, 9, 10, 11, 93.
Elizabeth, 9.
Hugh, 11.
John, 10.
Jone, 78.
Margaret, 93.
Mary, 9.
Prudence, 9.
Richard, 10.

Willand—*continued.*
  Sàra, 11.
  William, 5.
Willans.
  Edmund, 100, 103.
  Hugh, 100.
  Sarah, 123.
  William, 123.
Willet.
  Bennet, 96.
  Catherine, 96.
  Richard, 96.
Willett.
  Catherine, 10.
  Richard, 10.
Willey.
  Jane, 89.
  Thomas, 89.
Williames.
  Dennis, 49.
  Thomas, 49.
Williams.
  Dennis, 47, 50.
  Elizabeth, 24.
  John, 24, 38, 106.
  Joseph, 38.
  Mildred, 80.
  Susanna, 47.
  Thomas, 47, 50, 80, 118.
  Water, 94.
  [*Blank*], 50.
Williamson. -
  Jane, 39.
  John, 37, 39.
  Katherine, 39, 112.
  Martha, 37.
  Mary, 39, 112.
  Sarah, 37.
Willis.
  Elizabeth Evans, 138.
  Martha, 79.
Willond.
  Edmund, 93.
Wills.
  Edward, 116.
  Mathew, 105.
Wilsher.
  Susan, 87.
Wilsmore.
  Joane, 79.
  Thomas, 79.
Wilson.
  Josua, 103.
  Mary, 87.
  Mildred, 80.
  Rebecca, 103.
  Samuel, 87.
Windham.
  Edward, 52, 54, 55, 86, 119, 121.
  Elizabeth, 55.
  Elizebeth, 52, 55, 86.
  Francess, 54.
  Mary, 52, 119.
  [*Blank*], 54.
Wiseman.
  Ann, 57.

Wiseman—*continued.*
  Anne, 61.
  John, 57, 123, 128.
  Joseph, 59.
  Mary, 131.
  Olive, 59, 60, 61, 63, 124, 126.
  Sarah, 60, 134.
  Thomas, 57, 59, 60, 61, 63, 123.
Witham.
  Elizabeth, 61.
  Thomas, 61.
Wittam.
  Frauncis, 6.
  George, 6.
  Jane, 79.
  Thomas, 79.
Wittham.
  John, 6.
Wolly.
  John, 120.
Wolvet.
  Elizabeth, 83.
Wood.
  Alice, 59, 60, 61, 62, 63, 64, 66, 103.
  Elizabeth, 38, 59, 66, 124, 136.
  Ellin, 23.
  George, 26, 63, 127.
  Jane, 84.
  John, 64, 74, 86, 110.
  Jone, 83.
  Phillis, 74, 90.
  Rebecka, 118.
  Richard, 59, 60, 61, 62, 63, 64, 66.
  Sarah, 38.
  Susan, 86.
  Thomas, 23.
  William, 38, 61, 74, 90, 103.
Woodcock.
  James, 78.
  Mary, 78.
Woodfine.
  Francis, 111.
Woodhous.
  Edward, 45.
  Elizebeth, 45.
  John, 45.
Woodhouse.
  Edward, 44, 47, 117, 118.
  Elizabeth, 44, 47.
  Elizebeth, 86.
  Katherine, 44, 117.
  Mary, 122.
Woodland.
  Elizabeth, 88.
Woolard.
  Elizebeth, 122.
Wooilens.
  Anne, 74.
  John, 74.
  Richard, 74.
Woollins.
  Ann, 72, 73.
  Elizabeth, 72.
  John, 72, 73.
  Sarah, 73.

Woolly.
    Dorethy, 120.
    Dorothy, 54.
    John, 120.
    Richard, 120.
    . . . ., 54.
Woolmer.
    James, 134.
    John, 73, 138.
    Sarah, 73.
Woolvett.   ⸱
    Joane, 83.
    Richard, 83.
Worsegate.
    William, 133.
Wott.
    Sarah, 85.
Wrath.
    Elizabeth, 9.
    Georg, 9, 78.
    Margaret, 78.
Wren.
    Ann, 89.
    Robert, 137.
Wrenn.
    Ann, 57, 58, 123.
    Anne, 89.
    Damaris, 137.
    Elizebeth, 58.
    Olive, 89.
    Robert, 57, 58, 123, 128.
    Sarah, 128.
Wright.
    Abraham, 114.
    Anne, 110.
    Barbary, 78.
    George, 18, 20, 82, 110.
    Jane, 20.
    Mary, 114.
    Rebecca, 18, 20, 82.
Write.
    Ann, 30.

Write—*continued.*
    William, 30.
Writt.
    George, 107.
Wulpit.
    Elizabeth, 16.
    John, 16, 81.
    Mary, 16, 81.
Wyat.
    Grace, 77.
    Thomas, 77.

Yates.
    Bannister, 89.
    Mary, 89.
Young.
    Andrew, 89.
    Ann, 84.
    Anne, 106.
    Catherine, 88.
    Eleanor, 89.
    Elizabeth, 38.
    John, 38, 39, 102, 110, 118.
    Mary, 67.
    Robert, 67, 106, 107, 131.
    Sarah, 38, 39, 110.
    William, 88.
Younge.
    Allice, 105.
    Elisabeth, 83.

[*Blank.*]
    Ann, 89.
    Anne, 83.
    Elizabeth, 105, 106.
    John, 97.
    Katheren, 87.
    Mary, 105.
    Matthew, 102.
    Richard, 44, 116.
    Thomas, 87.
    William, 83.

www.ingramcontent.com/pod-product-compliance
Lightning Source LLC
Chambersburg PA
CBHW030841270326
41928CB00007B/1152